Theresa Cheung was born into a family of psychics and spiritualists. Since leaving King's College, Cambridge University with a Master's in Theology and English she has dedicated her life to the study of the unexplained and writing books to raise spiritual awareness of supernormal potential within ourselves and the world around us, as well as the very real possibility of life after death. The author of numerous best-selling mind–body–spirit books, including two *Sunday Times* top-ten best-sellers, Theresa's books and encyclopaedias have been translated into thirty different languages. She has never claimed to be a psychic, but sees the world around her with spiritual eyes and describes herself as an ordinary woman who has had extraordinary experiences.

Claire Broad gave her first message from the spirit world to a relative at the age of four and started to develop her ability from the age of twenty-one with the hope that through cultivating her skills she might help others and better understand the question of life after death herself. She has twenty years' experience working in various ways, including one-to-one private sittings, public demonstrations, public speaking and teaching. Claire is much in demand and her private practice is booked far in advance. She regularly runs workshops, teaching by herself and alongside colleagues at Lucis College. She is often invited as a speaker to spiritual-awareness centres and spiritualist churches and has demonstrated to sold-out theatre audiences. Claire has been accredited by the Institute of Spiritualist Mediums as a Registered and Approved Medium (RAM).

Answers
from
Heaven

Incredible True Stories
of Heavenly Encounters
and the Afterlife

THERESA CHEUNG
AND
CLAIRE BROAD

piatkus

PIATKUS

First published in Great Britain in 2017 by Piatkus

3 5 7 9 10 8 6 4

ISBN 978-0-349-41302-0

Typeset in Bembo by M Rules
Printed and bound in Great Britain by
Clays Ltd, St Ives plc

Papers used by Piatkus are from well-managed forests
and other responsible sources.

FSC
www.fsc.org
MIX
Paper from
responsible sources
FSC® C104740

Piatkus
An imprint of
Little, Brown Book Group
Carmelite House
50 Victoria Embankment
London EC4Y 0DZ

An Hachette UK Company
www.hachette.co.uk

Death is not extinguishing the light. It is only putting out the lamp because the dawn has come.

RABINDRANATH TAGORE

CONTENTS

ACKNOWLEDGEMENTS

So many people to thank for making this book happen, but I would especially like to thank my lovely agent, Lorella Belli, who introduced my writing to Piatkus and my editor, Zoe Bohm, whose open-mindedness, understanding and trust have been heavenly. I'd also like to extend heartfelt thanks to all the people who contributed stories to this book and my readers, whose support these last twenty years has truly been heaven-sent. The world needs spiritual books – books that remind us we are far more than the material – and everyone who seeks out or reads them is an earth angel inspiring others by their example. Thank you for being you.

And while we are on the subject of earth angels, this book, from Chapter Five onwards, simply couldn't have happened without the contribution of Claire Broad. As I explain in the Introduction, I truly feel that her involvement is a major step forward for spiritual writing, and I could not be more blessed to co-author this book with her as she is quite simply a most remarkable and honest medium.

Special thanks to Dr Julie Beischel for taking the time to write a fascinating essay in the Appendix about her incredible research at the Windbridge Institute and for writing the Foreword. Both Claire and I draw inspiration from the research of Dr Beischel and could not be more honoured.

Last, but by no means least, I would like to thank my beautiful family, Ray, Robert and Ruthie, for their love and support as I went into self-imposed exile to write this book. A special thank you also to my little angel dog Arnie who lights up my life every day and monitored the entire project from my lap as I researched and wrote.

NOTE FROM CLAIRE

Firstly, thank you to all those in the spirit world who have borne the brunt of my limited understanding and frustrations over the years, yet haven't faltered in their unconditional love. Thank you also to those pioneers of mediumship and spiritualism now in the spirit world themselves, but particularly Jean Dynan and Dennis Jones. To my husband, Martin, thank you for being my rock, and to my beautiful girls, I love you more than all the stars. To my parents and extended parents, you are golden. To Sheila Thomas, words cannot express my gratitude for your teachings, and to my lovely students in our circle who carry the light out into this world, I thank you. Huge thank you and gratitude must also go to Zoe Bohm for taking a leap of faith in me – it means so much; and thank you to everyone at Piatkus who brought this book to life. Finally, my biggest thanks go to Theresa Cheung who is a true kindred spirit. You gave me wings so I could fly. I shall be forever grateful.

FOREWORD

When Theresa and Claire approached me about writing the foreword to *Answers from Heaven*, I was honoured to contribute to their project. It was my pleasure to be included in an appendix in Theresa's previous book, *Heaven Called My Name*, and I embraced the opportunity to work with her again.

With this book, Theresa breaks new ground and takes her work in an innovative and exciting direction. A combination of the compelling and personal stories she has collected and Claire's unique insights drawn from her experiences as a medium, as well as a broad overview of the relevant afterlife research, *Answers from Heaven* provides readers with a holistic view of this fascinating and often misunderstood topic.

As a research scientist who has spent the last fifteen years of my professional career studying mediums, the process of mediumship and related afterlife topics (please see Appendix, p. 301, for details), I consider this book to be an important addition to the popular literature. It will help normalise afterlife experiences and, hopefully, bring understanding and comfort as we all ponder one of the primary questions about our human experience: what happens after we die?

Dr Julie Beischel

INTRODUCTION

VOICES FROM SPIRIT

*The song of the voice is sweet, but the song
of the heart is the pure voice of heaven.*

KHALIL GIBRAN

I should be dead. I was heading towards a junction in my car behind a lorry intending to turn left, but then a voice from outside my mind told me to take the right path. The voice was so clear and authoritative I obeyed it without question. If I had turned left, you wouldn't be reading this book. I would have headed into a pile-up that claimed the lives of three people in the cars directly behind the lorry I had been trailing.

This incident happened a good twenty years ago and marked the starting point of my absolute dedication to spreading the word that there is more to this life than meets the eye. I still to this day can't explain that voice or where it came from. Prior to that I had always been drawn to a life in spirit and believed in heaven – how could I not, as I was born into a family of psychics and spiritualists? – but I had never had a paranormal experience of my own that felt utterly convincing to me. (You can imagine my frustration growing up surrounded by family and friends who could hear heaven when I sensed nothing at all.)

During my teens and twenties I studied the psychic world in great depth. I had an insatiable appetite for knowledge of all things spiritual and became like a walking paranormal encyclopaedia on meditation, psychic-development classes and workshops, shamanism, paganism, mediumship, astrology, spells, tarot, numerology, crystals and so on. I studied absolutely everything and it was all deeply fascinating, but all this learning didn't give me what I truly craved – direct personal experience of the afterlife.

There were glimpses along the way – powerful dreams, flashes of intuition and moments of divine awareness – but nothing that gave me the confidence and the certainty that heaven was real. Eventually, as I settled into my life as an afterlife author collecting stories from people all over the world – and feeling truly blessed to be in the fortunate position to write about what I love: the search for meaning in life – I began to see, with the benefit of life experience and hindsight, that heaven had been speaking to my heart and gently pointing me towards my work as an afterlife author, just not in the way I'd thought it would. I'll talk about some of the unexpected ways heaven has whispered to me and continues to whisper to me later in the book.

I began to understand that I was intuitive, but not a

medium. I was sensitive rather than psychic, but this 'psychic block' was all for a reason. It is extremely rare to get a full-blown encounter with the other side to remove all doubt. The great majority of us fall into that 'hopeful' category, and because I'm in that category myself and don't claim any special powers I hope that many people can relate to my books. Developing psychic powers takes years of dedicated training, and as writing is my gift – I've written close to 100 books about the psychic world and personal development and am also a busy mother of two – something had to give. It's impossible to have and do it all in this life. My spirit made a choice and that choice, I can see now, was to be a voice or a scribe for spirit: a believer, but not a practitioner.

Thousands of people from all walks of life have sent me their astonishing stories of afterlife experiences and I have included lots of them in my many afterlife books. I've also openly shared my spiritual journey and my fears along the way when heaven seemed so far off. I've talked about being born into a family of psychics and spiritualists, my frustration at not being able to see, hear or sense heaven when it was something I wanted so much, my struggle with depression, my doubts and the glimmers of hope when heaven shone through – including my elation in my early thirties when heaven finally gave me an answer, or my own personal proof. Prior to that I hadn't been able to connect with heaven, but hearing the voice of my departed mother in spirit and that voice saving my life on a busy motorway was a revelation. It was a one-off experience, though, and the more it fades into the mists of time, the more I start second-guessing myself about it. I long to have that kind of experience again, but nothing as dramatic has happened since. This honest approach has resonated with my readers, suggesting there are a lot of people out there who, like me, are inclined to believe but don't have direct personal experience of the afterlife. I care deeply about my readers and pray that each book I write helps them to trust themselves a little more, so they can find their own way to talk to heaven.

I'm aware that my books have followed a certain pattern – offering comforting reassurance that even if you can't always see it, or it doesn't seem rational, heaven is real. I've followed this pattern because it is all that I know and who I am. I hope this book offers that comfort too, but I also want to take things a giant leap further. Let me explain ...

A GIANT LEAP

During my twenty-year afterlife writing career two criticisms have constantly resurfaced, the first being that there is no proof and everything I write about is anecdotal, the second being that I'm not a psychic or medium.

This book will tackle both those criticisms head-on. First, the lack of proof. The place to find proof is in the world of science. I'm an academic with a Master's in Theology and English from King's College, Cambridge University, but am no scientist. Until the end of 2015, whenever the 'no-proof' criticism came up I was resigned to just sighing and simply saying that it was all a matter of belief. However, in 2016 the universe gave me an incredible opportunity to show the world that science and spirit are not as far apart as we have been led to believe.

While setting up my website blog and Facebook page I started to post quotes, stories and sections from my books. Immediately, the sceptics waded in with their battle cry of 'Where is the science?' I just said that for those who believe or have had afterlife experiences no proof is necessary, but a part of me wanted to be able to reply in a more substantial manner.

About ten years ago I compiled some encyclopaedias about the psychic world and included sections on science, but I didn't focus too much on it as the science wasn't really there or, if it was, it wasn't accessible. I was conditioned to believe that when it came to matters paranormal, science and spirit were incompatible. I decided to find out if that was still the case.

It most certainly was not. I found out that science has made incredible advances, especially in the field of near-death experience (NDE) and consciousness research. A 2014 study on 2000 patients from hospitals all over the world by Dr Sam Parnia, a leading resuscitation expert from the University of Southampton in the UK, proved that consciousness – spirit or soul – can survive body and brain death by three minutes. The research was so definitive that another larger study is ongoing. Parnia does not believe in life after death, but the frequency of NDEs reported prompted him to study them scientifically and search for answers to the extraordinary stories his patients were returning from the brink with.

As far as research about paranormal experiences and psychic abilities is concerned, look no further than the Institute of Noetic Sciences (IONS) in the USA. A team of highly qualified and respected scientists, doctors and neuroscientists there is currently leading the world in consciousness research. Their studies clearly show that paranormal experiences at the very least deserve credible scientific investigation because people have had them since the beginning of time and continue to do so. All these stories need to be treated as data and not dismissed, and what the team at IONS are finding is that when studied scientifically, in a large majority of cases there is reason to believe the explanation could be paranormal.

I was so in awe of what I uncovered in the IONS research library I wanted all my readers to find out about it – to show them that their beliefs and experiences were not just a matter of faith or anecdotal. I wanted them to discover that even science is beginning to consider the very real possibility that the afterlife is real.

Inspired by IONS, I invited the science team there to post a series of videos on my Facebook page explaining their research on channelling, precognition, energy healing, telepathy, mind influencing matter and, of course, afterlife encounters or experiences. To my delight they agreed. The response from my readers to those videos was awesome, with close to half a million views in a week and lead IONS scientist Dr Radin's book *Supernormal* jumping to number one on Amazon UK's charts for science and religion. (In recognition of my efforts, IONS awarded me a landing page http://noetic.org/theresa-cheung, which I hope you will check out as there are three free gifts there for my readers.)

What that science-meets-spirit week on my page demonstrated was that there isn't enough awareness of the giant leaps being made by science right now when it comes to researching the paranormal and that there is a huge appetite to discover meaning in life separate from religion. Since then, I have made a point of referring people to the science currently out there in my books and features, as often as I can. But for now, let's narrow the focus of all this exciting new research down to afterlife communication.

THE SCIENCE OF AFTERLIFE ENCOUNTERS

What happens when a person dies? Is it possible to communicate with the spirit of a departed loved one? Are mediums genuine? I've been trying to answer these questions in my paranormal books and encyclopaedias for over twenty years, most prominently in my best-seller, *The Afterlife is Real*, and my last book, *Heaven Called My Name*, but until a year ago I never mentioned the issue of whether there was any real science or proof. I have had multiple stories from my readers over the years, but I simply didn't know if there was any research to support that anecdotal evidence. I now know that the science is out there – we just aren't hearing enough about it.

My journey from promoting a simple message of belief in paranormal experiences to pointing my readers in the direction of genuine science began when parapsychologist Dr Cal Cooper, senior lecturer at the University of Northampton, got in touch asking if I could contribute reader stories (I get sent thousands) to his PhD research database. Dr Cooper is studying bereavement and afterlife experiences, as well as dreams about departed loved ones. The conclusion he has drawn is that in approximately 85 per cent of cases those who experience afterlife signs are better able to manage their grief. This was something I knew already from the stories my readers send to me. I've also experienced for myself and seen the comfort afterlife encounters, signs, dreams and experiences provide for my readers.

But what about actual scientific proof of survival?

Dr Cooper's study demonstrates the positive effects of afterlife communication and shows it is being taken seriously by the academic community, but his research doesn't offer scientific proof of communication from the other side in the same way that the Windbridge Institute is committed to providing. In partnership with IONS, the Windbridge Institute is rigorously studying the accuracy of the information reported by mediums.

I was fortunate enough to get an opportunity to interview lead Windbridge researcher Dr Julie Beischel for my blog and last book, *Heaven Called My Name*. Dr Beischel forfeited a potentially lucrative career in the pharmaceutical industry to pursue scientific research of consciousness with mediums full time. She dreams of scientifically approved mediums working with the bereaved to ease the excruciating pain of grief. I share that dream and was delighted when she agreed to contribute to this book.

As with all research, more work needs to be done, but promising data collected by IONS and Windbridge under blind conditions demonstrates that some mediums (there will always be frauds out there) can report accurate or detailed information about a deceased person without any previous knowledge of that person or about the sitter. All possibility of cold reading is removed. (Telepathy could be an explanation, but that phenomenon is equally compelling – and another book, perhaps, as countless stories are sent to me about that too.) One standout study, published by IONS and Windbridge in 2015, involved fifty-eight readings from twenty mediums and provides perhaps the strongest evidence yet for anomalous information reception by mediums.

AN HONEST MEDIUM

So far, research cannot determine for sure if life after death exists, but it can most certainly offer a deeper understanding of the infinite possibilities of human consciousness. Although I was born into a family of spiritualists, over the years I had lost my faith in mediums, having encountered numerous frauds along the way, but working with IONS and inspired by Dr Beischel I was encouraged to go to a demonstration again. I had the good fortune – or perhaps heaven-sent guidance – to immediately encounter the real deal when I witnessed the work of medium Claire Broad. As I sat in the audience, the information coming through felt way beyond chance. I saw the healing it was bringing to even those who didn't get a personal message.

Like many genuine mediums who shun publicity for fear it will pollute their gift, catering to their ego, not the needs of those who come to them, Claire had been working quietly without great financial reward for years. I felt it was time to try to educate my readers about genuine mediumship – to remove the fear, stigma and misconceptions – and so I asked her to do some video posts on my Theresa Cheung Facebook author page explaining mediumship. She thought long and deeply about whether she wanted to do this, as her first inclination was not to step into the limelight, but then – as she will explain later in the book – she felt a deep calling to spread the word. She agreed and her posts proved extremely popular. I took yet another leap of faith and asked her to collaborate on this book with me.

Claire's honesty and energy impressed me greatly when I went to her demonstration. Here at last was a medium who wasn't afraid to admit to a crowded room eager for news from the other side that sometimes she gets it wrong or a message doesn't come through. She compared mediumship to the Internet: sometimes there is flow and it all works; other times it gets stuck and you get frustration. In addition to her honesty what also struck me was how 'normal' – for want of a better word – she was. She didn't look like a medium or the medium persona that the media and movies have created. She was a lovely, extremely intelligent, fun-loving and eloquent woman.

Alongside working as a medium for twenty years, Claire had a promising career in the advertising industry, working at Leo Burnett and Disney, and is a happily married mother of two. In other words, she is the last person you would expect to be a medium, but a medium Claire most certainly is, as the messages that came through from the other side for an audience she knew absolutely nothing about were astonishingly accurate. She insisted that she was there for one reason only: to offer evidence of survival. The accuracy of what she was saying blew me away. How, for example, did she know that someone she was drawn to was adopted, or that someone else had just been diagnosed with cancer but was keeping the news hidden from family and friends? The 'How could she know that?' list could go on. As I sat in the audience I could see the comfort she was bringing not just to the three or four who were lucky enough to get a message, but to everyone present. They were witnessing proof of survival.

Later, when I spoke to Claire and asked her about the hows and whys of mediumship, she just laughed and said she really didn't know and hoped that one day science would be able to explain it to her. She also, again with refreshing honesty, told me that she has incredible doubts herself and often wishes science would explain what happens to her and why spirits talk to her. She said she sometimes even wished that she didn't have the gift because her life would be much easier, but from the age of four she has repeatedly heard voices from the other side. She told me that she feels called upon by spirit to offer evidence of survival, and if she hasn't been able to offer a client proof of survival by telling them something about a deceased person that she couldn't possibly know, she will offer a refund. She said drawing a blank does happen, but fortunately, more often than not, something valuable does come through and the many testimonies available online from people she has read for bear witness to that. She also said that she truly wished she could find a way to educate more people about mediumship, as so many have the wrong idea about it, but she didn't know how.

This was an 'ah-ha' moment. There I was, feeling a bit stuck with my writing about the afterlife after close to twenty years and wanting to get people talking and thinking about spirit in a new way. And there was Claire, feeling stuck with her mediumship after twenty years of dedicated work and not really sure how to move things forward for the greater good. In other words, I'd become a best-selling afterlife author, but not been able to offer my readers direct experience of psychic powers or an explanation of mediumship, as I've only caught sporadic glimpses in my life, whereas Claire had had a successful career as a medium, but was feeling frustrated in that she wasn't able to get her life-changing message of proof of survival after death out to significant numbers of people.

I knew in an instant that life was presenting me with the real deal – an honest medium – and I asked Claire to collaborate on this book. She would be a perfect voice for mediumship in the modern age. We both in our different ways felt that this book was meant to be and jumped for joy when our editor at Piatkus felt the same, taking yet another leap of faith in giving our joint proposal for this book the green light.

ABOUT THIS BOOK

So what's coming up in this book?

Using the true stories of ordinary people who have had paranormal experiences, or clients who have received proof of survival through a reading with Claire, we will outline the various ways that heaven is trying to answer our prayers and dying to offer us comfort. To protect their identity and to ensure confidentiality, the names of the people you will read about have all been changed, but the content is an accurate representation of their experiences.

Punctuated throughout with insights from both of our spiritual lives, as well as channelled wisdom from Claire, the book provides spiritual answers to some of life's eternal questions. For example: why is there suffering? What happens when we die? What is heaven like? And so on. Through reading this book, it is hoped that you will lose some of your fear of death, be able to tell if heaven is trying to contact you and see that the gap between science and spirit is closing fast. It is also hoped that you will see that mediumship is a message of eternal love and nothing to be feared, and that it is possible to receive answers to life's questions from the other side, either directly – as is the case for me – or through a genuine medium, like Claire.

It is very much a book of two halves.

Part One is written by me, Theresa, and focuses solely on direct communication with heaven without the need for a medium. The first chapter explains what an afterlife message or sign is and outlines the most common ones. Chapter Two looks at afterlife visions and dreams and how they also offer answers from above. The next two chapters narrate and discuss true stories of partners, family members, children and friends communicating from the other side, including afterlife communication from beloved pets and animals.

Part Two is written by Claire and focuses on mediumship. She tells her own story, shares client stories, offers advice about visiting a medium and tries to explain what she senses, feels, hears and sees in readings. Chapter Five explores how and why loved ones in spirit communicate. Chapter Six focuses on client readings where spirit answer questions and Chapter Seven is all about spirit guides – the wisdom brought through by them and how to connect with them. In Chapter Eight Claire answers a series of commonly asked questions about visiting a medium, while Chapter Nine stresses once again the life-changing benefits of believing in an afterlife and how you may access your own answers from heaven.

The book closes with a few healing words from myself, reminding you that you are a spiritual being having a human experience and that however you may decide to connect to heaven, the afterlife is real.

But the heavenly insight doesn't stop there, as the Appendix is a rich resource of suggested reading, bereavement with spirit support, mediumship or development training and online information, afterlife research and support and a link to online free gifts. You can also find out the best way to get in touch with myself or Claire directly.

Although there are definitely two perspectives offered in this book, it will become clear that neither is preferable to the other. They are simply different. If visiting a medium isn't for you, then it is still possible to have a direct link to heaven. Conversely, if you do choose to visit a medium, you can still find ways to hear heaven for yourself. But whether you decide to visit a medium or not after reading this book, it is our sincere hope that what you read will open your mind to the many different ways that heaven can send us answers and help you see that all of these ways can be equally magical and comforting.

AN ANSWER FROM HEAVEN

I can think of no better way to end this Introduction and set the heartfelt tone for the chapters that follow than this poem channelled by Claire. She wrote it after her beloved aunt died in 2009 – a sad passing that was followed by seven other close family members dying over the next five years. Through this painful period of grieving Claire's knowledge of the spirit world kept her strong. She knew in her heart they were still close by.

One afternoon, she thought deeply about her aunt and sent out her love. A thought came to her mind: I wonder what she would say to me now? No sooner had she finished that thought, than the answer came straight back to her. It came with an energy of its own, fully formed, and felt like it was instantly being downloaded into her mind. She knew she had to write it down, and with no time to find pen and paper she grabbed an old envelope and make-up pencil and scribbled away.

When she had finished, she read it back and could not believe what she had channelled from above. She found that the words spoke straight to her as truth; she had the answer to her question about what her beloved aunt would say to her now.

Over the years, these words have continued to give many people great comfort and when I posted the poem on my Facebook author page the reaction was beautiful. Here is that poem – an answer from heaven speaking with love directly to your heart:

What I would say to you now?

Even though you can't see or feel me
Know I AM there with you.
Though you will doubt this,
Know I never doubt you.
When you are lost, I shall shine a light and if you
       do not recognise it,
I'll work tirelessly to help you see it.
When it's hard to make a decision,
Think about what I might do, have clarity, be
       guided.
Though you cannot feel my kiss,
I'll kiss your spirit.
Though you cannot feel my hugs,
I'll place my arms around you.
When you are tired in life or have had enough of
       pain,
SHOUT out to me, I'll be listening.
When you feel lonely, STOP ... LISTEN ...
       FEEL

My energy IS there.
For there is no place or time I cannot be,
I love you now as I have always loved you, if not
  more.
And, while we are apart, I'll think of you often
  and always
Celebrate me, for I celebrate you
I miss you. I love you.

*To the well-organised mind, death is
  but the next great adventure.*

J. K. ROWLING

PART ONE

PART ONE

CHAPTER ONE

MESSAGES FROM THE OTHER SIDE

Those we loved never go away, they walk beside us
every day. Unseen, unheard, but always near.

ANONYMOUS

Although you may not be able to 'hear' or 'see' the afterlife, this doesn't mean it isn't real.

Have you ever suddenly changed your mind and done something amazing you never thought you would? That's spirit inspiring you.

Have you ever strongly sensed that someone was behind you, only to turn around and there is no one there? That's an angel watching over you.

Have you ever felt completely lost and then, for reasons you can't explain, everything changes and you are filled with a sense of direction and purpose? That's heaven sending you a message.

Have you ever felt alone and then a gentle breeze or a beautiful sunset or a smile or a stunning coincidence or just a simple change of heart from the inside out fills you with love and hope? Yes, spirit is reaching out to you again.

Have you ever lost your faith and doubted the existence of heaven and then rediscovered it when all hope felt lost? That's how spirit works.

SPIRIT AT WORK

In recent years I have on many occasions felt lost and alone and fiercely doubted that heaven is real. Sometimes there is a personal trigger for that doubt. For example, things in my life aren't turning out as planned or I'm disappointed or hurt in some way, but more often than not the trigger isn't personal but related to what I see happening in the world around me. Even as I type this, news is breaking of yet another inexplicable crime – in this case, the brutal murder of a seven-year-old girl.

My heart flies out to the mother and father and family of that innocent child, but I also can't help but compare this horrific reality with the message of a spiritual life being one of unconditional love, light, beauty and joy. Where were the love, light, beauty and joy for this angel baby? Why would spirit allow this to happen? I try to shut the questions down, but the harder I try the more they scream at me. A seed of doubt has been sown and I am helpless to do anything about it. And as the doubts gather strength, my belief in the message I am trying to send the world weakens. I've devoted my entire life to researching and writing about the very real possibility that heaven exists in this life and the next. Yet almost every day the reality of hell on earth feels more likely. Perhaps those who don't believe in heaven have got it right?

I've got an open mind and feel it is important for me as a spiritual writer to be aware of the beliefs of sceptics and atheists. I want to understand where they are coming from and, more often than not these days, I can actually see their point. I recently read a book called *The God Impulse* by Kevin Nelson, which argued that belief in heaven is simply something hard-wired into our DNA not because it is real but because it makes us feel better. According to Nelson there is absolutely no proof of an afterlife, but believing in spirit is something to be encouraged because it can bring comfort and strength and help us cope with grief. The argument that heaven is no more than a biological impulse is a logical one and on days when the voices of doubt are screaming at me I wonder if there might be something to it.

I'm hoping you haven't been too shocked by my frank admission that I sometimes have great doubts about the existence of heaven. And you may wonder, after what I have just said, how it is possible for me to still fiercely champion the voice of spirit in the way I do and have done in my books and, more recently, online through my Facebook page, where visitors draw comfort and hope from my conviction that heaven is real. Admitting now that sometimes I lose that conviction could have devastating consequences, but I want to reassure you that if I ever reached the point where it felt dishonest to write my heaven books and run my page I would stop.

I've been writing about heaven for over twenty years and during that time I have had pauses but I have never stopped believing completely. This is because on every occasion, just when I feel that enough is enough, I see the light again. Time and time again, whenever darkness and doubt threaten to overwhelm me, something always happens to convince me that I am on the right path and my doubt isn't the end but an awakening, the darkness before the dawn. I will have a vivid dream of a departed loved one that is just too realistic to dismiss. An afterlife sign will reassure me. I will receive an amazing story from one of my readers. I will read about something uplifting in the news. Or there will be a sudden and inexplicable shift within me that I know deep down is coming from spirit. Heaven calls out and my faith is renewed and stronger than before.

With amazing clarity in those moments of absolute conviction I see that I am trying to understand heaven in human terms. Why bad things happen to good people is something I will not ever understand in this life, and for good reason – because if I knew all the answers I would stop evolving spiritually and become complacent in the spiritual and human sense. For example, we know that a woman screams in pain during childbirth, but we aren't too concerned because we know it is because a baby is about to be born. In much the same way, if we knew why there was suffering, we would probably become equally nonchalant about it.

My periods of darkness and uncertainty also remind me that there is tremendous power in doubt because every time I doubt I am forced to try and find new answers or insights and in the process I do what I was born to do – I grow some more in spirit. I am reminded that doubt is a powerful spiritual awakening and that I am here on earth not to go to heaven but to grow to heaven. Sometimes growth, or shedding old skins, hurts.

There is always a wonderful return to love after periods of doubt. I see clearly that even when I doubt heaven is real it is very much alive within and all around me and drawing me closer. Like everything in life, I know that this beautiful clarity is temporary and in due course, I will probably feel lost and confused again, but I trust myself enough now to know that however hard it gets, and however much I doubt, I *will* pull through. The pain and sense of isolation will pass. I will continue to grow in spirit even when I doubt.

AFTERLIFE SIGNS

One of the most compelling ways heaven pulls me back from the brink during times of personal crisis is through afterlife signs. These aren't typically spectacular ones involving visions and voices – full-blown afterlife encounters can and do happen, but I must point out they are extremely rare. I include some stories later in this book that are very dramatic, but I want to start with subtle signs. I want to do this because we don't tend to hear as much about these or even not notice them, which is a tragedy because these are the ones we are far more likely to experience.

None of the people in the stories in this chapter actually saw a departed loved one or celestial being complete with halo and wings, but they remain absolutely convinced they received an afterlife message. And not only did it bring them great comfort, it also made them feel happier, stronger and more magical than they believed themselves to be. After reading this chapter, I hope that when heaven sends you one of these subtle signs – and trust me heaven will, time and time again – you will notice it and recognise it for what it is and not dismiss or ignore it.

What is an afterlife sign?

Before you can start to notice these subtle signs from the afterlife, you need to understand what they are. Afterlife signs, messages or 'calling cards' are direct, personal contact with the afterlife without visiting a medium like Claire as a go-between. They can offer incredible reassurance that death is not the end. As mentioned above, many afterlife signs can easily be missed or ignored because they are so subtle. This is tragic because they provide such inspiration. It's a bit like getting a letter from some who loves you deeply and knows you well, offering you the most profound, potentially life-changing reassurance and advice, but never reading it. Signs are deeply personal. Having collected thousands of stories from my readers, I'm tempted to say that literally anything that speaks to you on a personal level can be an afterlife sign if it makes you feel that a loved one is close by or a higher power is at work.

To give an example, Jade wrote to me a week after her beloved aunt died. They had been very close and she missed her greatly, but the most absurd thing gave her comfort and that was a box of tissues! Jade's aunt had always insisted on a particular shade of pale purple tissues that weren't too easy to get hold of. Feeling tearful in her flat one evening, Jade reached out to grab a tissue and could not believe her eyes. The tissue was pale purple – not quite the same shade her aunt had stipulated in her own home, but purple all the same. Jade always purchased white tissues as her boyfriend insisted on it, so this felt impossible but incredibly comforting. For the first time since her aunt's death Jade slept like a baby and felt so much better the next morning. But the story gets even more surreal, as the next morning, when she went to blow her nose, the tissues were no longer purple but white.

Jade asked me if she had been imagining it, but I asked her to tell me how seeing the purple tissue had made her feel. She told me that it made her feel as if her aunt was right beside her and wanted her to use the purple tissue to dry her tears. I told her that there was her answer from heaven.

This is the only 'heaven-spoke-to-me-through-a-tissue' story I have received, but I've included it to illustrate my point that it is impossible to generalise about afterlife signs. They can quite literally be anything. The common denominator is that you just know your departed loved one is close by and it brings you tremendous comfort. Don't ever dismiss your experience as chance or imagination. At the end of this chapter I explain in more detail why.

The top ten afterlife signs

Although, as I've said, almost anything can be an afterlife sign, I have found from the many stories sent to me over the years that some are more common or more likely to occur than others. Here are my top ten in no particular order, with a few stories to illustrate them.

1. Invisible sensations
Yes, the first afterlife sign I'm going to highlight is invisible! It's something you can't see, but you can feel it touch you. Interestingly, Claire tells me that during her demonstrations of mediumship, as well as hearing and seeing spirit clairvoyantly she also experiences these invisible sensations. Nothing illustrates this better than this story sent to me by Mick:

Kissed by an angel

I lost my daughter two years ago. She was only seventeen months and it hit my marriage really hard. So hard that my wife and I split up. I missed my daughter terribly when she passed, but after splitting from my wife the pain was unbearable. I felt so alone. I'm not ashamed to say – as I think tears in both men and women are a sign of strength not weakness – that many nights I would cry myself to sleep. I started to leave the TV on at night so that I would not feel alone as I'd hear the sound of voices.

Ten days after my wife moved out I remember waking up in the early hours of the morning and the TV wasn't on. There was no reassuring sound. I panicked, but then I felt someone holding my hand. My hand was outside the duvet. The hand was tiny and it felt electric and warm. I was wide awake at that point, but I pretended to be asleep as the tiny hand in mine was so comforting. Then I felt a gentle kiss on my hand. My daughter used to kiss my hand when I held hers. I knew it was her. I felt her all around me. I drifted off to a peaceful sleep and in the morning when I woke up I knew my daughter was alive somewhere and always would be with me. It is the most comforting feeling.

This happened two years ago and I can honestly say it helped me manage my grief. A colleague at work recently lost his teenage son in a road accident and my experience has really helped me help him. After my daughter died I thought I would never see or touch her again but now whenever I want to I close my eyes and I remember her tiny little hand in mine. It's blissful. In those moments it feels like she is alive again.

All the people who have sent me stories about invisible hands or kisses or other gentle touches know it wasn't their imagination and that they were experiencing something out of this world. How did they know it? They knew because even though they couldn't explain it, the experience made them feel better.

Perhaps the most powerful way this happens is when there is no physical sensation at all – just a feeling of bliss from the inside out, as Samaira describes so perfectly in her story:

Driving through

I visit my husband's grave every week. He's been gone for twenty months. It is the only thing I could think to do to ease the pain. It does help, but I had an experience which I hope you will share that gave me even greater hope and comfort.

It happened when I was driving home from work one day. I passed a Burger King and it made me think of my husband as he loved Burger King. I didn't — mainly because I'm a veggie — but I loved seeing him happy, so just put up with it and had a veggie burger. I was hungry so decided in his honour to have a veggie burger. The moment I stopped my car and turned the ignition off I got this incredible feeling of love. It started right inside my chest and spread all over my body. It was beautiful. It was like having a hot chocolate on a cold winter's day. I shall never forget it. It is my proof that my husband walks in spirit beside me and the love we shared doesn't die.

2. Scent

This next subtle sign is invisible too. Heaven will often speak to you through a scent that is either instantly recognisable to you or completely unfamiliar. In either case there is no logical explanation or source for the scent. It tends to unexpectedly appear and then vanish just as mysteriously, but it leaves the experiencer with a profound sense of inner calm. Usually, the scent is something that you can connect with a departed loved one, such as their perfume or cigar smoke, but I have had many stories sent to me too about the unexpected scent of flowers, typically roses or other beautiful scents — like vanilla, jasmine, lavender, mint and strawberries — when there is no recognisable source. This doesn't surprise me as our brains process scents in the limbic system (the system of nerves and networks in the brain concerned with controlling basic emotions) in the same way as we process intuitive or psychic feelings and thoughts. Scents are also powerful because they trigger memories. Here's Darren's story:

Warm bread

The night before my grandmother died I smelled a strong scent of warm bread when I woke up at about 5 a.m. one morning. My grandmother lived over 200 miles away and what I smelled was exactly how visiting her cottage felt when I was a young boy. There was no explanation for this scent as I was living in student digs at the time and we all existed on takeaways and beans on toast. Nobody baked bread and the kitchens were locked at 10 p.m.

I knew my grandmother was ill, but she had been for several months and doctors had said she wasn't close to death and could well pull through, so I wasn't actively thinking of her at the time. A few hours later, when I was on my way to college, Dad rang to tell me she had passed. It's been months now since she died, but I still tend to get a random smell of warm bread. It tends to happen most when I am alone or in my room, and I know it is definitely not coming from somewhere else or outside. I know it is not someone baking bread. I feel as if my grandmother is trying to let me know that she is close by. Sometimes the scent is so strong, especially when I'm feeling low or lonely, and I wonder if she is trying to tell me something specific, but I haven't figured that out yet.

I wrote back to tell Darren that his grandmother was and is telling him something very specific. She is telling him how much she loves him and trying to reassure him through her love of baking that he is never alone in spirit.

3. Appliances

When I first started collecting afterlife stories I would receive accounts of lights flickering, doorbells ringing, jewellery boxes playing or clocks inexplicably ticking again after years of malfunction or not working at all. Indeed, the phenomenon of clocks stopping when a loved passes over is incredibly well documented. Spirit adapts itself to the age we live in, though, and increasingly today the stories I am being sent are more likely to be about TVs, computers, laptops, phones and mobiles sending texts or messages for which there is no rational explanation. Nothing illustrates this better than Jenny's story:

Call from heaven

One Saturday morning I slept in longer than usual. I'd been working late the night before and needed to catch up on my sleep. My mobile rang and I ignored it, thinking whoever it was would leave a voice message. Five minutes later it rang again. I was awake now, but when I reached for my phone it stopped ringing. I fell back into bed and after about a minute it rang again. This time I was ready for it and I answered straightaway. It was my father. I was delighted to hear from him. I loved the sound of his rich and warm voice – always have. He asked me how I was doing and when I told him I was working too hard he reminded me that nobody on their deathbed remembers how much time they put in at work.

What they think about is the connections they made and if they and those they loved were happy. I laughed and asked him how he knew all that and he said, 'Trust me, Daisy' (his nickname for me) 'I know.' Then he said he loved me and always would and hung up.

When I put my phone down it felt like I had just done the ice-bucket challenge. I felt a profound sense of shock and wonder that I had not thought to question the call. You see my father had died six, yes, six years earlier. Then it hit me again. My father had died six years ago that day. I had completely forgotten it was the anniversary of his death. Wow!

I called my brother and he said I was imagining it. He told me to check my phone records. I did and at 7.05 and 7.12 and then again at 7.14 I had received calls from a number listed as 'Unknown'.

Of course, there could be a rational explanation in that Jenny was dreaming and the calls were spam calls, but the perfection of the timing speaks otherwise. For Jenny this was a phone call from heaven. Even if a rational explanation could be found, the call felt real for Jenny and gave her much-needed hope and comfort – and anything that does that is spirit-sent in my book.

William certainly believes his call was from heaven:

A life-saving call

My lovely daughter, Claire, had been very ill. I was in my car driving when my mobile rang. I stopped my car and looked at my phone, but there was no number showing, no name or anything to say I'd had a call. I then thought it perhaps might be Claire trying to get hold of me for something. I wasn't alarmed; I just thought I'd go over to her house and see if she maybe wanted some shopping.

I got to Claire's, and walked into her house to find her doubled up in agony on the living-room floor. I rang 999 and as a result, she had a life-saving operation that night. It turned out she had a burst ulcer. My wife and I sat in a room all night at the hospital not knowing if Claire would come through it. The doctors told us it could go either way.

Mercifully, she came through the operation and during the following years regained her health and is now doing fine, but if my phone had not rung while I was driving I would not have gone to her house and found her. Claire did not call me. I'm convinced she wouldn't have survived if my phone hadn't rung while I was driving. That call came from heaven without a shadow of a doubt.

4. Sounds

Sounds are a truly beautiful and extremely common afterlife sign. Sometimes music is heard inside a person's head that they have never heard before, but it is mesmerising. More commonly, you may hear a familiar song or piece of music playing that reminds you of someone departed or reassures you that you are not alone, but being guided from above. In her demonstrations, Claire sometimes hears familiar songs and music associated with a departed loved one. This next story from Wendy illustrates this beautifully:

Stranger in Paradise

When my grandfather died a few months after my grand-mother I was really upset. They had been more like parents than grandparents to me and we were very close. My mum wasn't around much and my dad was never around, so it was left to me to clear out their house. I found it really upsetting and could only manage an hour or two at a time.

One day, I was feeling particularly emotional, so I decided to have a cup of tea before I got started. I thought it would be a good idea to put the radio on as some music might distract me. I switched on the radio and the song 'Stranger in Paradise' was playing. It's a beautiful song, but not at all recent, so it was out of the ordinary to hear it playing on a radio station. But what made it really speak to me was that it was my grandparents' song. They had played it at their wedding. It was very special to them and was popular when they first met. I can remember them playing it and getting all misty-eyed with each other and my grandmother humming it as she did the household chores when I was a small girl. You could say this was just a fabulous coincidence, but for me it was much more than that. It helped dry my tears of sadness and replace them with happy memories. Wherever they are, I'm sure my grandmother and my grandfather wanted me to hear it.

Another commonly reported afterlife sign involving sound is a high-pitched hum in the ear. (This gentle and short-lived high-pitched hum should not be confused with the painful and constant grating of tinnitus; if the latter is the case, please visit your doctor.) If you unexpectedly hear that sound, which typically only lasts under a minute, instead of rubbing your ear to make it stop, take a moment to relax and think of it as heaven downloading sublime love and wisdom to you. This often happens to me when I am working on my afterlife books, in particular when I write up an achingly beautiful or inspiring story. It is almost as if heaven is singing along as I work.

5. Words

The afterlife can speak through the written word. Books with the perfect advice for you may appear at the ideal time – magazine features too, online articles or even posters, car-registration plates or T-shirt designs. Or perhaps you may overhear a conversation, hear something on the radio or see something on TV or online that offers the right advice, mentions something that speaks directly to your heart or reminds you of something a departed loved one would say. Don't dismiss this as coincidence. In the next chapter I discuss 'coincidence' in more depth and share several stories that show that it truly is the language heaven speaks.

As you're reading this book I'd like you to think about how it came into your hands. Was it was given to you by a friend or relative or loved one, or did you go into a bookshop and were somehow drawn to it, even though you had no intention of buying an angel book. Or perhaps you literally stumbled across it or found it left behind on a Tube, bus or train. I love it when people tell me about the 'surprising' and unusual ways one of my angel books, or books by other angel or spirit authors, ended up in their hands, and I don't feel surprised at all. Believe me, the fact that you are reading this book now means it found its way into your hands for a reason. Just like a white feather, a cloud, a butterfly or a coin it is an afterlife calling card and you were guided to it and are meant to read it.

6. Objects

This category of afterlife signs involves inanimate objects moving or appearing at the perfect time to offer comfort and hope that a loved one is nearby. The object can literally be anything of personal significance to you, but those most commonly reported are pictures, coins and jewellery. This story from Lucy involves all three:

Three wishes

I'd just come back from a trip to Ireland with my husband. It had been a break spending time with my family who lived there; the only sadness was that my mum wasn't feeling very well and had not been able to leave hospital to spend time with us.

When we got home we unpacked and went to bed fairly swiftly. Around 2 a.m. I woke up to the sound of a gentle thud. I switched the night light on and saw that a picture of my mother with me and my two brothers had fallen from the wall and slipped down the back of a chest of drawers. My husband joked that it was my mother making her presence felt because she couldn't spend time with us in Ireland.

The next morning when I got up I pulled the chest of

drawers out to pick up the picture. Fortunately, it hadn't smashed. Just as I was about to push the drawers back I noticed that there was a pound coin there, so I picked it up and smiled. Mum always used to tell me that finding coins was a sign heaven was close by and it would be a great day, so I picked it up and put it in my jewellery box. When I tried to close the jewellery box something was stopping it from shutting properly. It was a chunky pearl necklace, a gift from my mother to me on my fiftieth. I pulled it out and decided to wear it.

At that moment I got a call. It was from my brother. His voice sounded weak as he told me that my mother had passed away in the night. It took a while to sink in, but I'm convinced my husband was right and that the picture and then the coin and then the necklace were my mother in spirit making her presence felt.

7. Intuition

Sometimes departed loved ones can speak to us through a feeling of just knowing or intuition. This is when you simply get a hunch about something or someone and later you realise that your hunch was spot on. If you follow your intuition, you feel deeply grateful, but if you ignore it and find out later it was right all along, you regret that you didn't trust yourself more. It's often hard to tell the difference between intuition that is heaven-sent and fear that is very human, but in general intuition is gentle, positive, direct and energising, whereas fear often expresses itself through harsh and long-winded self-criticism. In short, intuition doesn't require endless explanations or make you feel bad about yourself. You just know. Fear specialises in debate, uncertainty and insecurity.

I'm hoping this next story sent to me by Naomi will illustrate the difference between knowing when your intuition is speaking and when it is fear doing the talking:

STOP

I love nothing more than spending a day cycling to new places. I don't cycle for speed or as a sport – more because it takes me to beautiful places and I love the freedom and the fresh air.

One Saturday afternoon I decided to try a route my friend at work had recommended. She told me there were some very hard climbs, but then when you reached the high point it was all downhill and absolutely glorious scenery.

My friend was right. The initial climb was tough – very tough – and when I got to the top I felt a bit weak, so I got off my bike for a bit to rest my legs and have a drink. It was so beautiful up there I stayed a bit longer than I perhaps should have done, as even though it was March it was getting dark fairly quickly. I got on my bike and started to cycle downhill; cycle isn't really the word, as I just sat there whizzing down at speed. There was nobody around, so I pulled off my helmet and let out a 'woo hoo' or two as I felt the breeze hit my hair. I must have been about a third of the way down when I got this incredibly strong feeling that I needed to STOP.

I immediately pulled on my brakes and got off my bike to see if there was anyone behind me. There wasn't. I walked for a while feeling puzzled and a couple of cars drove past. With the cars safely past I got on my bike again and started freeriding down. There it was again: that overwhelming feeling that I needed to stop. I really didn't want to stop as it was such a breeze hurtling down the hill, but it was impossible to ignore.

Getting off my bike I had this powerful sense that my aunt was close by. I can't explain it, but as I walked down the hill it was like she was walking right beside me. I think I got my love of the outdoors from my aunt as when she was alive we used to go for long walks and talk about life, the universe and everything.

I'm so glad I did walk down because within a few feet of getting off my bike there was a sharp bend and then a series of massive potholes in the road. Of course, there's no way of telling whether I would have spotted them in time to avoid them, as by now it was dusk and visibility was not great. If I had gone over those potholes at the speed I was travelling without my helmet on I may not be writing this story to you today. You never know what is around the next turning.

If Naomi hadn't listened to her intuition here she is right that the consequences could have been deadly. Her story shows that sometimes heaven can speak to us through a powerful inner sense whose sight reaches further than our eyes can.

Mandy shudders to think what might have happened if *she* had not listened to her intuition:

Front-seat driver

My husband, myself and our one-year-old son had been to see my parents, about a forty-minute drive away. On leaving, instead of placing my baby in his baby capsule I decided to hold him in the front of the car with me to go home. I have never done this – apart from the illegality of it, it is certainly not a safe practice. I have no idea why I did it, but I just had this overwhelming sense that I had to. I thank heaven I listened to my intuition because about seven minutes after leaving my parents' place Glen stopped breathing. Thankfully, we were only about one minute from the local hospital. They got him breathing again, but he was admitted to hospital for four days. He had had a febrile convulsion and his temperature would not return to normal. Had I placed him in his capsule it would have been too late to revive him as we still had another thirty minutes or so to go and we would have just assumed he was sleeping the whole trip. I am forever grateful for the way it turned out that night.

The next story, from Sheila, also shows the power of intuition at work and how important and healing it is to simply trust it.

The other side

My sister Joan died last year, but I swear I heard her speak loud and clear to me. I was in my daughter's garden preparing to plant some potted flowers and all of a sudden I heard Joan say to me, 'Plant the flowers on the other side.' It sounded just like her and was her tone of voice. I looked around and there was nobody there. Then I heard her voice again. This time she said, 'Don't plant your flowers there. Plant them on the other side.' I rubbed my ears and wondered if I was going nuts, but thought I may as well go with it and went to the other side of the garden. As I did, I heard my sister laugh. I planted the flowers and had to give it to my sister — they did look beautiful where she had suggested. When I finished I heard her say: 'The best side, you'll see.'

Hearing my sister speak like that freaked me out a bit, so I went inside to have a cup of tea. I reasoned to myself that it was simply my imagination and I remembered how when we were young Joan and I used to have great fun playing in our garden. It made me smile.

When my daughter came back home I was still in the garden. She had my little granddaughter with her. The two of them noticed the new flower display immediately and shrieked with delight. It turned out that my granddaughter's beloved hamster had died last week and she had been really upset about it. Nobody had told me, but you guessed it — they had buried the hamster where I had planted the flower display. It was a beautiful moment for all three of us.

My daughter asked me how I knew and I just shrugged it off as coincidence. I didn't tell her I had heard a voice from the best side telling me where to plant the flowers as she might worry about me hearing voices. I'm so glad I can tell you and your readers because you will see that something awesome was going on here.

As psychic coach and intuition expert Jo Angel (see Appendix, p. 326) explains in her story below, intuition is a superpower we all have but don't necessarily trust – because we don't trust ourselves enough.

We need to talk about Jenny

I often get a gut feeling about a person, place or relationship straightaway. Over the years I have learned to trust that gut feeling. Here's one example.

About fifteen years ago, I moved house away from my circle of friends. After I moved, one of my friends told me all about this woman she had met and how she was such a great spiritual person, etc. Her name was Jenny and I heard only marvellous stories about her.

My kids had gone to stay with friends near our old house and had met Jenny while they were there. They also came home raving about how lovely she was. I was really looking forward to meeting her and a part of me wished I had not moved so far away as she sounded so much fun. She also sounded incredibly supportive, as my friend had hit some financial troubles and was going through a very hard time. Jenny was on hand to help and lent her money and looked after her children so she could take an extra job.

A few months later, they were all coming to visit for the day and I was so excited to spend time with my friends and finally meet Jenny. But when they arrived and I gave Jenny a hug, I had the strangest feeling. It was as if my entire body was telling me to be very careful of her. This shocked me as

I always look for the positive in people. My face and body language changed a little and I had to pull myself together quickly before the others noticed.

We were all catching up and had a nice little party atmosphere going, but my eyes were being constantly drawn to Jenny, who was chatting away as normal. I was so confused. Was I jealous? Had I turned into a spiteful person? I had quite the battle going on in my head. My intuition was sending me a warning sign.

When it was time for everyone to leave I waved my goodbyes, closed the door, turned around and leaned against it. My family were looking at me strangely. 'I do not trust that woman at all,' I said. I was met with confusion as to how I could have come to that conclusion. My children adored 'Auntie Jenny' as they called her. But nobody was more confused than me.

A couple of months went by and, to cut a long story short, a few things came to light. Jenny had been stealing my friend's money all along, and then lending her money that in effect was her own. She had been feeding my friend's small child and pushing food into her mouth to make her sick – so much so that she had started to refuse to eat food. She had been trying to sabotage her small business and then been the one to save the day, etc. The list was horrendous and the police had to get involved.

I knew it! I had not gone mad, but my instinct that day had been screaming 'Be careful!' as soon as I set eyes on her. I had received this information through my intuition and this was a powerful lesson for me to not doubt it or myself.

Can you remember a time when your intuition has been so powerful as to warn you of something?

Also belonging in this intuition category is the sensation that someone is watching you or standing or walking behind you when there is no one there. If this happens to you, first of all check that you are safe and that you aren't indeed being followed – but if you find that nobody is there, don't panic or think you are losing it. Quite the opposite: what you have sensed intuitively is heaven watching over you and that is a beautiful thing, so relax and feel only gratitude and love.

8. Nature

This is perhaps my favourite category of afterlife signs and every time I read another story it feels like the first time and I'm filled with a sense of joy and expansiveness. There are infinite possibilities for heaven to use natural signs to speak to you, but the most common involve feathers, clouds and rainbows. Here are a few stories to illustrate how these signs can appear:

Always beside you

I was beside myself with grief at my mother's funeral. I didn't think I could get through it and was thinking of leaving, but then I saw this brilliant white feather on the floor beside my feet. I picked it up and when I did I felt stronger. The tears were still there, but with the feather in my hand I was able to get through it. I've still got the feather today. It isn't quite so white and shiny as it was when I found it in the church, but to me it is the most beautiful thing I own. It's Mum telling me she is always beside me. I've found other feathers since, but none as beautiful as the one in the church.

My sign

My daughter died at the age of nine. Part of my heart died that day too, but something happened that did give me hope that one day I might see her again. After her funeral, as we were driving home, I looked at the sky and there was a cloud in the shape of angel wings. I really hope that was my sign.

Pot of gold

After my husband died three years ago I was cut wide open. I missed him terribly. I went to grief counselling, but that felt like an out-of-body experience in that I didn't connect with what I was saying and my mind and heart were with my husband. Then something beautiful happened. I woke up one morning missing him beyond belief and looked out of the window and there was the most stunning rainbow; but not just one rainbow – two.

I instantly remembered my husband a few years ago jumping up and down with excitement when he saw one when we were walking our dogs. As I looked at the rainbows I felt his excitement all over again. It was like he was there with me. Previously, I hadn't felt that sense of awe that he did and jokingly said, 'What's the point of rainbows as nobody ever finds the gold?' And he told me that we weren't meant to find the gold because that would mean we wouldn't catch the beauty of the rainbow. His wisdom didn't sink in then, but it did now. I can't explain it, but I felt closer to my husband than ever before when I saw the double rainbow that morning. I understood him. I felt his awe. I felt his love and that feeling has never gone away.

Butterflies, birds and wild animals also fall into the nature category and you can read about those delightful afterlife signs in Chapter Three, where I discuss pets and animals from heaven.

9. Numbers

Numerology is an intriguing esoteric science that you may want to research for yourself as it does seem that numbers carry with them spiritual energies. Have you ever noticed repeating numbers in your life? If you have, this could be heaven talking to you through the medium of numbers.

The numbers could be ones that remind you of departed loved ones – their birth date, for example, or their age when they passed. They could also be numbers that are personally significant to you. For example, if you are born on the eighth of the month, you may see the number 8 everywhere and each time it gives you pause for thought. But the number I get the most correspondence and questions about is repeating number 11s. So many people have written to tell me about the 11.11 phenomenon it could be the subject of its own book.

The number of times I have glanced at my watch or mobile and seen that the time is 11.11 or noticed that I have received a significant email or text at 11.11 is always a source of great delight to me because I just know now that this is heaven sending me a gentle sign, reminding me that I can experience heaven in the present moment. Indeed, whenever I see the 11.11 sign I always try to stop what I am doing and take a few moments to reflect and send thoughts of love and gratitude to departed loved ones in spirit. It doesn't have to be 11.11 though. I've also had letters about other repeating numbers and when that is the case I also urge the people who have written to me to do some research into the spiritual significance of numbers that repeat to see if there are any life lessons to be learned.

Also in this category of afterlife calling cards are significant dates – dates that have tremendous personal significance to the person involved. This short story from Linda speaks for itself:

Not random

For Christmas 2007 my partner bought me a women's health book. The first page I turned to randomly was pregnancy. We had been trying to get pregnant for two years with no luck, but in January 2008 I found out I was pregnant. My beautiful daughter was born on 18 September2008, my late mother's birthday. A couple of years later we tried for another baby, it took over four years and I finally gave birth to another beautiful daughter on 6 February 2015, the date my mother died.

10. Earth angels

The last, but by no means least significant afterlife calling card is one that may surprise you and that is heaven reaching out to you through the compassion and kindness of other people. Every time someone in your life goes out of their way to help or to show compassion and kindness – and particularly when that person is a stranger you have not met before and don't meet again – heaven is sending you a clear sign that you are loved from above. Here is a beautiful story sent to me by Angelina:

Don't believe it

A few years ago, I was getting some petrol from a service station and I noticed a lady sitting in the car beside me with her head in her hands. She had two dogs in the back and a child of about ten asleep in the seat next to her. I didn't think much of it, but when I came back from paying for my petrol she was still there in the same position. I gently knocked on the window and asked if she was OK. She looked up and I could see that her mascara was running down her face. She told me that she had lost her purse and couldn't pay for the petrol. Her phone battery was dead and she couldn't call anybody. I didn't think twice. I offered her some cash to pay for her petrol. She asked for my address to send the money back and told me that I was an angel.

As I drove home I realised that I couldn't afford to give away the cash and that the chances were I might never see my money again, but in my heart I felt good about myself. Two days later a letter arrived and the lady returned my cash. She also put an angel charm in the envelope and a short note. She wrote: 'Its people like you who make me believe heaven is real. My husband died a month ago and I'm still in shock. I miss him greatly. He always used to tell me to bring my purse when I went out just in case he forgot to bring his wallet. He never forgot his wallet and I got into the habit of going out without my purse. I forgot on the day you rescued me. This may sound strange but what you did made me feel that my husband hasn't gone.'

This story is close to my heart as it shows how the simple actions of others can truly change lives. It is also a reminder that heaven works in mysterious ways and we all have within us the potential to be a light to inspire, comfort or guide others in their moments of need. A few kind words or deeds can truly change lives for the better, and when lives are changed for the better we catch a glimpse of heaven on earth.

I love this story sent to me by Donna as it illustrates this 'be the loving change you want to see in the world' point simply and beautifully.

Five minutes

I walked past a homeless man just sitting quietly on the street. I looked at him and thought he looked hungry, but knew I only had five minutes to buy him something or I'd miss my train home and have half an hour to wait for the next one. However, I remembered in your book that if it was an act of heaven, then things would work out, and as he was sitting so close to a Tesco Express I felt it would be mean to walk past and not buy him something. So I bought him some food and treats for his dinner, but because the cashier had to check the price of a previous customer's items, I was stuck in the queue for over five minutes. I was convinced I would miss my train home, but when I handed the man the bag of food, the look on his face and his gratitude were worth it and I didn't care if I missed the train as my heart felt so content and full of love.

Of course, when I got to the train station my train was late, so I still had three minutes to spare, despite having taken longer to get to the station, so it must've been meant to be. I would have regretted not stopping if, when I got to the platform, the train was ten minutes late.

It served as a simple reminder that little things can make a big deal to someone else and I will try to do this more from now on.

The lesson in Donna's and Angelina's stories is that *you* can be an afterlife sign or calling card for anyone you encounter in your life, reminding them that there is a heaven. Perhaps you can be an instrument of the extraordinary kindness and inspiration that can help others feel as if they have been touched by a miracle. So the next time you want to see heaven or an angel on earth, try just looking at your own reflection.

EVERYDAY MIRACLES

A miracle is defined as an extraordinary event that can only be explained as divine intervention. It is often thought to be extremely rare but, as the stories above show, unexplained events are far more likely than we think. You could say that all the stories you've read so far are simply luck or making too much out of too little, but for the people involved what they experienced was nothing short of a miracle – an everyday miracle, but a miracle all the same.

The world we live in today is increasingly dominated by science. In some ways science has become the new religion, and one of the arguments against belief in an afterlife is that it isn't scientific. In the world of science, where everything must be proved and logically explained, there is no room for miracles or the unexplained; it dismisses afterlife experiences as being purely anecdotal or only for the deluded and wishful thinkers. But, as I explained in the Introduction (see p. 6), I have made it my mission through my collaboration with IONS in recent years to show that miracles are not just for believers – they are also for scientists.

Science, by definition, is the search for truth and surely that search must include all experiences – even those that can't be seen, don't seem logical and can't be recorded in a laboratory. There is just too much anecdotal evidence out there about the existence of an afterlife for science to continue to dismiss or ignore. People are having these experiences and feelings of closeness with heaven that transform their lives. In any other field these would be recorded as data and science needs to study them. As the stories in this book bear witness, there is something at work in our lives that goes far beyond simple biology or brainwave instruction and physics. There is something other, something deeper and something greater than ourselves at work.

The gap between science and spirit is closing fast and

quantum scientists are having to come to terms with the notion that this life is not as simplistic as we thought. The indications are that our consciousness is capable of existing independently of our bodies and of linking to something greater than ourselves that is eternal. Not only are we capable of miracles, but the universe is too.

Miracles don't always happen but they can and do happen. Sometimes they happen in answer to a prayer, on other occasions they happen when we don't expect them. They aren't always dramatic and newsworthy as this chapter has shown and are more likely to be the small unexplained things that make us smile from the inside out, but whatever form they take they are part of that great and invisible power that connects us all.

EXPECT MIRACLES

Hopefully, what you have read so far will encourage you to expect the unexpected and see everything that happens to you as a potential heavenly sign card, pointing you in the direction of healing and love. You will pay attention to the deeper meaning behind everyday things that you may previously have dismissed. You will listen more carefully to what is being said around you. Music will speak to your soul, chance encounters won't feel random any more and the events in your day will be filled with significance.

In my humble opinion, miracles are not about belief but about recognition. I truly hope that as you read this book – starting right now – you will consider the unique miracle of

DNA that you are: you are one of a kind, there is no one on earth like you and never will be again. Consider the thread of your life and how sometimes things have just felt meant to be. Reflect on the astonishing stories you read in this book. The more you recognise and acknowledge that miracles are real and can and do happen all the time – not just to other people, but to you too – the more you will experience them. And the more you will see that everything and everyone, yourself included, is touched by heaven.

> *Perhaps they are not stars in the sky, but*
> *rather openings where our loved ones shine*
> *down to let us know they are happy.*

INUIT LEGEND

CHAPTER TWO

DREAMS AND VISIONS FROM HEAVEN

*While you are asleep angels have
conversations with your soul.*

ANONYMOUS

You've seen in the previous chapter a snapshot of some of
the everyday ways in which the afterlife can whisper to
you. Many of these gentle signs are typically very subtle
and could easily be missed if you didn't know where to
notice them. Hopefully, reading this book will ensure you
don't ever miss messages from heaven again, but you may
be wondering why heaven chooses to reach out in such an
understated way. Why doesn't the afterlife make its presence
felt more clearly?

After my mother died this was a question I asked the spirit
world relentlessly. My mother was the one who educated

and inspired me about the afterlife. She truly lived and breathed it because in her early twenties she had actually died and gone to heaven in a near-death experience (NDE). I believed her completely. Many times when I attended spiritualist meetings with her I saw those who had lost loved ones being comforted by mediums. I was convinced that death was not the end, but a wonderful new beginning and that when I would inevitably lose a loved one my belief would be a source of strength and comfort.

Surely, if the afterlife was real my mother, of all people, would find a way to comfort and guide me, but in the first few years following her death all I got was deafening silence.

FINDING MY WAY

My mother crossed over when I was in my twenties. Until then, the death of a loved one had been very much something that other people experienced. When friends shared their grief with me I was a tower of strength. I would tell them all I knew about the afterlife from my research into near-death experiences, that their departed loved ones were in a better place and that they should feel happiness for them because they were graduating from this life to a peaceful and blissful life in spirit.

Sometimes I could see that my energetic conviction comforted them, but there were also the odd occasions when I could tell that my words were not encouraging or inspiring them. It made me feel sad that I couldn't offer the support and reassurance I wanted to. It was only when my mother passed that I understood why my words must have sounded hollow and perhaps even harsh. For example, I used to tell people that intense and prolonged grieving might hinder the smooth transition to spirit of a loved one, but when I experienced grief myself I saw how unfeeling that advice was.

Grief is an inevitable and natural human reaction to the loss of a person's physical presence and no amount of talk about the afterlife and near-death experiences can take away the pain of that loss or the urgent need to cry and scream. When my mother died the grief was like a tidal wave. I begged her to send me a sign to take some of the pain away, but I got nothing. I couldn't see, hear or sense her. I had no idea why she would disappear like that and leave me utterly and unbearably alone. That silence plunged me into the deepest doubt. I questioned all my beliefs about the existence of heaven – about everything I had based my life philosophy on. It was a true crisis of faith. Perhaps this truly was all there is? Perhaps heaven wasn't real?

Growing up in a family of spiritualists and blessed with the finest education, I was an expert in the theory of spirituality, but when confronted with my own personal tragedy it was obvious that I wasn't equipped to deal with bereavement. Talking about heaven was one thing, but it was a totally different matter when life called me to test that belief.

With the benefit of hindsight, I can now see that my mother's death and the intense grief that followed was a spiritual awakening. Nothing that I had learned, researched and witnessed in spiritualist meetings, at university and working in a hospice had prepared me for my true education, which began after my mother died. That education would eventually take me to where I am today, where heaven is a reality for me, but before I could get to that point I had to experience the dark night of the soul and the painful self-examination and questioning that it triggered.

In the immediate aftermath of my mother's death – the first few days – my strong belief in the existence of life after death sustained me. There was so much to do and organise, and at the funeral I smiled and celebrated her life, happy that she was now in heaven. My mother had often told me not to cry at her funeral, but to rejoice at her graduation and that is what I did. After the funeral I kept myself furiously busy with sorting out her clothing and other personal items and all the routine organisation that has to be done when a person leaves this earth. I only kept a few treasured items as I didn't feel I needed many physical reminders. I told myself she was alive in my heart and spirit. I bought a beautiful box and stored those items under my bed.

As the weeks turned into months, everybody remarked on how strong I was and how well I was coping. What I didn't tell them was that for reasons I couldn't understand I would sometimes get this sudden impulse to cry. I would also laugh when it wasn't appropriate or say things that truly didn't make sense. Sometimes I'd wake up thinking it was the weekend when in fact it was a weekday. Or I'd wander into a shop and forget why I was in there. Gradually, things began to get very confusing for me.

In the evenings, I would often grab the box containing my mother's items, take them all out and arrange them around me in a circle. I felt a need to see a photograph of her or read one of her letters because I was beginning to forget what she looked and sounded like. I needed to be convinced that she had been real. Then, in those moments, my heart would break. The sense of loss was unbearable and it would hit me like an avalanche that I would never see her physical form again. I would never hear her voice or her laugh or have deep conversations about life, the universe and everything with her. My life had changed for ever because she was no longer in it. I'd weep for hours before drifting into a heavy and dreamless sleep.

I kept asking my mother to send me a sign to prove to me she was still with me, but there it was again – that deafening silence.

Ashamed to admit to anyone that I was feeling wretched, I smiled through my teeth in the company of others. But alone, I would cry with all my heart. This went on for a few months, eventually leading to full-blown depression. If you've ever experienced depression, you will know that it is hell on earth. It is like living in a painful fog. Life loses all its colour and energy and you can't see any way forward. Some days, even keeping my eyes open felt like too much effort. I'd look in the mirror and see a lifeless, corpse-like face – a reflection of my internal distress, with no expression, as even frowning took too much effort. At work and during the day, when in the company of others, I'd function on autopilot and managed to continue to hide my pain, but when I was alone, the emotional pain can only be compared to a hammer hitting a bruise over and over again. Sleep was a respite when I got some, but many nights I'd just stare at my clock and the hour hand that never seemed to move. After two or three months of this non-existence, I felt that my spirit had died. I was a zombie. I believed in and felt nothing.

Then, one night, when exhaustion had finally taken over, I fell asleep and had a dream. It wasn't a particularly dramatic one. My mother simply came into my bedroom and started picking up things from the floor and tidying. I tried to talk to her, but my mouth wouldn't open. She didn't seem to be aware of me and I think she was humming to herself. She looked pretty and vital and very unlike the woman who passed away riddled with cancer. Although the dream was not extraordinary, it was incredibly realistic and for a few precious minutes when I woke up, I thought it was real and that I'd hear my mum calling me from downstairs asking me if I wanted a cup of tea. She never called, of course, and the pain hit me hard again.

That dream was a small comfort, but it wasn't enough for me at the time. I wanted much more. I wanted to actually hear her voice or see her in a vision. I did not realise then that this dream was my mother reaching out in the only way she could. Several other similar and extremely realistic dreams followed and with each one I found myself making a small step forward in the days after. For example, I'd do something positive for myself like going for a run or getting my nails done. Without even realising it, I began to see light at the end of the tunnel and slowly but surely, I started to pull myself out of the darkness. In time, I was able to get back to the business of living with energy. I even found the courage from within to ask for help in the form of bereavement counselling.

What is remarkable about my dark night of the soul is

that instead of resulting in a total loss of faith it just made my fascination with the other side even stronger. I realised that I didn't have psychic abilities to see or hear heaven, but I could seek out other people who did, so I could learn from them and grow. I started to gather together afterlife stories and experiences, and as these stories transformed into best-selling books, I found an inner peace that had been lacking before. Perhaps it was my destiny to be a messenger of the afterlife, a defence for the existence of heaven, even if I hadn't experienced it myself. After all, isn't the definition of faith to believe without proof?

It wasn't until a few years later, when I had completely let go of my insatiable desire for proof of my own and realised that in life we get what we need and not what we want, that my mother made tangible contact with me. I heard her speak to me directly first in a dream and then, the next day, when I was awake. On both occasions she told me to take the right path and – as I explained in the Introduction (see p. 1) – I believe her spirit voice saved my life.

After that dramatic afterlife encounter I realised that heaven had been talking to me all my life through dreams and intuition and coincidence, but I just hadn't tuned into the messages because I had been fixated on receiving more obvious signs. I needed to experience loss and a severe crisis of faith to gain this deeper spiritual under-standing. This isn't to say that we all need to be plunged into the depths of despair and doubt before heaven talks to us. Some people are blessed with a resilient person-ality and don't let grief stop them in their tracks. They find comfort and meaning through carrying on, but the experience of grief forced me to be still and to look within for comfort.

I thought depression was my enemy and I needed to work through it as soon as I could, but heaven wouldn't let me do this until I stopped denying my feelings of loss. I needed to mourn my mother fully. I needed to doubt everything I had been taught to trust in, so that if ultimately I chose to believe in heaven it wasn't because I had been given 'proof' by an afterlife sign, but because my heart made the decision to believe without proof. I needed to stop looking outside of myself for answers and enlightenment. I needed to find heaven within me – to look deep into the darkness of my soul and discover my own sense of meaning. In the words of Camus: 'In the depth of winter, I found there was in me an invincible summer.'

All these years I had been waiting for the afterlife to simply reveal itself. I'd thought that if I studied hard and learned the correct techniques, my psychic powers would materialise suddenly. I simply didn't realise that psychic development is about the growth of the whole person and is a lifelong process of learning to trust your instincts and discover your inner light. It is also about learning to love yourself unconditionally and letting go of fear and the belief that there are always going to be answers. It is about understanding that doubt can actually bring you closer to heaven because when you doubt, you are forced to search within for meaning and grow spiritually – and the purpose of our lives on earth is to grow in spirit.

Once you get in touch with your inner light and realise that heaven can be found from the inside out, you can begin to see and hear heaven all around you. On very rare occasions you may experience a dramatic vision or encounter, but far more productive for your spiritual growth is heaven whispering to you through a white feather or other everyday signs, or through a thought, a feeling, a coincidence or a dream – because this encourages you to seek heaven within the only true and real place to find it.

With the benefit of hindsight, I can now see that dreams were perhaps the only way my mother could have reached out to me at the time because I simply couldn't have coped with anything else. If she had appeared in a less subtle way this would have prevented me from adjusting to her physical loss and growing in spirit. I would have wanted to see her clearly over and over again and I wouldn't have moved forward with my spiritual development. I would have got stuck.

MORE THAN A DREAM

At the risk of repeating myself, you do need to fully grieve the loss of the physical presence of a loved one before you can enter into a new relationship with them in spirit, and the chances are that the first way they will reach out to you will be in a dream.

Dreams, along with the gentle signs mentioned in the previous chapter, are extremely common heavenly calling cards. According to Claire, they may in fact be the preferred way for spirit to reach out to us, as they are safe and comforting and unlikely to cause alarm. The sad thing is that we so often dismiss dreams or don't remember them, but I hope after reading this book you will never let memories of your dreams of departed loved ones slip away unrecognised again. You will treasure them as the gift from heaven they are.

Often, when people get in touch to tell me that they haven't been able to sense their departed loved one the first thing I ask them is whether they've had a dream about them. More often than not they say yes. I then have great joy in telling them that this is their loved one reaching out to them. It is bliss to see the look of recognition and comfort in their eyes.

If you are one of those people who say you never dream – think again. We all dream; it's just that some of us are better at remembering our dreams than others. It is estimated that even if we can't remember them we have 100,000 dreams over the course of our lives. The only reason most of us think we don't dream is that we haven't got into the habit of remembering them as soon as we wake up.

You need to remember a dream immediately on waking because if you do or think about anything else, it will fade. I highly recommend keeping a pen and paper beside your bed, so you can write down whatever you can recall as soon as you wake up, even if it doesn't make sense at the time. More often than not, when you read through it later you will see that there's a hidden message there.

Answers from heaven are constantly being given to you in your dreams and all you need to do is remember them. Dreams have enormous potential to comfort, guide and inspire and I truly hope this book will alert you to it. Becoming more aware of your dreaming mind will awaken you spiritually and reveal to you another reality that has infinite possibilities. Many great artists, writers, musicians, inventors and scientists have got their inspiration from dreams. Paul McCartney's 'Yesterday', for example, came to him in a dream. In rare cases, dreams can also save lives, as you'll see later in this chapter when we talk about premonitions.

Something else I've noticed as I enter my fifth decade is that the older you get, the more dreamlike life feels. Perhaps this increased awareness of an alternate reality is to prepare us for when we eventually pass over and transition from our physical form into pure spirit. And yet, despite being such a potentially powerful link to the other side, dreams can often seem incredibly hard to understand or interpret. This is because they speak to us in a different language. And if you want to speak a different language you need to spend time learning it.

The language of dreams is one of symbols. You need to remember the symbols in your dreams, and that applies to everything from the people who appear in them to landscapes, colours, animals and objects, as well as the theme – for example, flying or falling. All these things are symbols. There are loads of dream-symbol books out there – some of which I have written myself – which give you generic interpretations for common dream symbols. This is a great starting point to get you thinking along the right lines, but there are limitations, as dream symbols have to be interpreted personally. For example, if you are a dog lover, the appearance of a dog in your dream could symbolise unconditional love and companionship; but if you are afraid of or dislike dogs, your dream dog will represent something sinister. So you are the best person to interpret your own dream symbols.

Every single night your dreaming mind sends you symbols to help you understand yourself and your life better. Your dreams can be amazing tools for self-awareness because they can help you to focus on your hopes and fears and challenges, so you can deal with them better in your waking life. I think of dreams as an internal therapist, as they can often help you to see a new way forward or to role-play different scenarios, so you can experience them and their consequences in safety.

The majority of your dreams should not be interpreted literally but symbolically. For instance, if someone you love dies in a dream, this does not mean they are going to die, but that your relationship is changing in some way – that there will be endings, but also new beginnings. Thought and self-analysis are required to find the hidden messages in symbolic dreams, but it is certainly worth the effort, as they can contribute greatly to your self-understanding and spiritual growth. However, the most powerful and transformative messages from heaven – which are often delivered with urgency and clarity – are what I call night visions.

NIGHT VISIONS

Night visions make up less than 1 per cent of our dreams and you may only have a few, if that, in your lifetime. They are very different to symbolic dreams. Whereas symbolic dreams have a surreal feeling, night visions are crystal clear. Symbolic dreams tend to have confused and overlapping plots, but night visions have a clarity with a beginning, middle and end. In fact, they are so clear cut and obvious you have no choice but to interpret them literally. They also have a very realistic feel, but by far their most defining feature is that you don't forget them on waking. You may even wake up thinking you are still in your dream. You will also remember your night vision for months, even years after you had it.

We've all had those unforgettable dreams at some point in our lives and if you close your eyes, you can still recall the images. I'm convinced these dreams, which usually involve visits from departed loved ones, are answers from heaven.

Night visions are not to be confused with nightmares. Nightmares are caused by stress, fear and doubt gaining the upper hand in your life. Sure, they are memorable too, but they lack the clarity of a night vision and they are certainly not messages from heaven, which would never alarm or frighten you. A defining feature of all afterlife signs is that they always comfort, inspire, guide or positively energise in some way. Night visions certainly do that.

The stories in this chapter fall into the category of night visions. In each case the person who sent me their story told me that their dream was so clear and comforting it was impossible for their heart and mind to forget. The majority of these night visions involved meetings with a departed loved one.

Elaine had a night vision about her departed mother and

it transformed her life, completely easing her pain. She woke from her dream feeling joyful and optimistic after months of deep and dark grieving.

She's always there

I lost my mum very suddenly in 2003. I had moved out of the family home on the Friday and my mum passed on the Wednesday. It was a huge shock. It was a couple of days after her death that I actually managed to go to sleep and that's when I saw her. I was walking up a lane in my dream and it was beautiful. I can still see it to this day. The sky was the brightest blue you could see and the flowers were all bright in colour and I can still smell the flowers if I close my eyes. As I was walking admiring the beauty of that day, I looked over and I saw my mum walking towards me. She looked amazing and so well. I just stared at her and said, 'Mum, what are you doing here? You're dead.'

'Elly,' she said, 'I'm OK. I just need you to know, OK?'

I said, 'Yes,' and she replied, 'I need to go Elly, I will see you again.' We both said goodbye and walked away. That was thirteen years ago, but I can still remember it as if it was yesterday. I believe she took me to where she was just so I could see how beautiful it was and how she was well. For a few years my mum would appear in my dreams. We would have conversations with each other, giggle and laugh. It's been a while, but I do believe that if I need her she's there.

Katrina also found comfort and meaning again after she had a dream about her departed baby.

Another life

Last year I lost my son, James. He died when he was just ten weeks old and it almost killed me. My boyfriend and I split up – we couldn't work through our grief – and I lost my joy and energy. I limped through the days, but a few days ago I had this stunning dream. It was extraordinary.

I heard James crying in my dream and went to his cot to pick him up. When I got there he reached out his arms to me and smiled. I picked him up and held him and this is the amazing thing: I smelled him. His glorious baby smell. It was pure bliss. Then I laid him gently down in his cot and the two of us just stared at each other. As we did, I saw him grow up from baby to old man. I saw myself taking him to school for the first time, I saw him become a teenager and a man and I saw him marry and have children. I saw him live his life. I saw him laugh and cry, and then I saw him die, and I was with him in that moment too. It all felt incredibly real, and I wonder if there are alternate realities out there where unlived lives get their chance to live. I guess I won't know until I cross over, but what I do know is that after that dream the weight of sadness has lifted and I am able to function again. Seeing James live such a full, rich life in spirit has encouraged me to make mine as full and rich. I just know that is what James's spirit wants me to do. He wants me to live. The thought of that dream brings me such comfort and joy.

I wrote to tell Katrina that I was sure this was her angel baby reaching out to her to let her know he was still alive in spirit. I was convinced because the night vision had brought comfort and joy – and for me, anything that does that is heaven-sent.

It's a happy moment whenever I read a story about a reunion with a departed loved one in a night vision. I love telling the people who write to me that they have received an answer from heaven and it is more than just a dream. I try to explain to them that when we fall asleep our conscious mind switches off, allowing our unconscious mind to take the driving seat. With our unconscious mind taking the lead, our egos – and the fear, anxiety and guilt that go with them – cannot close and block our minds as they do when we are awake. And in much the same way that the love in our hearts connects us to heaven, our unconscious mind is also a gateway to the other side.

Patrick sent me this moving story about how a night visit from his grandmother not only brought tremendous comfort, but also inspired him to start *The Big Seance Podcast* (see Appendix, p. 329).

Grandma Van

I don't remember dreams often, so this was very significant. The details are unclear and I really wish I would have jotted down whatever I remembered after I woke up. I had either dreamed or astral travelled to the living room of my late great-grandmother Van Zandt (whom I called Grandma Van).

In my dream/astral experience/whatever it was, I was clearly in the presence of my Grandma Van. She was sitting in her chair in the corner of her living room. She and I clearly both knew that I was dreaming and talking to the spirit of a dead person. She was explaining something to me and I'm pretty sure I remember her trying to calm me or telling me not to be afraid. I woke up with the dream still vivid in my mind, told myself I was going to remember it and then promptly went back to sleep.

I'm so frustrated that I didn't document it. I'd love to be able to have some kind of validation that I truly had a visit from or visited my Grandma Van. Or ... maybe it was truly just a dream. I believe that our soul leaves our body all the time while we sleep. I think we visit with our spirit guides and other entities as well. I like to think we get special advice and a 'heads up' on events we're about to experience when we wake up. To my knowledge, this is the first time I remember having such a pronounced experience and, in hindsight, it probably inspired me to investigate the paranormal for myself and run my own podcast on the subject.

Over the years I have noticed that a lot of the stories sent to me tend to occur around special days or anniversaries, as if departed loved ones in spirit want to be there sharing memories with us. This is Sonia's story:

Loved from above

I believe I have had a couple of visitation dreams. I lost my grandparents many years ago and was extremely close to them both. I lost my uncle in 2012 and that was a very difficult time for me, as again, we were very close. The couple of dreams I have had involved my uncle and my grandparents.

The dreams were so vivid, I didn't feel as though I was asleep and the next day I was filled with such a happiness inside. I am always talking to them and have pictures of them in my room, so they are the last people I see before I go to sleep at night.

The last dream I had was very close to my uncle's anniversary of passing in July this year. I was also suffering with shingles and felt quite unwell. I asked him if he would come and visit me in my dreams and said how much I missed him. The dream was so clear, he gave me the biggest hug that seemed to last for ever and when he let go I was left with his smile. It's as though he knew I needed to see him. It's a wonderful energising and inspiring feeling to know you are loved from above. I have read about visitation dreams and believe this was one.

Sonia wasn't deep in grief when she had the vision, so it wasn't a lifesaver in that way, but she did long for comfort and reassurance and the vision gave her a sense of energy and optimism she may have been lacking in her life before.

Is it possible to induce a night vision? This is a question I'm often asked and my answer is yes. And no. Yes, in that you can increase the likelihood of a night vision by thinking about your departed loved one just before you go to sleep and making a concerted effort to remember and record your dreams, as this will send a clear sign to the afterlife that you are preparing the way. And no, in that there is always a possibility that you won't have a night vision, even if you ask for one or are diligent about remembering your dreams. This isn't because spirit doesn't want to connect with you, but because the time is not right for them and for you. Often, I feel it is because they want you to find your inner strength first – because when you do that you become a clearer channel for heaven to connect to.

Always remember if you aren't sure if you had a symbolic dream or a night vision that a night vision will be incredibly vivid and feel real. You may actually find it hard to believe you are dreaming. You will also have a sense that this was something more and the personality of the departed loved one will be immediately recognisable. And as mentioned before, the sure-fire confirmation that you have been touched by heaven is that you will feel comforted and uplifted. That feeling – as if you can fly – is the hallmark of heaven.

Jordan sent me this story about night visions experienced by his family members:

People in white

When my grandfather was about to pass he said he could see his decreased family members around his bed waiting to collect him. He was holding his hands out to them the whole time and looked really peaceful and content. Years later, when my nan passed she was in a hospital bed and told me and her family that she could see her deceased family members around her bed waiting to collect her. After her funeral, everyone came home to find a large, fluffy white feather on the doorstep at home. Then, a day before her neighbour/friend died just recently, a white feather all of a sudden floated into our conservatory and I wondered, was this the angels' way of letting us know that they are near and coming for her? Also, I keep having vivid dreams of them all dressed in white. Then my auntie woke one night to find a lady in white standing at the end of her bed, who said, 'Hello, I'm your nan who died before you were born,' and then just disappeared again. That night vision brought peace and healing to my auntie.

Psychologists are quick to explain away such dreams as wishful thinking, natural pain relief or part of the grieving process, but if that is the case, why doesn't everyone who loses a loved one have them? Also, it is extremely unusual for such coherent, vivid and comforting emotions to be born from such negative emotions that grief inspires. The only explanation, as far as I am concerned, is that the dream comes from above.

I've been sent many stories of parting visions in which the dreamer is unaware that the person they see in the dream has died – stories like this one sent to me by Ruby:

Night shift

I started my working life training at a large general hospital in Johannesburg. Trainees would spend three to four months in different wards, e.g. medical, surgical, ENT, etc. with twenty to thirty beds per ward. One ward was for private patients, local dignitaries or senior medical staff, housing only one to two patients. I did my first spell of night duty, which I didn't enjoy, as one of the patients, an elderly doctor, would not allow anyone but me to attend to him. While I ought to have been flattered, it was tiring as the good doctor kept me on the hop.

I never slept well in night quarters, as it was difficult to get the room dark enough to induce sleep. In the early hours of the morning I had a dream that felt so real about the doctor. I was walking past his ward when he called out to me. Entering the ward, I was surprised to see how fit and well he looked. His face was aglow and he'd sprouted a head of thick grey hair (in reality he was as bald as a coot). As I stood beside his bed, he gripped my hands tightly and told me he was going away. I reassured him that it was all right, that there was nothing to worry about. Managing to loosen his grip, I jerked myself free, whereupon I woke up. Glancing at my watch, noting that it was only 2.15 p.m., I finally managed to fall asleep again.

The next evening, I was sitting out on the bench in the nurses' home garden, chatting to the girls coming off day duty, when one of my friends spotted me. She was on day duty in the private ward and looked absolutely bushed. She parked herself next to me. 'Lord, what a day,' she said. 'Three deaths, one after the other!'

'How is my doctor doing?' I asked.

'His was one of the deaths,' she answered.

With that, I remembered my dream. 'Do you know what time he died?' I asked. 'I'm not sure,' she answered, 'but it must have been around two-fifteen because I'd just got back from second sitting lunch.'

You'll notice the words 'felt so real' appearing again here in Ruby's story, as that is the hallmark of night visions, along with a clear beginning, middle and end (in contrast to symbolic dreams which are fragments of unconnected images).

Light years ahead

Dreams of departed loved ones appearing to people who don't yet know they have died belong to another category of night visions known as precognitive dreams, and they appear to warn of or predict future events. Sometimes these dreams are waking ones. For example, one of Claire's clients told her the story of a woman in a hospice who was suffering from dementia and seemed to know when someone was about to die: whenever she started counting there was a passing. These unexplained stories are yet more proof that heaven is real because when we sleep the boundaries between our conscious and unconscious merge, enabling spirit to transcend the laws of the everyday and bridge the gap between this world and the next as well as past, present and future. From the NDE accounts I have read (more about them in Chapter 4) it becomes clear that in spirit there is no concept of time as we understand it here on earth.

In heaven, those who have glimpsed the other side through NDEs or afterlife encounters have seen that life is eternal. They also say that the concept of time as we comprehend it simply does not exist. Time is not real. Time is a creation, an illusion. There is no time as we experience it when we are alive. Our souls exist beyond time. Einstein suggested that time only exists to stop everything happening at once. What he meant here was that the concept of linear time (things happening one after the other in a straight line) is something created by our minds to allow things to happen in an orderly manner; without time there would be chaos. His theory of relativity showed that time is not constant or linear and can be changed or altered by the speed and direction of a moving object.

This new perspective on time that NDE accounts reflect can have a tremendous impact on the way we live our lives on earth. When we consider that from the perspective of heaven our life on earth could be over in a fraction of a second, and that events may be happening at blinding speed or occurring simultaneously, but that they have been slowed down and reordered in our minds (as we live in a physical rather than a spiritual universe), we may begin to understand that a ninety-year lifespan on earth may take place in the blink of an eye in spirit. So perhaps the reason why some of us don't feel a strong sense of connection with departed loved ones or receive a sign is because the departed only feel they have been gone a few moments, or have not left at all, and they know you will be together with them again in the blink of an eye.

To return to precognitive dreams, like night visions, they are extremely rare. More common I have found are dreams or daydreams that are not accurate descriptions of the future, but warnings of some kind, offering the dreamer a chance to change the course of events in order to avert potential disaster. The dreamer recognises in real life what their dream has forewarned and this prompts them to make changes. Of course, you could say that such dreams are simply intuition at work, especially dreams that save lives, but I am firm in my belief that intuition is the voice of heaven too.

Precognitive dreams may be rare, but they have been documented many times. For example, a number of people had dreams of towers burning and crashing down before 9/11, and many of the passengers on the *Titanic*, which sank in 1912, had premonitions about the ship going down. Some of them didn't get on board because of them, but others ignored them – again, we have grown accustomed to dismissing our dreams, even those that are clear and vivid, because science has encouraged us to think in this way. So they aren't recognised as premonitions until the event or tragedy has occurred.

One of the most fascinating kinds of precognitive dreams are those about meeting children before they are born. They often include accurate information about a child's future personality or appearance, sometimes even before conception. Mountaineer Aron Ralston, who amputated his own arm to save his life when he was trapped between a boulder and a rock wall for over five days, had a spectacular vision of his unborn child. (His story of survival against the odds was made into the Oscar-nominated movie called *127 Hours*.) During his ordeal, when he thought he was going to die, he had a vision of a small boy who encouraged him to fight for his life. At the time, he wasn't even married, but months later he met his wife and they went on to have a son called Leo who fitted the description of the boy he saw in his vision perfectly. Ralston is quoted as saying that 'Love at its deepest point is what connects us'. His accident and the vision of his unborn son that saved him became a turning point.

Sensational stories like Ralston's offer yet more proof that we are spiritual beings having a human experience and our spirits can cross the boundaries of time and space, life and death. In our dreams we have the opportunity to connect to something greater than ourselves. Doctors and scientists may use their own terminology to explain such experiences, but none of this can encapsulate the truth for the person concerned. For them, no words or explanations are needed because they know they have been touched by heaven.

If you've ever experienced the joy of first love or becoming a parent, if you're a mountaineer who scales new heights, or perhaps you're an athlete who achieves their personal best, you will know the feeling of being out of this world or touched by heaven. If you've ever suddenly and inexplicably found new hope and peace after a period of depression or heartache you will know what I am talking about here and you will know that what you felt was real and heaven-sent.

SIXTH SENSE

People who have clear precognitions or flashes of profound intuition are often said to be psychic or to have a sixth sense, suggesting they experience something that does not conform to the laws of physics. But the only reason something is described as psychic or paranormal is because we don't yet understand it. In other words, you don't have to be a psychic to have premonitions or night visions. All you need to do is pay more attention to your dreams and your intuition and the coincidences in your life.

Sixth sense, psychic power, clairvoyance and telepathy are

terms often used to describe this supersense – the cumulative power of all the senses: sight, hearing, taste, touch and smell – but perhaps the simplest way to describe it is intuition. And remember, as we saw in the previous chapter, intuition is an afterlife calling card.

We all have intuition, but most of us aren't aware of it. Centuries ago, our psychic ability would have been more finely tuned, as it would have helped us escape from danger, but with the advance of technology we rely less and less on our intuition, and like a muscle, the less we use it, the weaker it gets. So rather than being something that some people have, intuition is something that others lack. The potential is there within all of us; it is simply a forgotten art that needs to be rediscovered and developed.

If you have ever experienced any of the following or just felt that you might have, this is your sixth sense speaking loud and clear:

- You dream about something or get a hunch or gut feeling and it comes true and turns out to be right.
- Sometimes you just know what someone else is thinking.
- Perhaps you think about someone and then they call or text.
- You walk into a room or space and know when someone is angry, upset or excited before they speak to you.
- You have a sudden feeling that you should – or should not – go somewhere and then find out later that you should have listened to that feeling.

I sincerely hope that after reading this book you will pay more attention to the gentle voice of your intuition or sixth sense and think of it as a voice of comfort from above. It is easy to distinguish intuition from fear because your intuition will always feel warm and uplifting – or protective, in the way that a loving parent would protect a child. The message will also be simple, in contrast to the voice of fear, which is harsh, critical and involves endless explanations that clatter around in your head.

COINCIDENCE

Coincidences appear like chance or random events, but to those who experience them they can often feel like synchronicity or part of a carefully orchestrated plan for their lives. Heaven prefers to reach out to you with gentle and subtle signs and will not try to dictate your life or interfere with your free will. Instead, it will try to open your heart and mind and gently guide you with signs to a path that will lead to your happiness. And the way that heaven chooses to do that is through coincidence.

When wonderful coincidences happen we tend to ascribe them to luck. For instance, when we just happen to bump into the right person at the right time or we find ourselves in the right place at the right time we thank our lucky stars. But this isn't a matter of random good fortune – it's heaven talking to us. So the next time you notice a coincidence in your life, even if it is a trivial one, open your mind to the idea that it is a heavenly calling card. And the more you pay attention to coincidences and feel gratitude for them, the more likely they are to happen.

You may have noticed that all the stories so far in this book have a common theme, and that is clarity coming out of confusion, order coming out of chaos, pain evolving from hope and certainty emerging where there was doubt. Many of us today feel confused and uncertain and it is all too easy to believe that everything that happens to us is chaotic and random.

Atheists cite chaos theory as the answer to anyone who believes their life is more than just a series of random events. But in the last few decades scientists have discovered that there are subtle patterns to chaos. Take the miracle of DNA, for instance, or the human circulatory system, or the intricate design of a snowflake. There is nothing random here – just a perfect design in which everything has a place, function and purpose. To illustrate the point further you need only look at the natural world where patterns and an unexplained intelligence can often be seen. Take salmon, for example, just how do they find their way to their spawning grounds every year?

So even scientists are slowly beginning to accept that there may be an underlying order to everything. I'm sure you have heard of the butterfly-effect theory, whereby a single occurrence – no matter how insignificant – can change the course of our lives for ever. (The flap of a butterfly's wings changes the air around it enough to create a feeble air current that sets off corresponding changes in the environment until a tornado breaks out two continents away.)

From a spiritual perspective, the butterfly effect points

to the universal truth that we are all connected and the smallest or most trivial action can have potentially huge consequences further down the line. It could also signal the importance of and interconnection between our thoughts, words and actions. Although scientific theories have yet to acknowledge a spiritual power, theories like this, along with quantum science, suggest that scientists are beginning to recognise the interconnectedness of the universe.

It is at times like these that you might begin to seek a way to live that is more harmonious, more fulfilling and more meaningful. And one way to do this is by expanding your vision of life and raising your awareness and consciousness to understand the guidance from your higher, spiritual self.

One thing I know for sure is that when it comes to after-life signs, whether they occur when you are awake or asleep, heaven can send you answers in the most unexpected ways. The messages may be subtle and gentle but that does not make them any the less powerful and life changing. Indeed, they may be more transformative than the more dramatic signs we will cover in Chapter 4 because in order to start noticing them they require you to arrive at a place when you can sense the connectiveness of all things. Sensing that divine connectivity is the key to spiritual growth and an awareness of the eternal reality of heaven in this life and the next.

TALES OF THE UNEXPECTED

Opening your mind and your heart and recognising that heaven can speak to you through the language of coincidence, the voice of intuition, subtle afterlife signs and vivid dreams will bring a real sense of meaning, magic and infinite possibility into your life. In the words of the English romantic poet Blake, 'You will see heaven in a wild flower,' and 'the world in a grain of sand'. You will notice the sun, moon and stars and admire the shape of a cloud or gaze in awe at a rainbow. The possibilities for heaven to speak to you through this beautiful world are endless.

The theme of heaven revealing itself on earth will continue in the next chapter with stories that celebrate the connectivity of all living things and the eternal bond created by unconditional love – in whatever form that may take.

No person is truly alone. Those we have loved
echo still within our thoughts, our words,
our hearts, our spirits and our dreams.

ANONYMOUS

CHAPTER THREE

LIVING AND LOVING CREATURES IN SPIRIT

Until one has loved an animal, a part of one's soul remains unawakened.

ANATOLE FRANCE

Miracles come in many forms and I couldn't be happier than to devote this chapter to a category of afterlife communication stories that aren't taken as seriously as they should be – those involving beloved pets and animals. I truly believe there is a spark of heaven in every living thing and that they are all connected. Later in the book Claire also references animals in the spirit realm and how you can connect to and draw inspiration from them.

Having received countless letters over the years about animals and the spiritual healing they bring both in this life and from the next, I felt it was time to devote a whole chapter to them. From what I have read, it has become clear to me not only that it is possible to connect to animals in the afterlife, but also that in this life animals can teach us spiritual lessons of unconditional love, healing, compassion, loyalty, trust and patience – and by so doing, offer us a genuine glimpse of heaven on earth.

Glen sent me this adorable and deeply spiritual story about his dog:

My black dog

It's ironic that Churchill called depression his black dog because a black dog – a Labrador – saved my life, and possibly that of my unborn son too.

About ten years ago I went through a very acrimonious divorce. I still loved my wife, but she had moved on and found someone who she loved more. We didn't have children, but we had Samson, our two-year-old Labrador. We both loved that dog, but as my wife had bought him we decided it was best Samson stayed with her. Adjusting to life on my own after five years of marriage wasn't easy and after a month of pain I had a breakdown. I seriously didn't want to go on living. I remember lying on my bedroom floor crying. I might have stayed there crying for days if the doorbell hadn't rung. At first I ignored it but the ringer was persistent, so I eventually dragged myself away. It was my wife – the last person I wanted to see. She had Samson with her and he looked very thin – and anyone who has a Labrador will know they don't like being thin. My wife told me he just wasn't eating and it might be because he missed me. She was at her wits' end and asked if I could take him for a week to see if he would eat.

I shrugged my shoulders and let him in, closing the door on my wife. Then I realised I didn't have any dog biscuits, so I had to get dressed and go to the supermarket. Samson settled on the sofa and when I came back he was lying on his back; it looked really funny and against my will I smiled. Two hours later, he had eaten the entire box of biscuits and wanted to go out for a walk. I had no choice but to take him. We walked for an hour and it felt good to get some exercise and fresh air. I think you know where this is heading, Theresa. Within weeks I was feeling better and Samson was getting fatter. When my wife came to collect him she could see how happy he was and I became his sole owner.

Samson gave me a purpose. He loved and needed me and I felt capable of taking care of him. He would get me up on mornings when I felt like I couldn't fact the world and he made me smile every time he got excited about the most trivial of things – a walk, a toilet break, a piece of chicken. He was the miracle I needed. He just accepted me as I was. He wanted to be with me, even when I was feeling miserable. Samson saved my life – of that I have no doubt.

Two years later, I got married to a fellow dog walker I kept bumping into who owned a delightful brown Labrador. Samson may also have saved the life of my unborn son. My wife was eight months pregnant at the time and it was about four in the morning when he came bounding into our room and pacing backwards and forwards. I thought he needed to relieve himself, but he didn't want to go out. My wife sat up and gave me a look that needed no translation. She was bleeding. I rushed her to the hospital and my beautiful son Tommy was born. I can't be sure, but if Samson hadn't woken us up my wife might have slept through the bleeding.

Last year Samson passed away in my arms from a malignant growth that would not shift, despite two operations. I felt like I lost both my arms and legs. Just before he passed and he stared into my eyes for the last time I asked him to be sure to never leave me and he never has left my heart. His death was more painful than my depression, but also the most beautiful spiritual experience. I felt deep, deep gratitude to the universe for sending this angel to me in my hour of need. I just need to think of him and he is with me every day. I scattered his ashes on our favourite park walk and keep a few of them in a locket that I wear close to my heart. That is where my black dog, Samson, will always live – in my heart. I miss him endlessly but his love is all around me and within me.

Dogs are often said to have a supersense when it comes to their owners being in danger and I have read many stories like Glen's in which dogs save lives or give their owners a reason to live. It breaks my heart every time I read media reports of dogs turning on their owners and injuring or killing them. The stories are horrendous, but more often than not it is the way these dogs are treated by their owners that is the problem. The older I get, the more inclined I am to believe that if we continue to treat animals with cruelty, we will perpetuate suffering and perhaps even suffer the consequences ourselves. In spirit, it is possible that our treatment of animals and lack of respect for them is stunting our spiritual development. We only develop spiritually when we honour and respect all life forms, including animals. In the words of Ghandi, 'The greatness of a nation and its moral progress can be judged by the way its animals are treated.'

Darcy sent me this next story about another popular household pet that was able to sense and heal her owner's physical and emotional pain.

Journey's end

My mum died last year from liver cancer. She was very strong and did not complain, but it was clear that she was in a lot of pain. I didn't want her to go to a hospice so I cared for her at home. I was warned that in the final few weeks and days it would get very traumatic. My brother and I were worried about how we would comfort her, but drew strength from our prayers.

About a week before Mum died she was on very high doses of morphine, but there were moments of lucidity. It was unbearably heartbreaking. One morning, I was in the kitchen making what must have been my hundredth cup of coffee – I'd hardly had any sleep in the weeks preceding – and I heard a meowing outside the back door. I opened it and there was this straggly cat standing there. Normally, I'd have closed the door quickly to stop the cat coming in, but something – whether it was tiredness or intuition, I don't know – made me hesitate. The cat ran straight upstairs and went into my mum's bedroom, jumped on her bed and curled into a ball beside her.

My mum was sleeping peacefully, so I tiptoed to the bed and tried to take the cat away, but he just jumped over my mum to the other side of the bed. The movement must have woken my mum as she opened her eyes. When she saw the cat she smiled and shook her head at me as if to say leave things be, so I retreated and left the two of them sleeping together.

For the next two days this cat never left my mum's side except for mealtimes – we fed him white fish – and to go to the toilet outside. My mum had been very unsettled and uncomfortable, but now with the cat curled up beside her she seemed much more peaceful.

When Mum died we decided to keep the cat because he found a new job – for want of a better word – and that job was to comfort Dad. Dad missed my mum terribly when she was gone, and the cat seemed to sense that and was his constant companion.

Stories like Darcy's reinforce my belief that there is an unexplained and possibly mystic connection between animals and humans and that it manifests itself very strongly when we are at our most vulnerable and needy. Darcy's cat gave her parents great love and affection and her story is proof to me that sometimes heaven will reveal its love through animals, in much the same way that it reveals itself through afterlife signs or dreams.

CALL OF THE WILD

If you want to catch a glimpse of heaven, spending more time with your pets, if you have any, is one of the easiest ways to raise your spiritual vibration. If you don't have a pet, then spending more time in nature or a local park is another way. As we saw in Chapter One, nature is one of heaven's favourite places to send a sign. You truly can feel heaven in the breeze or through a departed loved one kissing you with a raindrop or whispering to you in the leaves or singing a song of love through birdsong. We are all familiar with stories of domestic animals like dogs and cats sensing danger and saving lives, but sometimes wild animals can do the work of angels. I love reading incredible true stories like this one recently reported by NBC:

Three lions

In Ethiopia young girls are at risk of being kidnapped and forced into marriage, but for one twelve-year-old girl three lions intervened. She had been taken by seven men with the intention of one marrying her, but what the abductors didn't know was that a group of three lions had been following and watching them the whole day. When the men started to beat the girl they charged at the men and chased them away and proceeded to guard her and protect her until the police arrived to find her. As soon as they saw the police they ran away. According to wildlife experts it is possible that a young girl crying might sound like a lion cub, but whatever the reason, the girl was lucky to have three angel lions watching over her that day. The animal kingdom never ceases to amaze.

I have a big file of stories that have been sent to me about wild animals and how they have been able to ease the grief of those who were missing departed loved ones. Birds, most commonly robins, appearing at the perfect moment or being unusually tame can be uplifting afterlife signs or bringers of healing and comfort. And in the case of this next story, sent to me by Kasha, Heaven chooses to sing through wild animals.

Angel bird

My husband used to call me his angel and when we had our daughter, Poppy, he called her angel bird because she had such a tiny appetite and ate like a bird. We were a very happy family until my husband died in 2006 from prostate cancer. I was devastated, but needed to carry on for Poppy. I also sensed him all around me and in the love for my daughter he was alive. It was different for his mum though.

I'd call in on my mum-in-law every day after work to have a chat and make sure she was eating OK. She seemed to hardly eat at all. Sometimes she'd go for days with just a scone for sustenance. I'd bring food along, but she hardly touched it. It broke my heart to see her like this. She used to be so vibrant and alive. One day, in yet another attempt to get her to eat, I decided that we should all eat in the garden as it was a lovely, sunny day. I brought Poppy along; she loved playing in her grandparents' garden – it was much bigger than ours.

Something very special happened that afternoon. We were sitting on the patio watching Poppy play when this wild little bird, a robin, I think, flew down beside Poppy and let her pet it for at least a minute. Curious, I got up to see if it would let me pet it too, but it flew away. I sat down again and the bird reappeared and allowed Poppy to pet it yet again.

It was extraordinary – but even more extraordinary was my mum-in-law's reaction. She looked at me and told me it was her son, my husband, saying goodbye to us and his daughter, his angel bird. How often does a wild bird let a child pet it without flying away? The bird wasn't injured and my daughter wasn't throwing breadcrumbs down.

From that day on my mum-in-law got some of her spirit back, and she died with a smile on her face because she knew her son was waiting for her.

For Lynne, the appearance of a young and vulnerable robin at her side brings to mind her father's love for her, even though they had a troubled relationship.

I remember the good times

My father's favourite bird was a robin, and robins have featured in my life in amazing ways.

One late summer, I was walking down a quiet road when I heard a trilling, chirruping noise that seemed to be following me as I walked along. I turned around to see a young robin, too young to be away from its parents. I ushered the little bird into a garden and hoped its mother would come and find it before long.

My father came from a broken home, abandoned at just three years old and brought up by his aunt in a tiny Welsh village. I will never know why he was so violent to me and I never asked. It's complicated, but when I saw that robin I felt his own vulnerability and I remembered the good parts, the fun times and his love for me.

Birdsong can bring deep comfort during times of grief as it somehow captures sacred sounds that can link you to heaven. If you ever want to feel divinely inspired or connected to something higher, take a few moments to calm your mind and listen to the birds singing. I've also heard stories of insects like butterflies communicating messages of hope. Although butterflies are insects they belong in this chapter as they are living beings, loving creatures with a message of love and light to share too. Here's Shirley's story:

Beautiful things

I lost my husband five years ago, following a long and painful battle with cancer in which I nursed him at home to the bitter end. The night following his passing, I slept soundly for the first time, having come to rely on light sleep so that I could be aware of his needs during the night, if required. That night I dreamed that we were in a bird hide (we were avid birding enthusiasts) and I spotted a large tortoiseshell butterfly on the floor. I pointed out the butterfly to him and bent down to pick it up, but as I did so it grew larger and larger until it was so big that when I picked it up it spanned the width of both of my hands. I then set it free through the open window.

My first thought upon waking was how unusual the dream was in that it was so clear and strong in my mind and completely different to how I felt on waking from other dreams. As I went downstairs I noticed that two sympathy cards had been put through the door and when I opened them I saw that they were identical and had the same butterfly on the front. Later that morning, the district nurse called to see me and handed me a card; before even opening it I said to her, 'Does this have a picture of a butterfly on it by any chance?' She confirmed that it did, saying that she usually buys cards with flowers on them for female bereaved and had no idea what had drawn her to the butterfly card. It was, as you will now guess, the very same card as the two others I had received, so my mantlepiece looked a little unusual with the three identical butterfly cards on it. I took the butterfly connection and the dream of the growing butterfly to be a sign from my husband that he had finally been set free and was now whole again.

It is important to bear in mind, as Shirley's story illustrates, that messages from heaven delivered by living animals are not restricted to those that appear in their physical form. They can bring messages and teachings to you in your dreams, in pictures or in the words of others. They can appear in your thoughts to bring you a message, in stories, on the TV or even in adverts or posters.

A few years ago, when I was going through a confusing period in my life and wasn't sure which direction my spiritual writing should go in, I walked past a shop with a spectacular poster of an eagle and the following words underneath it: 'Rise above, see the bigger picture.' The eagle really spoke to me. I was getting too involved in running my Facebook page and struggling to keep up with the number of messages and stories I was being sent, wondering where it was all heading. I needed to see the bigger picture and think about why I was actually writing spiritual books – which was to remind people we are spiritual beings having a human experience and not the other way around. It was soon after seeing that eagle poster, with its caption constantly on my mind, that I had the idea to invite a medium – someone who channels information from heaven – to co-author this book.

DO ANIMALS HAVE SOULS?

Today I'm convinced there is a piece of heaven in every living creature but this wasn't the case when I was grow-ing up. At school I was taught the survival-of-the-fittest Darwinian notion of life on earth and there certainly wasn't any room for love and compassion there, but as the stories in this chapter show, animals – both domestic and wild – can act with compassion and love. They can feel and give love just like us and they also have souls – souls that are immortal.

Whether in human or animal form I'm sure love has the power to cross the boundaries of space and time and I have a huge collection – numbering thousands now – of stories sent to me by people who believe they have been visited by animals from the other side. I have had personal experience of this when I sensed my beloved cat brush her body against my legs a few weeks after she had passed. The experience was incredibly comforting and would later inspire me to write a book about psychic cats. Today I own both dogs and cats and am sure that the intense and loving bond between us will survive death. I often think that if my pets don't meet me in heaven, it won't feel like heaven!

The more stories I read about afterlife communication from animals the more certain I am that it is possible for pets to reach out to us from beyond the grave. This is a view Claire shares and she confirms the presence of animals in heaven later in her section of the book. I hope that whether you are an animal lover or not, as you read this chapter you will be comforted by the possibility that there is life after death for animals and that our loved ones never really die, regardless of their species or size.

The next three stories suggest that just as heaven is real for both humans and animals sometimes beloved pets can reach out to us from the other side to send us reassurance that their love is eternal.

Mark is certain that the bond he created with his dog has continued despite her passing. His story shows that when pets live they make us smile and when they die they leave a permanent smile in our hearts.

Dreaming of Treacle

I've been blessed to take care of the most amazing dogs in my life. They are all miracles in their own way, but I want to tell you about Treacle. She was a gorgeous lovable retriever and I probably felt closer to her than any dog I have had. I was the first person to hold her – well catch her – as she was born and the last to hold her as she died with her head in my lap.

Treacle brought magic to my life for eleven years and taught me so much about unconditional love and simple joy in the moment. A couple of weeks after her death I met Treacle on the rainbow bridge in a very vivid dream. In this dream she took me flying over the earth and we ran together in fields. Before she died she could barely walk, but in my dream she was so nimble. During the dream she was telling me telepathically that she was OK and could now run free again and heaven was amazing. In my dream Treacle had a friend – a small brown and white pug I had never seen before.

The next day I went to work and told my colleague about my dream and the dog with Treacle. When I described it she said she could not believe it because it sounded just like her dog that had died a year ago before she started working with me. She showed me a photo and it was exactly like the dog I'd seen in the dream with my Treacle. That was all the proof I needed and need to show that heaven is real for humans and for pets.

Like Mark, Lucy knows that the bond between her and her cat, Kyle, is unbroken by death.

It's fine

My cat, Kyle, died around two and half years ago. He was my cat, but lived at my mum's house as I had left home. We'd had him and his brother since they were kittens and when my dad was diagnosed with cancer my boyfriend and I gave them to my mum as a comfort for her.

Kyle had been ill for a couple of years and he was put on tablets to prolong his life. He managed two years, but then he began to go downhill. One day, he was rushed to the vet. He was in a bad way and we were told to expect the worst. I went to visit him and he looked strangely content, purring as soon as he heard my voice, and happy, even though he couldn't move as both his back legs were completely paralysed. He had been holding on for a couple of days. The next day, I rang the vet really early to ask if I could bring some food in for Kyle as he hadn't been eating. At that moment I knew something was wrong as the receptionist put me on hold, then told me that Kyle had just been put down as he had taken a turn for the worse in the night and been in pain.

I was devastated and kept busting into tears throughout the day. I felt guilty that he was all alone when he died and I wasn't by his side and I kept thinking that he would have thought I didn't love him because I wasn't there in his final moments. We were really close when he was alive – he used to flop down in my arms and liked to be cradled like a baby and nudge and curl up by me when I was upset.

Anyway, that night my boyfriend and I were lying in bed and I just burst into tears and blurted out how I was feeling and how I loved Kyle so much. My boyfriend tried to reassure me that Kyle would give me a sign to let me know he was OK, but I didn't believe him.

Before I fell asleep, I prayed to Kyle that he would give me a sign to let me know he was OK and said that I was sorry I wasn't there when he died and that I loved him. I eventually fell asleep and then, around 4 a.m. I woke up, startled by Kyle's mum, who lived with us. She was making this odd noise/meowing sound right by my face, as if she had been woken up too. She was licking my hand and nudging me, being overly affectionate. She was never usually like that. She wasn't an affectionate cat like Kyle had been. It was like she was trying to talk to me, but I had this feeling of comfort and a weight lifted off my shoulders and a sense of happiness. It was like it was a message from Kyle, through his mum, to let me know he was OK and he knew I loved him. The next morning, I felt happier, as I just had this feeling Kyle had contacted me. And as I was walking to my mum's house, the path I walked along was scattered with tiny white feathers, almost like someone had burst a pillow down from heaven. There were hundreds of them.

Kyle was only seven when he died – so young. It feels like he was only brought onto the planet to give comfort to my mum a year before my dad died, then to help her through the death/grieving process and then, when I saw him at the vet he just looked at me as if he was thinking, It's OK. I've done what I needed to do. My job is done on planet earth and I'm happy to go now. It's fine. Almost like this was his purpose in life.

Sam also feels that his cat, Poppy, returned in an unusual way to say one last goodbye.

Right by your side, always

I have had numerous cats in my life, but one of my favourites, Willum, had to be put to sleep in 2010. I was very upset, but knew it had to be done. He was a distinctive-looking cat – I'd never seen another one like him. About three months later, I was still missing him. It was the middle of July and the back door was open. I looked out into the garden and I saw a black cat exactly like Willum – he had his back to me but he was sitting under the prunus tree, and right next to him was my other cat, Poppy. Poppy would never tolerate another cat in her vicinity, so this was definitely strange. So there they both sat, right next to one another, like they always used to, with their backs to me. My brain was telling me it obviously wasn't him, but I can still feel the euphoria that I felt on seeing him. It was like he had returned from the dead! I walked out into the garden to try to get closer, and he disappeared through the hedge. Usually, when I see a new cat in my garden, I see it again and again. I had never seen this other cat before and I have never seen it since.

ANIMAL TRANQUILLITY

As I was writing this chapter, I found myself – by heaven-sent chance – to be in regular contact with Tina Read, who is an animal healer. Her work is so inspiring and her stories about animals so comforting that I asked her to do a regular post on my Theresa Cheung author page on Facebook. Her weekly posts are proving to be a favourite and it does not surprise me. Here is a selection of just some of the magical stories she has shared about her life and work and the animals that inspire her.

Sparrow

On one of my first visits to Feline Care Cat Rescue a tiny dot of a tabby cat, who I later learned was called Sparrow, somewhat delicately climbed up onto my knee while I was in reiki meditation. Within moments, she was sleeping peacefully and did not wake up until it was time for me to leave. Despite her frail stature and being seriously ill, she still managed to boss everyone around and was rather a character! Molly, who runs FCCR, knew when the time had come to call the vet and she wanted to make Sparrow's last day full of all the things she loved. Molly and Sparrow had cuddles and she tucked into her favourite food; afterwards, Molly snuggled up with Sparrow on a duvet on the floor and spent the last few hours with her until it was time for her to pass peacefully over the rainbow bridge to be with the angels. When I visited the cats last week and was in Sparrow's area, I felt her presence very strongly indeed and believe she is now a guardian angel to the other cats while they are in the special-care unit.

Lucky

Some things are simply meant to be. My husband and I were not thinking about adding to our pack, but one

Sunday afternoon we were both on Facebook and looking at the same rescue page, which was for German shepherds. There was a pair of deep brown eyes staring at me from the screen and I felt an immediate connection. The dog was elderly, around fourteen, and certainly not a German shepherd – perhaps a bit of pointer in there somewhere and tan feet like a shepherd! I mentioned Lucky to my husband and he was looking at the same post at that moment. We both knew straightaway he was meant to come and live with us.

We soon found out that Lucky had had a difficult life with very little love or care. He had a few health conditions, but despite being told he needed a quiet retirement home he seemed to rush around like a young pup, enjoyed his food and all the TLC he was now getting. He was the life and soul of the party! He was happy with his new pack and set about making up for lost time. We had the most amazing six months together jam-packed with happy days and so much love. I wished it could have been six years, but I truly believe he did everything he had missed out on.

During his last week or two my husband and I took it in turns to sleep downstairs with him and one night his eyes told me he was ready to make his journey over the rainbow bridge. It was hard to accept, but I could not ignore what I felt in my heart and we arranged for the vet to visit. We took him for a potter in our paddock with our other three dogs and took some photos. In each of these there were streams of light following Lucky.

After Lucky passed, I felt his energy so strongly and the joy of freedom from a frail body. Six months later, we fostered

Nelson, a blind German shepherd. After six weeks, he went off to his new home, only to unexpectedly return to us a few days later on the exact date that Lucky had arrived with us a year earlier. If ever there was a sign from Lucky that Nelson was meant to stay that was it. Needless to say, Nelson is a much-loved member of our family and has now been with us for two and a half years. We are very blessed that Lucky is watching over us all.

Tiny souls

In October 2014, I spent two amazing weeks in my role as a Shelter Animal Reiki Association reiki practitioner and teacher at Tree of Life for Animals in the Rajasthan area of India, or TOLFA as it is known. A few days before I was due to return home, Rachel, the founder of TOLFA, asked me to share reiki with some tiny puppies, who were orphans and very ill indeed.

When I entered the room my heart opened so wide seeing these tiny souls, I had to take a deep breath and centre myself, so I could be in that space of love. I spent some time sharing reiki with them that first afternoon and returned again the next day. On my second visit, only two of the puppies remained. Again, we shared a peaceful space of love and compassion. As I got up to leave, the smaller of the two puppies unsteadily walked over to me and kissed my hand. I felt he was saying goodbye and felt so much love coming from his tiny body. On my final day, only one puppy was still alive. He was so poorly, but clearly fighting with everything he had. I settled in to share reiki with him and a wave of complete peace came over me. I could sense the other puppies like tiny angels flying around us in the space and sending us so much love. It was the most beautiful and loving experience you can imagine and the tears of joy streamed down my face.

That afternoon, I said my farewell to the lone little pup, not knowing what his future held, but having complete faith that his siblings would be with him no matter what. A year later, I was speaking to Rachel and mentioned the puppies. I was delighted to hear that the little pup had grown into a very handsome adult dog and now had a wonderful forever home with a retired TOLFA team member and was living a happy, healthy and fulfilled life. I am sure to this day his siblings are blessing him with their love.

Apa

Apa was a beautiful and regal-looking dog with long legs and a beautiful sandy-coloured coat. Apa had recently passed away at a very good age, having shared an amazing life with her family since being rescued many years earlier. She was truly loved and cherished. This was obviously a very sad time and her family asked me to go and see their other dog Calin. I settled next to him and he quickly relaxed. I went into a beautiful reiki meditation space with him, when I suddenly sensed a loving presence in the room and felt immediately it was Apa. I opened my eyes to see Calin staring at a particular spot by the sofa. At this exact moment, there was an incredible wave of pure joy, bliss and heaven. There were tears rolling down my cheeks and the feeling was so powerful, but in a truly peaceful way. Calin and I were bathed in this love which we knew was being sent by Apa. It was such a blessing to be able to tell her family that Apa had connected with us and how free and full of love she was.

Fred

Fred was a gorgeous terrier who, despite his small stature, had a huge character and the ability to bring joy to everyone he met with a simple look and some well-timed tricks, including standing on his back legs, which never failed to raise a laugh. Judy, his guardian, and I always joked that he was a Zen master – he had such knowing eyes and was truly an old soul. I had shared reiki with Fred and his doggy family for many years on a regular basis, and when he journeyed over the rainbow bridge I felt consumed with grief as he had become extended family to me. The unusual thing was that suddenly, this grief was cleared from me in a flash – it was like something magical washed over me and took the pain away. From that moment I could not feel any sadness at all. I believe this was one of Fred's parting gifts to me. For those first few weeks, when I thought of Fred I would see pure white feathers – this could be at any time and anywhere and I always knew without any doubt they were coming from him. Fred is truly an animal angel and never far away from his wonderful family.

ANIMALS AND THE AFTERLIFE

I'm deeply grateful to Tina for allowing me to include her beautiful stories in this book. She is an angel on earth for animals and details about how to connect with her and learn about her inspiring work can be found in the Appendix (see p. 326). Tina also helps owners to deal with pet bereavement and continue their loving bonds with pets after they die. There is so much need for this as from personal experience I know that the loss of a pet can be a huge blow to the heart, but you are just expected to deal with it and move on. Taking time off work to grieve because your dog has died is not considered acceptable but, as anyone who has lost a beloved pet will know, the impact of their loss can be devastating.

This story, sent to me by animal healer and friend Fiona, shows that when animals die they sense the closeness of heaven.

Tiffany

The morning of 9 March 2012 started normally enough. My horse's greeting, followed by her polishing her breakfast off, was no different to any other day. But as I led her from the stable to her field, her back end started to wobble sideways. I put her in the field and immediately rang my vet.

As I waited for the vet to arrive, I stayed in the field with my horse. She stood in front of me, her head resting on my shoulder, then every few minutes she would walk in small circles, whinnying at the same time. But it was not a distressed or pained sound – it was her happy, greeting whinny. I was immediately reminded of my nan a couple of years earlier. Hours before she passed away, she talked about a little boy and girl standing by her bed. Intuitively, I now felt that Tiffany's mum had come for her, and I was saying goodbye. It made me cry, as I realised this was the end of our twenty-six years together.

This pattern of behaviour continued right up until the vet walked up the path towards us, about an hour later. As she did so, Tiffany started circling all the way up the field, collapsing near the gate. She had held on long enough and now it was time to go. The timing was perfect. The vet was able to quicken the dying process. She reckoned it was neurological.

I had lost my horse in literally the space of a couple of hours. Although it was distressing for me at the time, I knew this was the perfect way for Tiffany to pass. At thirty-four years old, she still had incredible energy and it was difficult to view her as an old horse. Having a long, debilitating illness would not have suited her. This is the way she would have wanted to leave, and from what I witnessed, there had been no pain or suffering – only the love of a mother who had arrived to take her daughter home.

If the stories in this chapter have moved you, chances are you have animal-communication skills and the ability to connect to your pet, soul to soul. This is the place where miracles can happen because pets through their love can touch our souls. Loving a pet, therefore, means that you are touching heaven. The love pets offer us in both this life and the next is unconditional and eternal. They can protect us, guide us, calm us, comfort us and love us when we need it the most. Heaven answers our prayers in many different ways and, as the stories in this chapter have shown, for people who feel connected to animals those prayers sometimes come with fur, feathers, whiskers, wings and tails.

CHANGE OF GEAR

So far, you've read eclectic stories, both gentle and inspiring, about some of the most common answers from heaven, and you've discovered that heaven can speak in countless ordinary but extraordinary ways, including through the love of a beloved pet. All these answers are ones that you will, at some point in your life, have experienced − even if you didn't recognise them as a sign from heaven at the time. If you don't believe me, ask yourself these questions:

- Have you ever dreamed of a departed loved one?
- Have you ever found yourself thinking something was a wonderful coincidence?
- Have thoughts of a departed loved one flooded your mind when you least expected it?
- Have you ever felt an overwhelming sense of love and joy for no particular reason?

Chances are you will have experienced at least one of these in the course of your life and I hope, from now on, you will know that when these amazing things happen heaven is calling you. I hope also that all you have learned here about other common but often ignored afterlife signs will help you find your own ways to receive answers from above every single day of your life.

There's going to be a change of gear now. The stories in the next chapter are far more dramatic than those you've read so far because they are rare examples of afterlife encounters that are anything but subtle, showing, for reasons that are simply unexplainable, how heaven chose to reveal itself in a way that left absolutely no room for doubt. They are quite simply powerful, bold and clear statements of eternal love from the other side.

> *I swear I think now that every living thing*
> *without exception has an eternal soul. I swear*
> *I think there is nothing but immortality.*

WALT WHITMAN

CHAPTER FOUR

LOVE FROM ABOVE

Unable are the loved to die. For love is immortality.

EMILY DICKINSON

It's impossible for anyone, even a medium like Claire, to know for sure what happens when we die. Some people believe we simply breathe our last and our light goes out and there is nothing. We are gone and the only thing we leave behind for those mourning us are memories. Some believe in reincarnation and that our spirit keeps returning to earth in a different human form to learn lessons and carry on growing spiritually. Others believe in some kind of an afterlife, perhaps where we are rewarded or punished for our actions on earth.

Then there are those who believe that our consciousness, our spirit or that spark of life within us survives the death of our bodies and continues living in an invisible dimension we can't fully understand in our human form. In other words, we are spirits in human form. If you've ever seen the body of someone who has recently passed, as I did several times when I worked in a hospice many years ago, there is an overwhelming sense that even though their body is still there, their spark, their essence – or whatever it is that makes a person unique – has gone. The body simply looks like clothes that aren't being worn. Try as they might, scientists still haven't been able to create that spark of life and it remains a mystery. But from all the afterlife stories I have read and researched over the past three decades I'm more convinced than ever that when a body dies that spark of life continues on in another invisible realm.

Far from denying the existence of an afterlife, modern science may actually be pointing in its direction. Basic physics tells us that everything – you, this book, your phone, your car and everything and everyone you encounter – consists of energy that vibrates and how that energy vibrates determines its form. Obviously, this is way too simplistic, but the point I'm making is that we are all energy: your body, your mind and your thoughts too.

Is it such a leap of faith, then, to suggest that when our bodies die, the energy created by our thoughts and feelings – which you may call spirit, if you prefer – carries on in a non-physical, invisible dimension? And is it possible that sometimes we can tune into that eternal energy of the departed?

It most certainly is, according to the countless numbers of people who say they have been touched from above and have had an afterlife encounter. Thousands of people have sent me such reports and their experiences bear witness to the very real possibility that in some cases and under certain circumstances the strength of the energy between two people who love each other can make communication between this life and the next possible.

This communication or connection can happen in countless different ways. You've already seen how it can happen in afterlife signs, dreams, intuition and coincidences and now you are going to see how it can take place in less subtle ways, including partial and full-blown apparitions, when a person is not asleep but wide awake. In each and every case the messages from the other side are ones of comfort, hope and love or a recognisable answer from heaven that offers reassurance that those we have loved and lost have not gone away but are still sending their love and watching over us.

FAMILY CONNECTIONS

The stories that follow were all sent to me by people who have had the most astonishing afterlife contact with a departed family member. They all prove that the love between family members can not only be a source of strength, comfort and joy in this life, but may also reach out to us from the other side. This story from Craig shows how the love of a mother and wife can transcend space and time.

Taking him home

My mother died in November 2000 of breast cancer and my father died in February 2004 of stroke. The day before Dad died, I was due to be at his house to wait for workmen to come and fix the doors, so we could get a wheelchair through them and he could come home to die. I got up in the morning as usual, and when I went into my living room, there was my mum sitting on the sofa! She looked just the same as the last time I'd seen her when she was healthy, dressed the same. She turned her face towards me and smiled. I blinked – and she was gone.

I did what I'd got planned to do at my father's house and came home. The day after, I had a call from the hospital to tell me my father had taken a turn for the worse. Now, Dad and I had already agreed that I would not go and be with him at the end; he didn't want to die in front of me, bless him. So I stayed put until I got the call telling me he had gone. I am convinced my mother had visited me to tell me she was coming to take Dad home and was really looking forward to it.

Penny's story follows on next and it is a beautiful illustration of the enduring connections families share and how a beloved father made sure his daughter knew he was alive within and around her.

One night

My father died twenty years ago. He was the best person. I always felt he would put everything right and would be there to protect me. He was my rock and my 'go-to' person. He died out of the blue from septicaemia, after being bitten by an insect. I was devastated and felt deserted and lost and alone. He did appear in my dreams, but they were frustrating dreams where someone would tell me he was on the phone, but when I grabbed the phone he hung up; or my mother would tell me he was hiding somewhere odd, like in a suitcase, but when I went to open it I woke up. The dreams really caused me anxiety.

Then everything changed one night. I was woken up by the doorbell ringing. My partner continued sleeping and I couldn't wake him. I went to the hallway and I could see through the glass panel in the front door. I saw my departed dad standing there. I wasn't shocked or surprised at all and opened the door. He smiled and walked past me, and strangely my mum was with him. My mum is still alive. He went into the lounge and sat down in an armchair. I sat down opposite him and noticed how young he looked. He was sixty-seven when he died, but he looked about forty. I asked him about this and he said he had chosen the age when he felt happiest. I told him how much I missed him and how sad I was. I asked him if he was sad and was missing us and he said no he wasn't sad at all and wasn't missing us. He was smiling the whole time. I remember little of the conversation that followed, but when he stood to leave I asked him if he would come back again and he said no, that he didn't need to come back. He left through the front door with my mum, who hadn't said anything during the visit. At no point was I scared.

The next thing I know I am sitting up in bed barely able

to catch my breath. My partner woke up and I told him everything and he believed me. I sometimes wonder if it was a dream, but it felt so real and I remember being wide awake. From that day on I have felt so peaceful about Dad. I feel him all the time and he once again is my 'go-to' person when I feel troubled or am not sure what to do. I speak to him every day in my heart and when he does appear in my dreams he is alive and not on the phone or in a suitcase. I feel so blessed and now, after reading your book, I believe this was my dad seeing my pain and coming to me to help me through it.

Penny saw her father and knew that what happened was not her imagination or a dream. Her father truly spoke to her and underlined to her the miracle of eternal love. Jordan believes his grandfather appeared to him too:

Floating figure

My first experience was when I was around five years old and it happened at my grandmother's house. As I walked into the dining room, I saw a floating white figure without any features. I ran out to my nan in the next room and asked her about it, but she had been sat in the same chair all the time, so it wasn't her and nobody else was in at the time. So I asked her about it and she said, 'Don't worry. It was your grandfather who was wearing white when he died.'

Jordan was fortunate because his nan didn't dismiss his vision as fantasy or childish imagination or scold him for making things up. She believed him and this belief gave him confidence to explore and develop his psychic abilities and not fear or be ashamed of them.

It breaks my heart when people tell me that their early signs of psychic potential were laughed at or repressed by their family. Children are close to heaven because of their ability to suspend disbelief, and every parent who listens to their child when they talk about matters of spirit and what they can see, hear or sense nurtures not just their creativity and individuality, but their spiritual development.

ETERNAL BONDS

Of course, it isn't just the enduring love between family members that can transcend space and time. Whenever love is strong between two people it can cross the veil of death, as showcased by Lily in the next story.

Love goes on

Exactly twenty days after my husband passed away I was crying and talking to him and thinking that I cannot go on without him. The next morning when I woke up, I went to my balcony and looked down at my garden. I saw a small piece of paper with a message on it attached to one of our rose plants. I had never noticed it before when I was in the garden or looked out from the balcony. The first thought was that someone had left it for me, but I thought that all doors were locked, so it wouldn't be possible. I went down to the garden and took the paper and written on it was a poem saying that life and love go on. The most amazing thing is that the handwriting matched my husband's and the plant had a small rose – this plant had never before flowered! It was the first and last rose on this plant. And it flowered in one night! In addition, my husband loved roses! I also had other experiences with my husband over a period of one and a half years after his passing. One time, before I went to sleep, I was half awake when I heard his voice in my ears telling me not to cry.

Lily is certain that her husband orchestrated this beautiful message for her. She didn't have a vision, but it was a miracle for her. The theme of miracles and answered prayers can also be seen in this next story, sent to me by Julia.

Where are you?

I was at home on my own in the afternoon and had been feeling more upset than usual about the loss of a very dear friend and praying for some relief from the pain.

In my distress, I called out to him as I was crying. I told him how much I missed him and asked, 'Where are you?'

Suddenly, I felt an overwhelming sense of peace and calm come over me and I stopped crying and felt very peaceful. I smiled and thanked him in my heart.

It was so real and I know I had an angel with me that day. Since that afternoon, whenever I think of my friend, it isn't with sadness any more.

Yes, I miss him, but I seem to remember him more with

laughter and the tears are no longer there. I believe he is fine and that I will see him when it is my time to pass. It was a wonderful feeling of reassurance that day and I really felt healed.

Julia's story is out of this world, but also very much in it because she mentions something we have all done, whether consciously or unconsciously, and that is to pray. I hesitate to talk about prayer here, as it is so often associated with religion, but you do not need to be religious or go on bended knees to pray. Anyone with a loving heart can pray at any time or place. Prayer is simply a heartfelt communication with spirit and, as this next story from Carrie shows, it is possible that those on the other side can sometimes hear our prayers.

Something wonderful happened

It happened about twenty years ago and I've only told a handful of people, but feel it is something I was meant to share, but didn't know how. I have never needed convincing of an afterlife. I was a very lonely, only child, full of constant worry and despondency, but seemed to have had – from a very early age – a belief in the afterlife and I never truly felt at home on earth. I have had a few encounters with the spirit world in the past, but – like a lot of people – find it hard to 'live it' in my everyday life.

I was going through a particularly hard time. I was divorced with two small children and recently remarried, but knew this marriage was probably a mistake. I was a member of a church, but didn't feel welcome and when I put this to one of the elders of the church he told me I didn't 'belong' there and that I should 'go home and pray'. For weeks and weeks after this I prayed every waking moment for some sign that I did belong and I was meant to be part of this amazing universe. After literally weeks and weeks of praying and meditating, something wonderful happened.

I had gone to bed with the desperate plea for a sign still going around and around my head. Eventually, I fell asleep with my new husband fast asleep next to me.

I was woken to the sound of clapping, cheering, trumpets playing and a wonderful cone of beautiful warm, bright light enveloping me with the most amazing feeling of joy, peace and love I have ever felt. My arms were raised to the light and a voice I recognised, but had forgotten as my own spirit voice was saying, 'You came, you came.' In earthly terms, I have no idea how long this bathing in love lasted, but as the clapping and cheering began to fade, so did the light and then a beautiful white dove flew around the room and a voice spoke to me, but also somehow came from me, saying, 'Don't ever think we haven't got a relationship.' Eventually, everything gradually dimmed and receded and I found myself sitting up in a dark, quiet room with my arms raised, and my husband still asleep next to me.

I don't know what happened. All I can say is that whatever it was, my spirit recognised what was happening and I was 'me' but 'not me', if that makes sense. The 'not me' I recognised was a much more loving, spiritual being than the 'me' I have become.

I hope this all makes sense. As you know, it's extremely

hard to explain spiritual happenings in earthly terms, but I really felt a strong urge to share this with you.

We've all felt helpless at times. This may apply to your own life, if you have experienced bereavement or are suffering from depression. Or perhaps a loved one is seriously ill or there has been an accident or natural disaster, but practical help either isn't needed or you don't have the skills to give it. In those instances, I want you to know that there *is* something you can do. You can pray.

Prayer has incredible power and there have been scientific studies showing that patients who were prayed for had faster recovery times than those who were not. Considering that all matter (even our thoughts) consists of energy, it is entirely possible that this energy can be directed to achieve an outcome not just in this life, but to make contact with the next. This story from Michelle is a perfect example of this power, showing how departed loved ones can hear our prayers.

Waiting list

Last year, we moved house and sent our children to the local school. My daughter suffers with anxiety and at the time she hated school as she struggled with the work. Her new school was OK to start with, but her teacher left and then my daughter, who was six at the time, was getting bullied. She had no friends as there were only two other girls in the class and they didn't include her. They would shout in her face every day until she cried. The school was notified several times, but did nothing. Then it all came to a head as my daughter started acting differently and didn't want to go to school and one day finally broke down saying that for three months she'd always been on her own at playtimes.

That was the final straw. I applied to the school in the next village, where I work, but there were no places available and there was a waiting list, due to it being a good school and us being out of the catchment area. So I placed her on the waiting list, hoping for the best. I was told two children would need to leave for her to get a place. I felt disheartened ... what were the chances of two children leaving anytime soon?

So I still had to send her in and it broke my heart. There is nothing worse for a parent than sending your child into an environment which is unpleasant for them and you are powerless to help. After a month, I went to bed early one night, very tearful about the whole thing, and I prayed so hard to my dad that he would help my daughter. I said, 'Please, Dad, if you can hear me, please help your granddaughter get a place at my school, as it's breaking my heart. She's so unhappy, and I don't know what else to do!'

Three days later, the receptionist at my school came up to me and started saying something about a trial day for my daughter as a place had become available! I almost fell off the chair in shock. Two children were leaving at the end of term, so she had a place from the beginning of the next. What are the chances of that? I definitely don't think that was coincidence and I truly believe my dad helped make that happen. He was very protective when he was alive and I know if he was still alive he would have fought to the bitter end to protect his family and his granddaughter.

Nearly a year has passed and she's so much happier and confident and has loads of friends. She has also got the help she deserves with her learning issues, which the old school failed to provide.

Michelle prayed for a miracle, but in this next story from Lorella the miracle just happened. It wasn't prayed for or longed for, but it did save her life.

Without a trace

Late one night, I was driving home from my evening class in a rural area where there were no proper street lights. I drove very carefully as I was worried that I couldn't see properly. I was just about to turn around a sharp bend and, as I did, I saw a young boy wearing a school uniform walking on the side of the road. He waved at me. I slowed right down and waved back. I actually intended to stop because it wasn't safe for someone so young to be on their own at this time of night but, just at that moment, a car flashed around the bend incredibly fast and I know if I had been going at normal speed, I would have smashed into it for sure. Flustered, I hooted my horn but the driver speed past. I looked around for the boy and he had disappeared completely without a trace.

The next day, I told my friend at work and she asked me exactly which bend I was talking about and looked shocked. She said about two years ago there had been a horrible hit-and-run accident there involving a ten-year-old boy who was walking home from school.

So far, the stories you've read have been miraculous, but not typically a matter of life and death, as was the case for Lorella. She could not have known what was coming around the corner, but clearly heaven knew. Something with an awareness of future events intervened to give her a warning. I have personal experience of this kind of warning from above as you will have read in the Introduction when the voice of my mother in spirit spoke to me and saved my life (see p. 1). If you believe in heaven, you probably don't need an explanation, but if you want to speculate on how such things might be possible, then you might find your answers by remembering that we are all connected. Science attests to this and there is also the theory that time isn't linear and there is no past, present or future, just our perception.

These are mind-blowing concepts and there just isn't enough space here to discuss them, but I hope they will help you to see how the miracles you are reading about in this book are feasible from a scientific viewpoint. There is a possibility that our thoughts and feelings can cross the boundaries of time and space, life and death. But whatever the ultimate explanation, it is impossible not to be amazed, energised and profoundly inspired by the people in these next two stories. They believe they were saved by heaven.

Invisible hands

In 2015, I was doing some window cleaning with my boy-friend to earn some extra cash while I saved up for university. It was tiring, but I enjoyed it. I remember the day exactly that

I believed I was touched by heaven. It was 14 May at around 2 p.m.

I was laughing with my boyfriend about something – I like to tease him, so we laugh a lot – but this was a joke too far and I was shouting playfully to him as he was getting some more soap and sponges from the back of our van and I was climbing down my ladder, so I could move it and start on the next window. I was about halfway down and clearly not concentrating because my phone rang, and as I reached for it, I missed my footing and fell. Right before I fell and blacked out I remember a hand holding my head, so it didn't land on the concrete path.

The doctors told me that I had had a narrow escape because I could easily have cracked my skull. I told him that my boyfriend had broken my fall, but he later told me that was impossible because the first he knew about it was hearing me scream and hit the pavement. He ran over from the van and called an ambulance when he couldn't wake me. Not being a first aider, he felt it best not to touch me at all.

This is pretty incredible, right? But even more incredible is that my father died of a heart attack about an hour before my fall. The phone ringing had been my mother to tell me the terrible news. I think my father was there in spirit to break my fall. Can't prove it, of course, but it doesn't matter. It is my experience and it helped me cope with my father's death.

This next story from Amanda shows how her daughter saved her life from beyond the grave.

Stop now

Six years after my beautiful angel daughter died serving overseas in the army I was about to cross the road after doing some shopping. It was raining and the shopping bags were heavy. The lights turned to green, but as they did I saw my daughter – clear as day in the middle of the road – and she was holding a stop sign. I was frozen to the spot. Then she vanished, and at that instant, a white van sped through the red light. I've never forgotten that moment of magic heaven. I will carry it with me to my grave and beyond.

Cathy also felt heaven was watching over her. She believes she saw angels on two occasions:

I know it was real

My dear friend was dying and I was frantically praying for her when two enormous male-like angels appeared behind her and telepathically told me to 'let go'. I know it was real because of the enormous power radiating from them. There was no question of disobeying them because along with this power, there was the most unbelievable all-encompassing, pure love. There are no words that can describe this love. I 'let go' – I didn't really have a choice – and had the most wonderful sleep that I've ever had. My friend died three days after that. Later, I was persistently 'told' to tell her sister about this, but worried as I didn't know her her. However, an opportunity arose and I nervously told her. Her sister broke down in tears and thanked me profusely for telling her; she said she had been praying for a sign that her sister was OK. I had given her that sign.

Six months after my son, David, died, a pure white shaft of light came down on my left side and down this light came the most indescribable pure, perfect, divine and all-encompassing love. It was overwhelmingly beautiful and I knew it was from David. I was enveloped in a blanket of such great peace. David, when he had talked (he suffered from schizophrenia and this made communication difficult) invariably spoke about love being all important. How right he was. I felt like I'd been given a little glimpse of heaven that day.

Margaret believes angels visit her. Here's what she sees:

Always with me

I had my first angel encounter shortly after my daughter was born and I was very depressed. I had sobbed myself to sleep one afternoon and became aware of a sensation of being enfolded in what felt like wings and such a sense of being loved, it gave me a need to open my heart to God and my spirituality. Over the following years, I have seen orbs, had flying dreams and very vivid dreams where I conversed with my father and mother in spirit. I have seen spirits, but only once in that dreamlike state where I am not fully asleep or awake. I must admit to being afraid and I can recall the minute detail of these dreams, even though years have passed.

But the most wonderful experience to date happened

about six months ago. I was in Ireland (a very spiritual place, I feel) and I was in bed in that strange dreamlike state – neither asleep nor awake – when I opened my spiritual eyes and sitting beside me on my bed was this beautiful, elderly lady. She had silver-white hair and an aura of blue all around her to match her vivid blue dress. She said, 'Hello,' and held my hand and told me she knew my gift made me feel afraid, but that she would always be there to keep me safe! She stayed with me a little longer and I wanted to stay with her for ever, such was the feeling of love from her. I asked her name, but I don't remember getting one. I fell into a deep sleep and awoke feeling so happy and blessed. I have no doubt she was my angel and hope I'll see her again, although I know she is always with me.

In her section of the book, Claire will give her perspective on angels. I'm often asked if angels are spirits of departed loved ones. In the strict sense, an angel is a celestial being that has not incarnated on earth, whereas a spirit is a departed loved one. But in my mind, any spiritual presence that brings feelings of comfort and joy is angelic and from heaven. I therefore tend to use the terms angel, spirit and spirits of departed loved ones interchangeably, although I know there are those who would disagree and some who believe there are hierarchies of spiritual beings. But I prefer to keep it simple and – whichever word you use – in one way or another you have been touched by heaven.

This next story from Tamsin offers astonishing proof that love is infinitely more powerful than death.

Hold on, stay strong

My nineteen-year-old son was in intensive care after a motorbike accident and I had been staying in a hospital room for four days, so that I did not have to travel home. It was important I was close to him as his life hung in the balance. On 22 June last year I had the most amazing encounter or experience and I want to share it with you. I was sitting in my chair writing some thank-you cards to all my friends who had sent flowers and gifts to my room, when I got a strong smell of vanilla. I've checked since and none of the gifts I was sorting through contained any soap or perfume. The smell reminded me of my departed mother as she baked the best cakes.

Before I knew it, there were floods of tears running down my cheeks and I found myself rocking from side to side for comfort. The tears would not stop and I longed for my mother to be here with me as she was always so strong and warm. I needed to hug her and for her to tell me everything would be OK. After about an hour or so of sobbing, I calmed down and ran myself a warm bath. As I was running the water I heard a voice. It was my mother's voice and it was both inside and outside my head. She told me that I needed to cry and she had been right by my side and always would be. She told me my son – her grandson – wasn't ready to join her yet.

The next day my son made a dramatic recovery and four weeks later he left the hospital. I never stayed in the hospital room again as the doctors said he was no longer at risk of passing. My mother knew that and I feel her love and strength around me every day. I feel sad for anyone who does not believe in the afterlife as it is part of us all.

The love a mother has for a child can move mountains.
Rebecca's story is heartbreaking, but also deeply reassuring, as it shows that from before the cradle to beyond the grave heaven watches over us and guides us.

Silent night

The night after my baby was stillborn was the first time I felt heaven hug me. It is now eight years later, and as I relive the tragic day in my mind, I know now that my guardian angel hugged me with love and comfort and that I am worthy of that love and comfort.

As a parent of an angel, I do not want to forget one detail of my son's existence or death. He is a very special little boy who has brought many good things into my life because of his passing. Looking back at the night after he was born dead, I know that my angel helped me drift into the most wonderful and peaceful sleep.

Connor was stillborn late in the afternoon on a Friday and I was moved into a room on another floor, away from all of the happy new mothers. It was a ghost town with minimal staff and patients. I told everyone, including my husband, to go home. I wanted to be alone, rest and think about what was really happening. I had no wires, no tubes or anything hooked up to me, so there was no reason for me to be disturbed by nurses in the middle of the night. My room was quiet and as I melted into sleep, I felt a pair of warm arms wrap around me and lift me slightly from the bed. I also heard the words, 'Sleep in heavenly peace' and then I heard, 'Silent night, all is calm and all is bright.' And that was how I truly felt. All was calm in my heart and all was bright for my sweet child entering heaven.

The loss of a baby is devastating. It is a shattered dream and a shattered reality. Parents have to deal with the loss of their hopes and with the loss of their child. This is no easy task. Each baby or child that dies is a little angel, just a cloud away. Perhaps they weren't quite ready to take their place in this world just yet, for whatever reason that may be. Or perhaps they chose to give up this life and instead be reborn in spirit as a guardian angel watching over us. Or perhaps, as I like to think, they just needed to linger a while longer in the love, comfort and joy that is life in spirit. It's the same with the loss of a child or, indeed, anyone you hold dear. Heaven has called their name. They have done what they were meant to do in this life and it is time for their real life to begin in spirit.

DYING TO LIVE

An increasing number of stories sent to me in recent years fall into the category of near-death experiences or NDEs, when a person dies for a few minutes, but is brought back to life and has memories of visiting heaven.

NDEs offer perhaps the best proof we have of life after death. In most cases, they happen when a person's life hangs in the balance or their heart stops temporarily. Many lose their fear of death and are left with a life-changing sense of awe and wonder and absolute trust in the existence of heaven. NDEs are surprisingly common and in the overwhelming majority of instances, those who go through them are left with a new-found sense of wonder. Indeed, for some, like Elizabeth, below, the experience is so enchanting that all fear of death is gone.

All that I need

I contracted glandular fever, which left me with a rash all over my face and a swollen liver. I was having allergic reactions to everything I was eating and drinking. I had burning all over my body and didn't eat or drink for days. Eventually, I was admitted to hospital for dehydration.

I lay in the bed and my body felt like it was burning up. I believe I was near entering the other side and leaving this earth. I remember my spirit detaching itself from my body, like a ribbon had been cut. Amid all of the physical pain, I felt the most serene presence surround my scorching, ill body. It was cuddling me and I felt like I was in between worlds/dimensions. I felt I was near a tunnel – a pure light tunnel – and it was going to take me into it slowly and gently, so serene I wanted to go with it. I heard soft, whispering, angelic voices of calmness in my ears, saying my body was very ill and it wanted to be at peace.

I believe I was close to death, but I want to tell everyone there is nothing to be afraid of. I felt elements of the other side. The other side is peaceful; there is a sense of love and peace that no one could ever could find on this earth. I woke up the next day, the burning had relieved and the tunnel and presence had gone. I have learned a lot through my NDE and what spirit hopes for us on earth. It's not about the jobs, money or social status everyone strives to achieve. It really is just about the person you are, the good in you, the good you give and the love you carry. The way you treat others is what will meet you in heaven. Do unto others as you would be done to. That's all the scripture – all the guidance and all the inspiration I need.

Millions of people all over the world claim to have had near-death experiences that gave them a glimpse of the afterlife. These stories from people who have been to the brink and returned to tell their stories offer the closest data we have to date that there is life after death. These voyagers to frontiers unknown report astonishing glimpses of a world beyond, a world that shimmers with light, magic and love.

One of the reasons we hear more about NDEs now than ever before is improvements in resuscitation techniques. Increasing numbers of people declared clinically dead are being brought back from the brink. Typically, a person 'dies' for just a few minutes, but there are reported cases of people being 'dead' for up to ten hours. A decade or so ago, these people would have remained dead and not returned to tell their stories.

With the numbers of NDE accounts on the increase scientists can't ignore or dismiss them any more. They have had no choice but to research them and the possibility of the continuation of human consciousness after death that they present. Leading this research into NDE is Dr Sam Parnia and his team at the University of Southampton who, in 2014, published a study of NDEs experienced by 2000 people who suffered cardiac arrests at fifteen hospitals in the UK, US and Austria. This study offered the first tentative scientific proof that consciousness can survive bodily death for at least three minutes, and was so encouraging that another round of research is ongoing.

As is to be expected, sceptics naturally have a battery of counter arguments. As well as the chemical changes that occur in a dying brain, other explanations include NDEs being triggered by sleep disorders, medicines and drugs. False-memory syndrome, hallucination, wish fulfilment and temporary madness have also been put forward, but none of these explanations is convincing. For example, during a hallucination a person is out of touch with reality, whereas accounts of NDEs include accurate reports of what is going on in their immediate surroundings. Also, many NDEs occur when a person has a flat EEG, meaning they are brain dead, but if they have enough brain activity to produce a hallucination it would be registered by the EEG. Also, a dying brain or delirium are not convincing explanations as these would not be recalled as a positive experience or a spiritual turning point. In much the same way, mental illness typically leads to depression and an inability to cope with everyday life, whereas NDEs have the opposite effect and are likely to lead to a renewed zest and passion for life. Detractors have also failed to explain how people of different ages and from different cultures typically report very similar experiences involving a tunnel of light and meetings with departed loved ones. The 'wish-fulfilment' theory doesn't explain these similarities either. Surely people would have different memories from a tunnel or a life review? A beach at sunset, for example?

In addition, none of these arguments can fully explain cases in which a person has 'died' or been in a medically induced coma and reported seeing or hearing things like conversations of loved ones or relatives outside the room, or they've described what doctors were doing for several hours during an operation.

It is wonderful that NDEs are becoming a matter of debate in the scientific community because it shows that at long last they are being taken seriously.

Another type of afterlife encounter that convinces me there is more to us than our physical reality is out-of-body experiences (OBEs). This is when people have the sensation of leaving their bodies and floating or flying and seeing their body beneath them. They are a feature of NDEs, but can also occur during moments of meditation or even spontaneously. In common with night visions, the experience feels very vivid.

I've had several OBEs in my life. The first happened when I was thirty-five (like many psychic experiences, it came to me fairly late in life) and had just given birth to my daughter. I recall seeing myself asleep at night and noticing that my nightdress was back to front, which was indeed the case.

Quite a few people have sent me stories about OBEs happening when they are speaking, performing, running, walking, daydreaming, meditating or while drifting off to sleep. There's some crossover, I believe, between an OBE and a peak experience, where a person feels lifted out of their material body through feelings of unexpected bliss. In my opinion, both are heaven-sent.

Lara's experience convinced her that love cannot die.

Crystal clear

Back in 2004, my father was diagnosed with advanced liver cancer. The condition was at a stage where it was incurable and the doctors only gave him two to three months to stay with us on earth.

I am the oldest of three children and at the age of six I lost my mother. My father was an amazing man who raised all three of us from that point and I loved him with all my heart. The news that we were going to lose him in such a short space of time was devastating, to say the least.

He lived a twenty-minute walk away from me, a journey I had done so many times in the past, but as you can imagine this became more and more difficult. I visited him at least once, sometimes twice, every day. Sometimes the grief and sadness would get so overwhelming that I had to stand outside his house, cry away my tears as best I could and then regain composure before going in. It really was a trying time.

Then, one morning, I set out on my usual way, my heart heavy. I am not a spiritual person, but on this particular morning something made me look up, interrupting my heart-broken reverie. I remember feeling the warm sun on my face, closing my eyes and, remarkably, starting to smile. I had the strongest feeling that my father's love was part of the sun-shine and that, no matter what happened, he would always be with me, especially when the sun shone. It was literally a bright drop of joy within an ocean of sadness.

It suddenly became crystal clear; it was as if heaven had opened up to me, just for an instant, to reassure me that my father would be taken good care of and would always be around me. I wanted to share this because it proves, to me anyway, that heaven truly is accessible to the most ordinary of people.

Whatever anyone may say, the human brain is not the source of such experiences, just as a computer is not the source of the images produced. There is no conclusive proof that OBEs originate in the brain – in my opinion, they, like NDEs and night visions and all afterlife encounters (including the next story), are evidence that a part of us exists separate from our body and mind and that we are spiritual beings having a human experience. All those who have been through such events say they are incredibly powerful and a rich source of spiritual awakening. This beautiful afterlife encounter story from light worker Tania Poppleton (see Appendix, p. 327) just seems to sum up everything that this book is about:

Life carries on

When my ten-year-old son asked me one evening what heaven was like and was he going to die, I didn't quite know how to answer. After all, no parent wants to think of losing their child. But his questions were so out of the blue that I should have known then that there were plans for Leon other than what I expected.

Ever since Leon was a baby, I had been so over protective of him — as if I knew I wouldn't have him for long. I had an overwhelming feeling that our time together was precious.

One day, he decided to try on his sister's school blazer, even though he was a year away from wearing one. I found it so hard to imagine him being able to wear it. Call it mother's instinct or a sixth sense, but I just knew something didn't feel right.

We had just got back from holiday in the New Forest when Leon fell ill very quickly and ended up having to be put into an induced coma. We were given a room at the hospital to stay in and one night, when I was lying on the bed, just staring at nothing, absolutely numb to my core, something caught my eye. Some eerie-looking white smoke appeared around the light on the ceiling and then instantly I was directed to a shadowy orb near the wall. Suddenly, I heard a voice in my head say, 'We've got him; he's going to be OK.' I knew that voice was separate from me. It wasn't my voice or one I recognised, but I took it that my son was going to be fine and pull through. As it turned out, Leon passed away with a very rare brain disease called encephalitis caused by sinusitis. I was heartbroken and always will be until my time comes to be reunited with my son. Leon was an amazing fun, caring, bubbly character who everyone loved and life will never be the same.

I now realise that spirit sent me the most beautiful and

comforting message for which I will forever be grateful. They told me that they had received my son into the spirit world and he was safe. Through my grief, that message helped me to feel so reassured. I feel my son around me and have heard footsteps coming down the stairs, felt someone sit on the end of my bed and been woken by the brush of a kiss on my cheek.

As someone who was always very spiritual since childhood, I am even more so as the spirit world is where my son now is. I made it my mission to find out everything I could about it, but also to tell others to bring them comfort. There is so much more than we see with our physical eyes. We are made up of energy and energy cannot be destroyed. Life carries on in this beautiful place called the spirit world.

SPIRIT WORK

I want to close this chapter and my portion of the book with a magical category of afterlife encounters that are closely linked to OBEs, and I like to call them spiritual worker dreams. In these stories the people who have them say that when they fall asleep or meditate, their spirit leaves their bodies to undertake spiritual tasks. The tasks vary greatly, but almost always involve helping other people by bringing them comfort during times of crisis or helping their spirits cross over to the other side. Here's an example, sent to me by Lynn:

Incredible

I was visiting an old friend. We hadn't been in touch for years and I was looking forward to seeing her. We decided to meet at her house because she was looking after her mother who was frail and depressed following the loss of her husband, my friend's father, a month before. When I went to their house I got this overwhelming feeling of recognition. I had been there before. I told my friend that and she looked surprised as they had only been living there for five years, and in that time we had not been in touch.

When I was in their hall the sense of familiarity grew even stronger. To prove to my friend that I had been there before I told her that in her living room there was a painting of the Eiffel Tower and the sofas were green. It was then that the memories came flooding back. Her father had died in that room and I had been there. My friend confirmed that he had indeed died in that room on the green sofa. He had died from a sudden and unexpected heart attack when everybody was out of the house and it had broken her mother's heart that there had been nobody there. Theresa, you would not believe the comfort it gave my friend and her mother when I told them I remembered sitting beside him and holding his hand. I told them his passing had been frightening for him at first, but I had guided him towards the light and he was at peace now.

All my life I've been intuitive, but never have I had such an astonishing experience. It has encouraged me to join a development circle to see if I can work on my gifts. If I wake up in the morning feeling exhausted now, I never feel upset.

Quite the opposite. I feel fulfilled because somewhere and somehow I believe my spirit has been of service to others passing over.

Told you this story was incredible! I'm still coming to terms with it myself.

Lynn isn't sure why she was present and there to bring comfort to someone she didn't really know at all when they passed, but I believe it is to do with the connectivity of everyone and everything. We are all family in spirit. I also suspect that those who are drawn to matters spiritual or who have had afterlife encounters will also be drawn to helping comfort others in spirit in their dreams, so the next time you wake up feeling tired for no reason, perhaps you will have been on a spiritual assignment in your sleep. Such a wonderful thought that when we are asleep we all have the potential to become angels.

And equally wonderful is the reality that when we wake up that potential remains. Sally's story fits perfectly here.

Wake up

It often happens when I wake up in the morning, Theresa. I'm waking up to a new day and hear a gentle voice – can't tell if it's male or female – calling me. It always fills me with a sense of urgency and motivation. It doesn't happen every day, but when it does, more often than not, I have a very busy day. I'm a midwife and it's impossible to predict which days are going to be busier than others, but on the days my voice calls me I'm always fully awake and energised.

LOOKING FORWARD

I can think of no better way to move forward now than to hand over the remaining chapters of this book to the voice of a professional medium who has devoted her life to spiritual work and bringing comfort and hope to the bereaved.

Death, the last sleep, No it's the final awakening.

WALTER SCOTT

As I said in the Introduction, I've never visited a medium myself and don't intend to as I believe we can all find ways to have direct contact with the other side and I am content with mine. These last four chapters have borne witness to the tremendous comfort direct contact has brought me and can bring you if you open your mind and heart to heaven.

Previously, I have never included letters about experiences with mediums in my books, even though there are thousands of them, because my emphasis has always been on direct and personal communication with heaven. However, I preach open-mindedness in my writing when it comes to matters spiritual, and there is no denying that mediumship brings tremendous reassurance to many people and has done for centuries. I've been to Claire's demonstrations and been astonished and inspired by what I saw. So I hope when you read her story in the pages that follow your reaction will be similar. Every time you open your mind to new perspectives you grow in spirit. And in my view, there is absolutely no doubt that heaven is not a place you 'go' to but one you 'grow' to.

As always, I would love to hear your thoughts, so please do get in touch with me. For details about how to do so see p. 333.

I'll be back as the book draws to a close, but shall leave you, for now, in Claire's capable hands as she shares her remarkable story in the next chapter. Before that my favourite blessing:

Angels around us, angels beside us, angels within us.
Angels are watching over you when times are good or stressed.
Their wings wrap gently around you,
Whispering you are loved and blessed.

ANONYMOUS

PART TWO

PART TWO

CHAPTER FIVE

HEAVEN IS CALLING

If you have knowledge,
let others light their candles in it.

MARGARET FULLER

I was almost four years old when I passed on my first message from the other side. It happened as I busied myself playing with stones, water and a vase in a peaceful area of Richmond cemetery. Content to just play, I waited as my mum and my nan tended to my grandad's plot. He had not been gone long and the memory of his passing was still fresh in their minds.

As they readied themselves to leave, I suddenly became aware of my lovely grandad's presence. His endearing personality wrapped itself around me lovingly, and then he spoke directly to my mind, urging me to pass on a message to my nan. 'Tell Nanny Grandad says, "I love you, Iv".' The words played out and then repeated, and as they repeated, I was surrounded by a feeling of urgency.

Being so young, I had no concept of death or my own mortality. I had no cultural conditioning swaying my beliefs as to what was happening. I just knew this was Grandad, and so, without emotional attachment or question, I simply answered back in my mind that I didn't want to pass the message on. I was playing! The emotion and intensity of the message swept over me again. 'Please, Claire, tell Nanny, Grandad says, "I love you, Iv".' This time, slightly irritated, I gave in to my grandad's persistence. I stood up from my play and shouted across to my nan, 'Nanny, Grandad says, "I love you, Iv!".' The expression on her face was one I shall never forget. She was gobsmacked!

It turns out my nan herself had her own psychic experiences, and so she took this message seriously. As she would go on to tell me many times over the following decades, she knew that message to be true and she wholeheartedly believed it to be from my deceased grandfather for several reasons. My nan's name was Ivy Constance. She hated her first name, as it reminded her of poison ivy, so hardly anyone called her by it. I didn't know this at the time, though, because, of course, I called her Nanny, and everyone else I knew called her Connie or Mum. My grandad called her Iv, something I was too young to know.

My poor grandad was so ill through most of the first three years of my life. I only have one living memory of him and that is of him lying in bed at home, terminally ill. I didn't get a chance to build a relationship with him while he was here, so my nan knew there were too many layers to the intelligence of that short but poignant message for it to be explained away as just childish imagination. And on top of all this, how many preschoolers come out with that sort of thing, anyway?

As for myself, even at such a tender age, the experience stood out in my young mind as unusual and etched itself on my memory for ever. Needless to say, the impact the message had on my nan and Mum was even greater and they were convinced from that day on that my grandad was well and had, amazingly, reached out to them from beyond the grave. My grandad would go on to make further contact over the years that validated this encounter, but on this particular occasion it was so powerful that my nan talked of it right up to 2014, her ninety-second year, when she was at last reunited with the love of her life.

Of course, at almost four years old, I had no way of knowing that this simple message of love would go on to be a huge source of strength in my own adult years. There would be many times when I would doubt the validity of my own experiences and succumb to a crisis of confidence because mainstream opinion nagged away at the back of my mind. Each time, however, my mind would end up back on that day at the cemetery, and no matter which way I looked at it, I was forced to conclude that perhaps there's much more to life than many people acknowledge.

When I stop to think about it, it is little wonder that so many people in this world struggle to accept spirit communication as a reality. It just seems too good to be true, and in a cynical world where we learn to distrust for the sake of our own protection, I can see why, for some, it is more comfortable to remain in blissful ignorance than to open Pandora's box and find hope. But this is my invitation for you to do just that.

WHO I AM

My name is Claire Broad. As I enter my forties, I find I am secure and enjoy a loving family life. I'm deeply content being a mother and a wife. Everyone faces challenges in life, of course (and I write this with a smile because those close to me know that I'm prone to a good moan from time to time), but despite that, I count myself truly blessed because I am loved and because I have the chance to express love in return.

I concede that I'm conventional in many ways. I'm professional and not frightened of hard work. I am intelligent, creative, articulate, strong-minded and honest, perhaps too honest at times. I don't suffer fools gladly, but I am happy, compassionate towards others and passionate about life. I choose to stay open to the magic in it and, at the same time, remain very much grounded in the real world. There's nothing more grounding than motherhood. Kids are a joy because they have a way of making sure you keep it real and keep it fun, and my two have been my greatest spiritual teachers throughout my thirties in this respect.

Prior to becoming a mum, I held senior positions at Leo Burnett Advertising and the Walt Disney Company Ltd. So I've also learned how the corporate business world works and, I must say, I enjoyed many happy years in the advertising and entertainment industries and made wonderful friends along the way. In fact, I married one of them.

So you see, in lots of ways, I'm completely 'conventional and respectable' and fit right into society. There's just that one little fly in the ointment: I believe that the dead are not really dead at all and that they can and do communicate with us. I communicate with the dead!

It normally comes as quite a surprise when I tell people I'm a medium. I challenge the image in their head of what a clairvoyant is supposed to be because I don't fit the stereotype. For the past twenty years, though, I have chosen to quietly give my life in the service of spirit, raising awareness of the nature of consciousness, dedicating my time to developing and understanding my abilities as a medium, training others and providing comfort to those who seek it through one-to-one sittings and public demonstrations. I have put myself through an accreditation scheme with the Institute of Spiritualist Mediums to become a registered and approved medium because I felt it was important for the public to have some trust in my integrity, but I have not sought fame, or riches. Rather, I choose to live by the words of Albert Einstein, 'Strive not to be a success, but to be of value,' and make no mistake, if there is one thing I have learned, it is that the service of a genuine medium is very much in demand and of value, by those both in this world and the next.

HOW THIS BOOK FOUND ITS WAY TO YOU

I know this book has reached you with the assistance of unseen hands and I'd even go so far as to say you were destined to read it. I know this because since the very first time I walked into my local spiritualist church at the age of twenty-one, right up to current day, the spirit world has been directing me. My spirit teachers have consistently guided me, telling me they want me to write for them. Over the years, medium after medium would give me the same message, 'I'm being told you are to write for spirit. There will be a book and following this, there will be speaking opportunities. Through it you will teach many.'

This message was repeated so frequently that it reached a point where (I'm ashamed to say), I began to dismiss it. I'd simply heard it so many times and I couldn't see any real way of it actually happening. I also own that I deliberately chose to fly under the radar too, working quietly with those who found me through word of mouth only because I am not about ego, so did not relish the idea of drawing too much public attention to myself. It is only in recent years that I realised it was time to stand up for my truth, which is why you've likely never heard of me.

The reason for my change of heart came in May 2015 and then again in March 2016. I noticed that the urgency and intensity of the messages I was receiving from the spirit world were increasing, culminating in two very accurate messages from a truly exceptional shamanic healer. After describing my spirit teachers perfectly, she told me they were informing her that they wanted me to get their message out for them now – that it would be online at first, that I would write and it would lead to me reaching many more people. I was also advised that I should learn more about the science, that it was time to put my head above the parapet and to honour my responsibility to spirit because that is why I had come here. I was told it was a call to arms and that they would lead me forward, showing me the way. It was hard to ignore such a strong and passionate message.

I didn't have much time to mull it over, however, as very soon after, from out of the blue, I was contacted by Theresa Cheung. Martin Twycross, a fellow medium and tutor at the Arthur Findley College, had recommended me to her and she kindly invited me to join her popular Facebook page as a contributor. I knew this was exactly what my spirit teachers had been preparing me for and so I took a deep breath and, despite my trepidation of going more public, agreed to support Theresa's fabulous work.

I couldn't believe how things were playing out when Theresa put me in touch personally with many of the pioneering scientists and psychologists in this field, just as I'd been forewarned, and not long after that, the most wonderful opportunity came for me to collaborate on this book. In a short space of time, the prophetic message from my spirit guides played out complete and true. I was left in awe at their magnificent ability to manoeuvre things into play. More than ever before, I understood that there is a bigger plan and we are all playing our small part in it ... now that includes you too.

WHAT'S COMING UP?

What can you expect from the pages that follow? My spirit teachers want you to know for yourself the reality of spirit communication and how and why they communicate through mediums because they feel this knowledge more than ever would be helpful to the world. They teach me that we are becoming more and more separated from one another as we focus on short-term, material gains rather than seeking long-term, internal feelings of contentment and the rewards they may bring, and so instead of feeling greater internal connectedness to one another through the use of technology, we instead detach from one another in growing numbers. This results in us being at risk of losing touch with the eternal aspect of ourselves, which is detrimental to Earth. My spirit teachers therefore want me to impress upon you that life goes on and they want you to share in the joy of that knowledge – to release your fears, to have hope and to find peace.

In the chapters that follow, there are actual accounts of readings to give you a taste of how natural and healing a message from a spirit loved one can be. I answer some of the most common questions around mediumship and also explain about the higher realms of spirit, about guides and about angels. In addition, I provide my own personal true stories of afterlife communication, as well as pointing you to the scientific research available, so that by the time I reach the end, you will have been on a whistlestop tour of afterlife communication through mediumship – a tour that I hope will whet your appetite to explore more about this ancient and yet entirely modern subject because it is vast and exciting, there is so much more to learn and the rewards are many.

Mediums are not superhuman. We are absolutely no different from you; we just find it comes naturally to us to expand our minds and perceive alternative dimensions of reality. Through doing so, mediums may offer greater insight into an afterlife, as well as offering a highly valuable service to those in need of healing by assisting them to move through their grief more easily. Great mediumship doesn't require that people become reliant on a particular medium's abilities; rather, it renders the medium themselves unimportant and unnessesary, as through their work you become spiritually empowered yourself to transform the way you look at life. And in doing so, you may awaken to a greater reality and access your own connection with spirit. We are all going to die and so we all have a common destination. But through the exploration of mediumship we can understand more about that destination, our universe, the nature of consciousness and, ultimately, ourselves.

SPIRIT CHARADES

In Chapter Four, Theresa shared readers' stories in which people reported encountering the presence of their deceased loved ones, but what does it actually feel like for a medium when they communicate with a spirit? Well, for me it is an experience that is as real as the air that I breathe. Although it is an internal experience, I have felt it, seen it, heard it and known it, just as surely as I feel the air rise up through my nose and watch my chest rise and fall. When those from the unseen realms come close to me, I experience the encounter with my whole being. My mind becomes expanded and entwined with theirs and I am immersed in a midway dimension between two worlds, receiving concepts, emotions, intelligence and wisdom beyond my usual level of awareness.

Pause for a moment and visualise your own front door. Can you see it in your mind's eye? It's not a perfect vision, is it, yet you can still see it, and the more you concentrate, the more details you access. This is how a medium receives images clairvoyantly (clairvoyance meaning clear seeing), the difference for the medium being that they are shown people, objects or places that they have never physically seen before.

Similarly, have you ever woken up with a song playing over in your head? I'm sure you can testify that it can sometimes be so clear and persistent that there's no ignoring it, even though you're not using your actual ears to hear it. Theresa already touched upon this when she shared stories of people reporting hearing their names being called or even instruments being played as a way for those in spirit to reach us. Mediums experience clairaudience (clear hearing) in a similar way: as a spirit being blends with the medium's mind, then telepathically transmits into their awareness thoughts, words or even songs, the medium experiences internal hearing without the requirement to use their physical ears. Interestingly, this can seem so clear to some mediums that they feel they are actually using their ears to hear.

Finally, I'm sure you must have had the experience of walking into a room after two people have argued. Everyone knows that intense atmosphere that lingers in the environment after a disagreement. Even though both parties may address you warmly, the energy they've left behind hits your gut and you sense the true emotions behind their smiles. This is a form of clairsentience (clear sensing) and mediums have similar sensations when a spirit being connects with them and they become aware of that spirit's emotional well-being.

Mediums experience all of the above and more because we have trained to become highly sensitive to our environment. When I tune into a spirit intelligence, concepts, memories and emotions flood into my awareness and translate into actual physical sensations. At times, this can be so strong, I may become overwhelmed by emotion (which I'm clear is not my own), or I may feel sensations, such as aches or pains (that I otherwise would not have). To some, this may sound a little scary, but in actuality it isn't, as I'm quite clear this is just my body responding to the journey of the mind and that, ultimately, I'm perfectly fine. In a strange way, I find it reassuring because when the sensations are so strong, I can trust the communication and rule out the possibility of it being 'just my imagination'. Oftentimes, I marvel at the power of consciousness and far from feeling frightened I'm inspired and uplifted.

To truly understand the depth and reality of what I experience, you need to experience it for yourself and there, of course, is the rub. I have no way of making that happen. Communication between people in itself is always subjective and spirit communication through a medium is no different. This is probably one of the main reasons why science has had such difficulty studying it. All I can tell you is that it can be one of the most positive experiences you could ever have.

I affectionately describe the process as similar to taking part in a game of charades. When my mind links with a spirit intelligence, I observe and experience images, words, feelings and knowings as if the spirit being is acting out their communication to me and I am trying to make sense of a charade. Many people in spirit to tend to have a great sense of humour and enjoy making the connection, but of course, in reality this is not a game. I use this analogy only in the hope that it might give you a greater insight into a process that really is ineffable. My job then, is to interpret what is happening and to find the right words to articulate it in such a way that the recipient of my message can understand who is visiting them, which is no small feat.

I don't know how good you are at charades, but I have to say at times I don't think I'm always the best at it. I find it frustrating trying to find a way to express deep concepts with limited language and I put my hands up right now and say that I know there are times when I inadvertently misinterpret what the spirit world is sending me and get it wrong – in just the same way that someone might draw the wrong conclusion from a charade. For this reason, I am always open and honest with my clients about the process of mediumship and its pitfalls and I encourage everyone to keep a balanced mind when they receive a reading. In doing so, I advise clients to weigh up whether they believe by the end of the message that I've gone beyond chance.

Mediumship, like all forms of communication, works with energy. My body acts as a conduit and I receive information in waves. For spirit communication to be successful the conditions have to be absolutely right; when they are not conducive, communication fails, just as our Internet connection may fail us during that important Skype call. There have been occasions when I get absolutely nothing at all and others when, all of a sudden and for no apparent reason, the communication drops out and I'm left standing there like a spare part with nothing more to give. Ironically, though, in my view, this is what makes the experience more credible and I wish more mediums would be open and honest about their limitations.

When communication does goes well and the connection is clear I am often left in awe. It utterly amazes me that a complete stranger, whose name I don't even know, has entered into my day and I am able to be made aware of not only deceased loved ones who have gone before them, but I also gain insight into their lives and often the lives of others they hold dear.

The spirit world can be so successful at 'getting through', that at these times my clients are left without any doubt. I have become aware that when this happens, simultaneously the recipient of the message will often report feeling the connection personally for themselves, which has got to be the greatest connection of all. I remember one lady telling me that she'd found the session so comforting because during the whole sitting she felt as if her husband was squeezing her hand, which was something he used to do when 'alive'. Another time, a gentleman told me I'd taken on the mannerisms of his wife to such a degree that he felt he was looking at her through me. This unconcsious action on my part completely convinced him and he left very happy.

We should not ignore or underestimate the healing potential of a message. At its best, mediumship truly has the power to help people move through their grief. It helps the bereaved, motivates the lost and can be a catalyst for spiritual growth. Dr Julie Beischel at the Windbridge Institute and researchers at the Forever Family Foundation have carried out studies on the bereaved to establish whether receiving a message from a medium can be beneficial to a person's emotional health and the results have been found to be significantly positive.

For my part, I have a lifetime of evidence that points to the continuation of consciousness following physical death and I have witnessed the healing power of a message thousands of times. On that point, I must just take a moment to clarify something. There are two types of evidence in this world: evidence that is collected as data through scientific measurement and testing, and evidence that results from being witness to or having direct experience of an event (such as would be considered in a court of law). When I write about evidence of survival throughout this book I am referring to the latter; the only exception being where actual scientific research is being highlighted.

Beyond reasonable doubt

How can I be confident that the evidence points to consciousness surviving physical death when no one on the planet can profess to have the definitive answers about the existence of the Afterlife? A student of mine who is a lawyer by profession, informs me that when I deliver a message, the civil-law test *on the balance of probabilities* is frequently met. Furthermore, in cases where I can give information that neither myself nor my client understands, and the client must then go away and corraborate the information with other sources, the higher level of proof required for conviction in criminal courts – *beyond reasonable doubt* – is proven.

A recent and excellent example of such evidence happened when I connected a client to her mother in the spirit world during a personal sitting. After describing the mother in detail, so that my client could recognise and know it was her mother I was describing, I was shown by the mother in the spirit world a handbag that I strongly felt belonged to her. I felt this lovely mum making me aware that the handbag had not been disposed of since her passing and that if my client could locate it, she would find a ring inside the bag that her mum wanted to now gift to her. As my client had absolutely no knowledge of the bag, and could not confirm if the information was correct or not during the sitting, we had to leave the message there. However, she put the information to the test and, following the sitting, contacted her father and asked him to search the house for a handbag. To my client's amazement, he discovered the bag and inside was the ring! My client contacted me to let me know she was blown away by the discovery and is now the proud wearer of her mother's ring.

Cynics often argue that mediums research their clients

in advance, but this is an example where I could not have researched that information anywhere, as even the family were unaware of the fact, nor could I have somehow read the mind of my client or performed some magic trick. The information was not in her mind at the time of the sitting and the *only* person who knew about the ring and its location was my client's deceased mother who by now, both my client and myself believed *beyond reasonable doubt* was communicating with us.

Awakening to the truth

The enormity of the realisation that life goes on has, at times, been so tremendous it literally required a paradigm shift in me. Much of what I was taught at school, was brought up to believe through the media or heard preached in churches needed to be revisited and sometimes completely revised. It is not always comfortable to question your world view and to be open-minded enough to accept your own truth, even when going against the socially accepted norm, but the absolute beauty of the message, the revelations I received and the transformative power it contained once embraced, opened my heart and soul, expanded my thinking and enriched my life beyond measure. I wouldn't be without it. I have come to realise this knowledge has the potential to heal hearts and minds, to give strength and courage at times when needed and to inspire and motivate people to lead fuller, happier lives – because that is precisely what it has given me.

What a compassionate and peaceful world it might be if

everybody could experience that kind of spiritual transformation. And this is why I couldn't be happier that Theresa reached out to me to collaborate on this book, so that we can share our combined knowledge and bring our beautiful message of hope to as many people as possible.

THE MEDIUM WITHIN YOU

Would you believe me if I told you that you could be a medium? It is not an exclusive club. It has been forgotten that we all possess the latent potential to experience communion with spirit. Major religions point to the fact, but much of the original teachings have been lost in translation and many people who do believe in an afterlife have become extremely fearful, with some believing that all spirit communication is demonic, or that all those communicating from spirit are imposters, which simply isn't the case.

The vast majority of humanity has not consciously turned its attention to the fields of energy that exists within and around them, nor to the fact that they can and do interact with these fields frequently. Our sixth sense exists within our very make-up (I'm convinced within our genetic code) for good reason. If it was not supposed to be utilised, it would not exist at all. We evolved to use it because it aids our survival, and although there will, no doubt, be those who are more proficient in using it than others, I believe the world could benefit from us remembering that we can go within when we need to and purposefully connect with this aspect of ourselves.

Of course, there will always be people who dismiss the existence of an afterlife, no matter how persuasive the evidence and I have made my peace with that. I fully appreciate that some people will never experience an afterlife communication and if that were me, perhaps I wouldn't believe either. Others are happier not believing and that is good enough reason in itself. Perhaps what limits people the most, however, is the view that we are purely mechanical bodies and that the sum of all our life experience boils down to chemical reaction and exchange. This is currently the view held by many academics and while it may, at one level, be medically true, no one actually experiences their life like that – we have loving relationships and meaningful lives. The hard problem of scientifically understanding consciousness currently leaves people far more intelligent than me scratching their heads. They cannot prove how electrical impulses in the brain exchanging chemical reactions give rise to consciousness. On top of this, quantum physics opens up a universe of possibilities, leading forward-thinking scientists to consider that consciousness may be non-local to the brain. In other words, the brain may act as a sophisticated receiver to express consciousness, but it may not be its primary creator.

So although you may argue that you have never been aware of a deceased loved one's presence in the room with you, it's unlikely you would say that you have never experienced an inner sense directing you on how to handle a life situation. This sense is so common that we have named it – it's our gut reaction. You do have the potential within you to become aware of and consciously tap into a multidimensional universe within and around you, and this is precisely where your loved ones in spirit reside. Hence, as I've said, I believe we are all potential mediums/conduits of energy/receivers, with a conscious capability to interpret what we sense and act upon it.

IS THERE ANYBODY THERE?

So what is mediumship? Spirit communication via a medium in all its many forms is the ability for two separately identifiable intelligences – one incarnate and one discarnate – to blend both in energy and in consciousness to perceive one another. When this is achieved to a finely tuned degree, a bridge is formed connecting the dimension of the physical to those of the non-physical.

It was renowned physicist, inventor, futurist and electrical engineer Nikola Tesla who said, 'If you want to understand the secrets of the universe, think in terms of energy, frequency and vibration.' Therefore, the hypothesis is that both the spirit being and the medium must focus on blending with one another in all three of these ways. The spirit being slows down in frequency as it draws close to our earthly conditions and, at the same time, the medium must attempt to raise his or her own mental state and frequency to meet that of the spirit, enabling both parties to make an attunement, just like tuning in a radio.

I usually achieve this through meditation techniques, although over the years I've found the more I do it, the less preparation time I need, as my brain has learned to switch between different states of awareness more readily. Less practised mediums may need substantially more time to make a connection, that is if they manage it at all. This is because the aim is to still the mind completely and then to expand it, and that is not easy.

A lot of people start out keen to develop, but give up because they simply cannot calm their mental chatter. The mind just loves to talk to itself, interrupting all over the place like an unruly child! Mediumship, therefore, will always be a spiritual practice. It takes years to train the brain and to enlighten the mind to a level where a medium can attune to the higher frequencies of spirit and be in harmony with them.

Of course, the same is true for those in spirit. Just because a loved one has died does not mean they will be able to communicate or even want to. Many spirit beings find communication via a medium just as difficult. In the main, our loved ones are no different from how they were when they were physically here, albeit slightly more aware and informed; so, if communication wasn't their strong point when they were incarnate, chances are it still won't be when they are disincarnate.

I remember a lovely lady coming to see me for a reading. She wanted to know why her relative had been so difficult in life and why he'd left such a big legal mess for her to clear up. I didn't know her reason for coming to see me up front, of course, so I got frustrated when I just couldn't work out why all I could get was the image of a grumpy old man in a single-seat chair staring at me. He was being so tight-lipped, it was like trying to draw blood from a stone. I apologised to my client and explained what was happening.

'That's him!' she said, laughing. 'I know who you have and he always sat in that chair! '

'Well,' I replied. 'Whoever he is, he's making me aware he has no intention of answering your reason for coming.'

It was then that the lady filled me in, telling me she now had the chair and that she was disappointed her relative didn't want to communicate, but it didn't surprise her because that's just how he was in life. I felt I'd sent her away with a damp squib, but in its way, I guess it was an evidential message.

In contrast, when the connection is smooth and the ability of the medium is strong, there barely seems a difference between the medium and the spirit. The two become as one mind and information flows through seamlessly. At these times, witnesses to the connection really can be offered the opportunity to know their loved ones are well and just a thought away.

I read for a family once whose beloved relative had passed suddenly and left a huge hole in all their lives. No sooner had I arrived at their family home than a lady in spirit made her presence known to me. She was so keen to get back to her family and tell them she was fine and still with them that it felt as though she literally took over my senses. I felt as though I became her. She gave me her full name, her reason for passing and pointed out to me all the family members in the room. She was a colourful character, swearing and making everyone laugh by sharing their secrets – even embarrassing both me and her daughter by telling me about a tattoo her daughter had recently had done on her bottom! She urged me to sing sentimental songs and everyone was surprised when she told me she knew her grandson had been arrested since she'd passed. She affectionately gave him a right ticking off! No wonder this lady was so sorely missed. Her vibrant energy was unmistakable, and by the end of the session, even the sceptics in the room were convinced she'd visited. I've never received so many grateful thank yous in one evening because everyone felt they had been afforded a proper chance to say goodbye.

A TALE OF TWO HALVES

What I have described to you so far is known as mental mediumship. It is so called not because the medium is crazy, but because they stay consciously aware the whole time and blend their mind to that of the communicator. This is the most common form of mediumship and the one most likely to be experienced if you book to see a medium. But there are many different types, some of which are very rare indeed, and so before I finish this chapter, I would like to explain a little about mediumship in all its forms.

There are two distinct categories – mental mediumship and physical mediumship – and although they differ greatly, what's important to know is that all mediumship works in degrees, and so each form gradually morphs from another.

Mental mediumship

As I just mentioned, the most common form of mediumship is mental mediumship, so that's where I'll start.

Public demonstrations/one-to-one sittings Although mental mediumship takes many forms, these are by far the most popular. During the sitting or demonstration, the medium remains fully conscious and aware while relaying information. The intention is to provide an experience that presents evidence for the survival of consciousness after death, and this is achieved by the medium describing the recipient's deceased loved ones, conveying information that they did not know prior to the connection (provided by the spirit loved ones) and giving the spirit communicator's reason for linking. This particular form of mediumship has proven very popular in modern times and can be seen regularly on TV shows. It is also the form of mediumship I work with the most.

Psychic art Also within the category of mental mediumship, psychic art involves the medium blending with a perceived spirit intelligence and receiving guidance and mental images from the communicator that are translated onto paper. I have known people who say they can't draw a simple stick man produce works of art when inspired by a spirit communicator. Oftentimes, psychic artists work alongside mediums, so that while they draw or paint, the medium can bring evidence through to enhance the art. This can be a very powerful combination as two mediums work together to bring their joint description of a communicator to life. It is fascinating to watch the link unfold because both mediums tune into the same personality at the same time.

Automatic writing Similarly, automatic writing falls into this category too. The medium holds a pen and, resting it lightly on blank paper, allows their mind to relax and to become inspired by the spirit communicator. The medium's hand is then guided to write. It may surprise you to know that despite its poor reputation (largely due to the release of popular horror films in the 1970s), the Ouija board or talking board is a tool designed by spiritualists to enhance automatic writing and has been used to bring forward loving and evidential messages from the unseen realms since the 1800s. The true case of the 1928 airship disaster is a good example of this and I highly recommend that anyone who is interested in mediumship – or aviation for that matter – reads *The Airmen Who Would Not Die* by John G. Fuller (for details, see Appendix, p. 323). Similarly, the literary works of Patience Worth, communicated through the talking board to Pearl Curran in America at the beginning of the 1900s, are also a fascinating example of how the Ouija may be used successfully to channel.

Although I definitely do not advocate that inexperienced people, especially the young, 'play' with the board because by doing so they often throw open any old doorway to the spirit world, there are many operators, including myself, who have discovered that they can use it quite successfully and safely and receive beautiful messages of inspiration. So in an effort to create some balance and dispel some of the nonsense and fear surrounding all mediumship – and that includes the use of the Ouija – I ask you to bear in mind that the board is just a piece of wood or chipboard with a pointer, nothing more. It's simply a tool. Even scraps of paper and a glass may be used for automatic writing – and there's nothing evil about paper and drinking glasses. Any connection with the spirit world comes through you, regardless of what tool you choose to use, therefore it is your state of being and your intentions that are important, not the tool.

Psychotherapist and professional counsellor Karen A. Dahlman has gained a reputation as a world-renowned Ouija expert and has done much recently to dispel the myths and fears surrounding the use of talking boards. I would recommend that anyone who is inexperienced, but intent on experimenting with automatic writing, reads her book, *The Spirits of Ouija*, before beginning.

Channelling These days, nearly everyone has heard of channelling because it's enjoyed something of a resurgence in recent times. It differs from automatic writing inasmuch as the spirit does not influence the pen. Instead, wisdom is 'downloaded' into the mind of the medium and then written down or spoken, just in the same way you would if following dictation. Theresa shared with you at the start of this book the poem that was given to me after my aunt died (see p. 16) and this is an example of the helpful insights that can be obtained via channelling.

There are two different types of channelling: that which is brought through via a spirit communicator (as in the example of my poem) and that which is channelled from the medium's own higher mind. Many artists, musicians and authors display channelling ability. You hear it said many times that an idea came to a person fully formed and they rushed to record it while they were 'in the flow'. This is an example of creativity being channelled from the higher mind. One of my favourite stories about spirit-inspired channelling is that of Paul McCartney, who reportedly saw his deceased mum in a dream. At a time in his life when he was under immense strain, he dreamed she told him to 'Let it be.' She looked so well and it had such a comforting impact on him that he went to the piano and penned one of the greatest Beatles' songs ever written.

Trance mediumship Moving on, trance mediumship – as its name suggests – is the ability of the medium to enter into a deep state of relaxation and allow a trusted spirit communicator to assert a deeper, more direct influence over their mind. Mediums may enter either a light trance state, whereby at some level they remain aware they are speaking, even though they have no idea what will be communicated, or they may enter a deep trance state, allowing the spirit being to blend and overshadow their mind fully. When this occurs the medium loses conscious awareness altogether. For all intents and purposes, they enter a state of deep sleep before spirit beings are then able to communciate through them. In both these instances, the medium speaks in the first person as though the spirits themselves are talking. Interestingly, studies of the brain during trance mediumship have shown that, contrary to what we might expect, the brainwaves of the medium are highly active, despite their deep state of relaxation.

In Chapter Two, Theresa wrote about spirit loved ones communicating with us through our dreams and she wrote that I believe spirit beings find it easiest to contact us in this way (see p. 63). With both dreams and trance mediumship we can step aside completely from ego and our busy and logical minds and enter into a deep state of relaxation that allows us to become a purer channel through which the spirit world can transmit its messages, as our conscious mind makes no interferrence.

Deep trance is extremely rare, but when a medium shows an ability to work with spirit in this way, it offers the chance for truly stunning evidence of survival to come through. Famous trance medium Eileen Garrett was able to bring through astonishingly accurate information via trance state, which flummoxed even the most hardened investigators, including herself. She was extensively studied by Harry Price of the Society for Psychical Research, as well as many other psychologists and scientists of her time. Due to her own desire to scientifcally understand her ability, she went on to establish the Parapsychology Foundation and worked with scientists to research this field with the hope of finding greater understanding of what was happening to her.

Physical mediumship

The rarest form of mediumship is known as physical medi-umship and you will be very lucky indeed to experience it. As its name suggests, it is the experience of unexplained physical phenomena by all parties present while in the presence of the medium. As with mental mediumship, this can manifest itself in different forms, as follows.

Physical phenomena Mediums who manage to accomplish a state of deep trance may go on to become physical mediums and manifest physical phenomena while in a trance. Physical mediumship normally takes many years of dedication on the part of the medium, and often requires a harmonious group of individuals willing to commit to sitting with the medium regularly, perhaps for years on end, with no guarantee of success, in order for this form of mediumship to be fully developed. I believe this to be one of the reasons why, in our busy day and age, we don't hear of physical mediumship as much as we used to – people simply don't have the time for such a commitment, as perhaps they did in days gone by. Another reason, of course, aside from the fear of actual fraudulence, is the risk of being subjected to ridicule and accusations of fraud. This is why so many phyiscal development circles are kept quiet and away from public attention. It's likely more groups exist than we realise but we simply never hear of them. Two of the more well known physical circles in modern times have been the Scole Experiments and the Stewart Alexander circle (see pp. 323 and 324).

During seances for physical mediumship, sitters report witnessing all manner of physical events. There really is no end to what may occur, from changes in temperature or the switching on or off of electrical items, to old-fashioned table tipping or rare coins dropping from thin air and even full manifestation of spirit beings.

Transfiguration In transfiguration, while the medium enters a state of trance, it is as though a transluscent mask is superimposed over their face by the spirit world. The spirit beings then imprint their own faces on the mask, so that those witnessing the contact can recognise them.

Independent direct voice Here, the spirit world generates from the energy of the medium a substance known as ectoplasm and, remarkably, creates a voicebox from it that is independent from the medium's own vocal cords. As unbelievable as it may sound, the spirit beings then reportedly control the manufactured voicebox and sitters report actually being able to physically hear the long-lost voices of their loved ones talking to them in the room, sometimes at quite some distance from the medium. Whole conversations have been described in this way and although I have never personally experienced this form of mediumship, I cannot think of a better way to bring proof of survival, as the voice reflects completely the personality of a person and must leave the sitter in no doubt.

Medium Leslie Flint was by far the most famous medium of modern times to produce independent direct voice phenomena. What was unique about him was his ability to remain fully conscious while he worked. Disincarnate voices were heard by those present at seances, and because Leslie Flint remained aware, it meant his own voice could sometimes be heard interacting with his sitters at the same time as the spirit voices were heard. This made the argument for ventriloquism unlikely. Flint was studied extensively and subjected to many tests, such as holding a measured volume of pink water in his mouth throughout the whole seance while being tied and gagged. In this test he had to return from his mouth the same amount of pink water at the end of the seance as was measured in the beginning – a test that he passed.

Although independent direct voice mediumship may be extremely difficult for some people to accept, I have spoken to people who attended seances with Leslie Flint and they all testify to the validity of his mediumship. If you'd like to find out more about this unusual medium, you can listen to the recordings of his seances at the Leslie Flint Educational Trust and make up your own mind (see Appendix, pp. 315 and 323).

Spirit manifestations Medium Helen Duncan was famous for producing not only direct voice phenomena, but also full-body manifestations of spirit beings. Those who witnessed her mediumship were astounded to see their deceased loved ones fully appear to them. During the Second World War, at a time when many mothers were desperate to learn about the fate of their young solider sons, many turned to Helen Duncan for assistance. At one sitting, the spirit of a sailor with the name HMS *Barham* on his cap manifested. Obviously, the family contacted the British government to receive confirmation of this sailor's death, however they denied that the ship had even sunk. Helen Duncan was subsequently arrested as a spy. When it was later confirmed that the ship had indeed sunk, she was jailed for nine months under the Witchcraft Act, prompting Winston Churchill himself to get involved in protecting her interests.

Although fraught with pitfalls, there is no doubt in my mind that physical mediumship at its best has the power to give those who witness it complete and total confidence that the spirit world is real.

Sadly, however, by its very nature, it also opens up the door to fraudulence and therefore strict controls must always be in place. It is usual for both the sitters and the medium to be thoroughly checked before entering the seance room. Once they have all entered, the doors are locked and the medium is tied and bound to their chair. (They may also be blindfolded and gagged.) Historically, seances are often done in complete darkness. The trouble with this is that sitting in darkness heightens a person's nerves and imagination and invites pranksters and fakers to tamper with the seance room. Many mediums argue that they must sit in the dark because ectoplasm is light sensitive, but with so many accusations of fraudulence surrounding physical mediumship, some physical mediums are now trying to eliminate these risks by working in low light, therefore affording sitters a chance to see what is happening at all times. With the invention of infrared cameras too, there can be further control.

One thing is certain, if sitting in the dark, precautions are an absolute must and I would advise anyone seeking out a physical medium to keep a level head because, sadly, even recently fraudulent conduct has been exposed within the movement. Questions you could ask, for example, may be as follows. Would video footage of the seance be readily available to you afterwards if you were to ask? Are checks carried out, in front of the sitters, on all the chairs and equipment used before the seance commences? Are all members of the seance checked on entry and phones removed? Are the doors locked from within so no one else can enter? Is the medium 'transparent' and just as keen as you are to discover evidence? Do you know the people you are sitting with, and can you trust them? How much are you being charged to attend; is it reasonable? And, most importantly, does the experience stand up to your own scrutiny? Don't just accept, explore!

Of course, if you receive personal evidence that's irrefutable, you hear a loved one you know speak or see a spirit manifestation, you'll know you've found the real deal. Focusing on the positive, I personally know humble, quiet, everyday folk who have sat in development for upwards of thirty years, week on week, with the same group of people, in the hope of witnessing physical phenomena and getting it. The stories these people tell me are remarkable. They have observed things I can only imagine and what strikes me most about all of them is their absolute conviction that the spirit world is real and the strength and comfort this gives them.

Finally, let us not forget that the genuine medium gets very little out of sitting in seance for physical mediumship. It takes a great deal out of them and normally they aren't even aware of what's going on. Unlike mental mediumship, physical mediumship can be hazardous to the medium's physical health, especially if the medium is not looked after properly by fellow members in the seance room. Most mediums attend seances for the passion of serving the spirit world and often to their own detriment. That has to stand for something.

FOLLOWING A CALLING

So with all the perils and pitfalls of mediumship, the backlash and accusations of fraudulence, why do genuine mediums still choose to do this work? The reason is simple: we have a loving, true message to share that we know has the potential to heal hearts and minds. This is our truth and we are committed to helping those both in spirit and in this life who seek our services. We are answering a calling.

There are many reasons why a client or a spirit being may choose to call upon the services of a medium, and the most common reason, resoundingly, is love. In the next chapter, I shall show you just how great a power love is and the strength of its eternal nature.

True love never dies, it lives on in
the people who believe in it.

ANONYMOUS

CHAPTER SIX

CONVERSATIONS WITH SPIRIT

Love is eternal; the aspect may change but not the essence.

VINCENT VAN GOGH

I don't always remember the content of my readings. As I free my mind of thought and enter an altered state of awareness, I often lose the ability to consciously retain what I'm receiving. I liken this experience to the dream state: just as we forget our dreams after being awake for a short while, so it is with mediumship. The experience just seems to slip away. This is one of the reasons why I record my readings for clients. There are also those occasions, of course, when the connection is so strong and the emotional impact on me so great, that I do remember my sittings.

The following stories are examples from the thousands of readings I have carried out over the years. Just like the stories

Theresa shared in Chapter Four, these messages illustrate the healing potential of mediumship, emphasise the convictions of the spirit world and demonstrate the phenomenal power of love and its imperishable nature. Client confidentiality has been protected, but I hope these accounts speak to your heart because this is where the true connection with spirit is made.

The innocence of love

Toby virtually bounced into the room and bowled me over. There was no mistaking this lad. A broad, beaming smile shone from his face and kindness and love radiated from him in innocent purity. He was a proper boy in every sense of the word and I could feel it. A beautiful-looking child with dark hair and gentle blue eyes, Toby had been born with Down's syndrome, and I knew it as soon as I caught a glimpse of his lovely, smiling face as it had been while he was 'alive'. My heart was lifted instantly as he brought joy to my being and flooded my senses with excitement.

His father, in contrast, sat next to me quietly, completely oblivious to the fact that the son he had come here to make contact with had already made such an impressive entrance. As we sat together at my dining table, he waited patiently, allowing me a moment's quiet, so I could focus on my surroundings and expand my mind. I began very carefully, despite Toby's enthusiasm, because this was a link I did not want to get wrong.

'I'm aware of a youthful male personality here with me,' I began. 'A boy who I feel can be no older than twelve years old because I'm aware he didn't make teenage years.' Toby's dad looked at me, but said nothing. So I took a relaxing breath and carried on: 'He has a beautiful face and I know he would have been born with Down's syndrome. He is absolutely engulfing me in his love for you. He knows you well and is extremely excited to be here. I feel he must be your son because there is such a strong bond of love and I'm very sorry for your loss if this is true.'

Toby's dad looked down at his lap and nodded, so I cautiously proceeded, keenly aware of my responsibility to do no harm. 'He's a beautiful soul – so full of fun and confidence,' I went on. 'There's a depth to him, a spirituality and wisdom beyond his years. He's coming forward with so much energy and love it's a privilege to meet him. I can well imagine he was a very boisterous boy and I must stress, he hasn't changed, but that's what's so charming about him. It lifts my spirits just to meet him. He's a stocky lad, boisterous, down to earth and funny. I can see he's got dark hair and beautiful blue eyes. Now he's showing me his forehead. I don't know what he's doing. Oh, he's trying to show me he had a scar there.'

His father, whom at this point I could not address by name due to the fact he had chosen to stay anonymous, shed a tear and took a tissue from a box I kept on the table. I squeezed his hand gently to let him know I cared. It breaks my heart when a child in spirit comes to me, not because they are suffering – they most certainly are not – but because as a mum myself I cannot imagine the unbearable heartache that a parent suffers in being separated from their child, and I do not wish to add to that suffering any further.

Mercifully, for me personally anyway, children are not the most common reasons why people come to see me, which is one of the reasons why Toby stands out in my mind.

I continued: 'I just heard the name Steven in my mind. No, hang on, your son is making me feel that isn't quite right. I've got something wrong there, but I can't get any more clarity on it. I'm sorry. He's showing me a football now and he's giving me a memory of watching and playing football and loving it. I'm not good with football teams, but I can see a light blue and white scarf here too. He's impressing upon me, "Dad". I interpret that to mean it's your favourite team. He's showing me you've got his scarf.'

'That definitely sounds like my son,' Toby's dad said, and I noticed his body relax and a look of relief cross his face.

'Well,' I continued, 'can you understand why he's making me feel he didn't mean to leave you? He's showing me a football and in my mind he's showing me himself running around outside. He makes me aware he went out for the day, but didn't make it home that night, and he's making me feel a wave of emotion now. He makes me feel he wants me to convey he's sorry he left this world too soon.'

'That's right, but please tell him he doesn't need to apologise; it wasn't his fault at all,' said my client.

'Oh, I don't need to tell him, he can hear you say that,' I said. 'He's right here and I can feel his gratitude for your words wash over me … now he's making me feel a sharp pain in my chest. I'm drawn to my heart and I feel like I'm falling. There's a heart condition here with him.'

'That's right. And he suffered heart failure while playing football,' Toby's dad replied.

'I'm so sorry to learn that,' I continued compassionately, 'but I feel he wants you to know, it was quick and he didn't suffer. He was already in spirit by the time help arrived. There was nothing anyone could have done. Now I hear the name Tim. Feels to me like Tim is spirit side too. He's saying his grandad was there to meet him. His grandad knew he was coming across and he'd been to see you already in preparation. I don't really understand what that means.' I paused as I pondered.

'No, that does make sense to me,' Toby's dad said.

'Ah, OK. Now I just heard there's two Ts in the spirit world.' I puzzled a moment. 'I interpret that to mean there are two people in spirit with names beginning with T, it's not just Tim. Oh, he's pointing to himself.'

'Yes, that's right,' Toby's dad acknowledged.

'Now he's moving on again; he's like a whirling dervish, this kid,' I said, laughing. 'Your son is showing me gardening and making me feel he's got his hands down in the mud. That brings him a lot of joy. He's making me aware that he's been doing this in the spirit world — gardening with other kids his age and making new friends. How lovely. Now he's thanking you for planting a rose bush in his memory. He makes me aware he knows you think of him often and he wants you to know his spirit body is whole. He's completely well and able and wants you to know that his life on earth was short, but he achieved what he needed to. He's being very realistic with me. He lets me know he was never going to be here with you too long. It wasn't necessary for him and he's very happy and settled back home in the spirit world.'

'It's such a comfort to hear all this,' his dad replied, but Toby was communicating with my mind so quickly, I had to carry straight on.

'He's making me feel that he's seen what you've done to his old teddy recently and he makes me aware that he likes it. He's also thanking you. I feel you've given him a new teddy too. Does that make sense at all?' My client nodded in affirmation and laughed out loud. 'I'm also picking up an anniversary of a passing in June. I'm going around the middle of the month. Now he's letting me know that he's with you all the time. That he looks after you now instead of the other way around and he sees you're doing really well, but he wants you to cry a little less and laugh a little more. I've just heard "old Bob", and he makes me feel he's looking after him for you too. I'm looking at a dog now. He makes me feel you'll laugh at that. He's saying, "Don't be so serious, Dad. Go out and find a lady and start enjoying life again, cheeky beggar!" Seriously, though, he feels it's all got too intense and life is for living. He's giving you his blessing to move on.'

'I feel he's trying to lift your emotions. Oh, my goodness, he's now dancing and singing here and he wants me to join in. Ha ha! Oh, no! I'm hearing the "Crazy Frog Song" over and over in my head. I'm going to have to ask him to stop that. He'll drive me mad!' I laughed and so did Toby's dad. 'He's trying to make you laugh. I hope you don't think that's insensitive of me, but your son is so full of life! He's quite a character. I've got the name of Jack now. Jack feels like a friend and not a family member. I feel I want to give Jack something. I feel like I want to shuffle a pack of cards.'

'No, I can't take that,' said his dad.

'Oh, OK. Well, he's blowing kisses to you now, which is usually my sign that he has to go, but I want you to know how much he adores you and those bonds will never die. He'll be with you always. What a beautiful soul.'

My client looked fit to burst with happiness and couldn't wait to fill me in at the end. He told me his name was Stephan not Steven. His son, who was called Toby, was twelve when he passed on 16 June, so the two Ts in the spirit world would be Toby and Tim. Tim was his own dad (Toby's grandad), who had died when Toby was a baby. In a vivid dream, a couple of nights before Toby died, Stephan's dad had stood before him, looking very well and healthy, and had spoken, saying he was doing fine, that he loved him and he would always look after the family, so he must not worry. That dream had given Stephan great comfort after Toby died.

He also told me that Toby was an active child, full of energy and he loved him for it – everybody did. He'd felt sad that Toby missed so much of life and he had wanted to know what Toby was doing now. Toby had answered by telling him he was meeting friends and gardening, something he'd always enjoyed doing. Toby's dad had indeed planted a rose bush in his memory after he died and he couldn't believe that Toby could actually see that. He was also a big supporter of Manchester City football club. Toby had chosen to support the same team as his dad and they often went to games together, so Stephan had kept his son's scarf.

He also confirmed Toby did have a scar on his head from an accident. And only the day before seeing me, he had given Toby's old teddy a clean-up and dressed it in a new football shirt he'd purchased. He also said that he had been to the cemetery and placed a new ceramic one on Toby's grave. He told me Toby had known a boy called Jack, but he hadn't a clue about any cards. He was amazed, however, about 'old Bob'. This was a dog from his childhood, and he had loved him very much, but couldn't remember having ever told Toby about him. He said Toby loved the 'Crazy Frog Song' and had played it constantly at one stage, driving him mad, and that having heard all this he felt confident Toby was well and could continue to be with him, which gave him great peace of mind.

I listened, amazed at the power of the love the two of them shared, and its ability to connect them beyond all time. I hugged Stephan goodbye, noticing he looked lighter and happier, but this wasn't quite the end of the story. Just a few days later, Toby's dad contacted me again to say he'd been in touch with Jack and found out that, yes, Jack did indeed have Toby's old football cards and had kept them as a keepsake. This small piece of information had proved to him beyond doubt that the connection was for real.

I myself had a lot to thank Toby for. He'd provided a great reminder that some of the best evidence of survival is the information we don't know and subsequently need to find out. As well as this, he gave me hope that even when the worst happens and a parent loses a child, their love connects them for ever. I knew they would never truly be separated and that one day they would be reunited.

Anita, a physiotherapist working for a busy hospital, came to see me after her husband died. Of course, I did not know prior to meeting her that her husband had passed, as I never ask my clients anything before they come for a sitting. Usually, the only information I have is their own first name and an email address, so it was a beautiful privilege to feel the love they shared wave across me as I began her sitting.

Soulmate connection

'I have a man here with me,' I began. 'Goodness, there's so much love for you. It's washing over me and my heart is literally filled with it. Words cannot do this love justice,' I said, feeling my heart would burst if the feeling got any stronger. 'This lovely man is making me feel so protective over you. He's literally wrapping his love around you. This has got to be your husband and I'm aware he didn't make old bones.'

I continued: 'He is so romantic towards you. He's showing me a red rose that he wants to place in your lap and he's thanking you. I feel you gave him one. He's also showing me champagne glasses and I feel he is celebrating an anniversary here. I feel the anniversary only just passed. He's so close. I know you must have had such a strong relationship. This is the kind of man who put you on a pedestal. This depth of love isn't always found in life; this is a soulmate connection without a doubt. What a gentleman he is, and I can tell he would have treated you like a lady!'

'Yes,' said Anita. 'My husband has died and he was everything you say, a real gentleman and my greatest love. It should have been our anniversary this week and I have been very upset thinking about it. I miss him greatly.

I did also place a red rose out for him in memory of our anniversary.'

'Well,' I continued, compassionately, 'I know it must be very hard to live without a love like this, but how lovely to have known it at all, and how nice that he can let you know he's celebrating with you still and that he's received the rose … Now he's making me aware there was a ring that you should have received, but didn't, and he wants to gift it to you now. It looks like a sapphire ring.'

'That's right!' said Anita. 'We had discussed a sapphire ring we'd seen and my husband said he would buy it for me, but we never got there because he took a turn for the worse.'

'Ah, I'm sorry,' I replied, before continuing: 'I'm now looking at a photograph that he makes me feel you keep beside your bed of the two of you on holiday, and he knows you talk to it regularly. He's making me aware you shouldn't feel silly about this; he can receive your sentiments. In fact, this was quite a surprise to him. I don't think he believed in all this. I feel like he had a logical, intellectual mind and there was no need for spiritual beliefs.'

'I do talk to that photo every night and send him my love. And you're right,' Anita answered.

'He's showing me a white coat now. I feel like he's a doctor. Ooh, I just caught a glimpse of the GlaxoSmithKline logo. Does that make any sense?'

'Yes, it makes perfect sense,' said Anita. 'I can't believe this. My husband did work for the pharmaceutical industry; he was a research scientist and he wore a white coat. He always said when you're dead, you're dead. I wasn't even sure if I should come here today.'

'Well, I think he's changed his viewpoint,' I joked, kindly. 'I know I can't prove this, but nonetheless your husband is showing me that when he died, he lifted out of his physical body and moved into the most beautiful garden. He is showing me a glimpse of the spirit dimensions – it's stunning. He's very content there. He is making me aware he was met by his mother and he was just in awe of his surroundings. Now I just heard the words "Halls of Learning". I believe he's telling me that he's been to a place where he can access the most amazing knowledge, like a huge library where there's all sorts of rooms for different kinds of information. He loves to spend time there.'

'That's amazing. I'm so happy, my darling,' replied Anita. 'And his mother has passed also. How lovely to know he is not alone—'

'OK, now I just heard the name Mary,' I interjected.

'That's his mother's name!' Anita exclaimed, looking really shocked now as the reality of what I was doing was beginning to sink in.

'And he's met the Browns?' I said.

'Goodness, they were our old next-door neighbours,' Anita said. 'They were both very elderly. Lovely couple.'

'Now, he's moving on. I've got a pain in my stomach here and I'm seeing a big C written across the air. I know he must have had cancer before he died. I'm in a bedroom. It looks extremely homely and he's making me aware that you looked after him right up to his passing. I interpret that to mean he was able to die at home. He's thanking you for giving him such a comfortable environment to die in. I know he wasn't talking near the end, but he's letting me know he felt safe and in good hands. I feel he was sedated, actually. He's giving me to understand that he does not want you to feel guilty. He's showing me that he died when you weren't in the room. He had to; he couldn't leave you otherwise. He loved you too much.'

Anita replied lovingly: 'This is all true. My poor husband had stomach cancer and I did everything I could to ensure he died at home peacefully. He was given morphine and so was not able to speak. I made him comfortable on the morning he died and I went to fetch a cup of tea. When I returned he had gone and I felt terrible for not being there for him.'

'Please let go of that guilt; it doesn't help you,' I answered, reassuringly. 'It was a moment in time. He knows how much you love him and he is fine now. It's an eternal love you share and nothing can break that bond. You are twin flames. It's only goodbye for now, not for ever.'

Anita looked at me as if my words were soothing unseen wounds.

'OK, now your husband is letting me see that he's never far away from you. He's laughing! He's lifting the mood. He's making me aware he saw you go to the supermarket yesterday, but you didn't buy any food; you came out with high-heeled shoes instead. I'm looking at blue shoes—'

'Oh, my goodness! I did!' said Anita, laughing.

'Your husband is with you often. He's letting me see that you have a white chair in your bedroom with what looks like a big red cushion and he visits to take care of you at night when you feel lonely. Is that true, do you have a chair like that?' I asked, interested to learn if I had perceived the information correctly. 'Yes!' Anita said, emotionally. She shed a few tears, but I could tell these were healing tears, so I gave her this moment to release the emotion.

'He's making me aware of your two children now. One girl and one boy. The boy is the youngest – although he's laughing and making me aware they're both grown up. He's congratulating your son. He's so proud of him. He's laughing again and making me feel it's about time. I'm looking at a wedding ring. Your son must have popped the question!' I said.

'Yes!' said Anita. 'Now this is getting really spooky. I just can't believe this, how would you know all this?' she asked, laughing.

'Please know that your husband will be there to see him get married. He wouldn't miss it for the world,' I said, tenderly. 'OK, I just caught a glimpse of him now for the first time. Tall man with brown hair – looks to me to be in his late sixties; would have worn glasses. I can see him blowing kisses to you. That's my sign the reading is coming to an end,' I said, touching Anita's hand and giving it a squeeze because I could see the disappointment on her face on hearing her time with her husband was nearly over. 'I'm going to say goodbye and thank him for doing such a terrific job with me here today. It's really not easy for those in spirit to make contact. What a wonderful man who clearly loves you just as much today as he ever did,' I concluded.

'Thank you, thank you. It's beyond words how I feel right now,' Anita said, kindly. 'I didn't know whether to believe in all this. You hear so many stories of fraudulence and I've always lived in a logical world. I never needed any spiritual beliefs myself until my husband died, but I've missed him so terribly, I thought I'd give it a go. I kept quiet and didn't tell anybody I was coming. I didn't know what to expect, but this has gone way beyond my expectations ... and I've got so many questions now,' Anita said, enthusiastically.

We spent a further hour together, Anita quizzing me and both of us discussing the science of mediumship. I shared stories about my personal experiences too, and by the end, I'd certainly whetted her appetite for knowledge. But, more than that, a seed had been planted that day. Anita's husband had set her on a new path of discovery and opened her mind to greater potential. She realised her life wasn't over and she must live well as her husband continued to do the same. And although their relationship was different now, it wasn't lost for ever. She would see him again one day, once she had completed her own reasons for being in this world.

Sometimes our loved ones in the spirit world find the most ingenious ways to get their message of survival through, and it's on these occasions, as rare and as special as they are, that I have really been able to appreciate that we don't understand all the workings of this universe and that, in some unexplained way, life does go on. I will share such an occasion with you now.

I'm sorry

I've had the great privilege to sit in a development circle for the past twenty years. In doing so, I've experienced some wonderful things. (In Chapter Eight, I shall write more about what a circle is and where to find one, but for the purposes of this story it's enough to let you know that a development circle is the name given to a group of people who come together with the intention of developing their own connection with the spirit world.)

This experience goes back many years ago now, when I was still in the early stages of development as a medium. I sat in the cosy room at the back of Hampton Hill Spiritualist Church in meditation. Although I was supposed to be following a visualisation at the time, I kept feeling as though there was a young man next to me. The feeling was so strong that I couldn't focus on the meditation, so I just sat in the peace, aware of his presence there with me. Being inexperienced, I did nothing more. I didn't even think to ask him who he was or what he wanted. I was simply intrigued by the fact I could feel a person standing next to me whom I knew wasn't physically there. (When you start out in development, the simplest of sensations are all new and interesting to you.)

It's normal in a circle to be asked to take part in an experimental exercise after the meditation, so students can practise linking with the spirit world. On this evening, the task was to pair up and to make a connection for your partner. We weren't to speak, but instead, we were to sit in the silence and just write down on paper all that we perceived. That way, there could be no interference externally and no ability to read the body language of our recipient for clues as to our accuracy. This would stretch our development. Once we had finished writing, we could then report back to our partner, and the hope was that they would be able to identify and understand the person that had been written about.

When my turn came, I shut my eyes and attempted to

establish a link with spirit. Once again, I felt this young man with me, and this time, because I'd now received further guidance from my teacher as to what was expected of us during the exercise, I could direct the communication a little better. I mentally said hello and asked him to tell me about himself. My ability was limited, but I wrote what I perceived in list form: young man about twenty-four years old, feels tall, brown hair, glasses, James, wears a biker jacket, feel he's sorry and wants to speak to Mum, wasn't able to stay in this world any more, all got too much, wasn't thinking straight, suffered with depression or mental disorder, feeling responsible for ending his own life, safe and well and much happier now, worried about Mum, wants to get through to her to put things right, will be with her always.

I was shocked at what I'd written as it seemed just too sad, but a circle environment is a safe one in which to learn, and so if I was to get any sad information, I was glad it was here, where I was with sympathetic learners. I bravely read my list of perceptions back to my partner, who honestly but compassionately replied that she couldn't place any of the information I'd written down. It made no sense to her. She knew of no one who fitted the description I had given and so she didn't believe it was meant for her at all. With feelings of disappointment at my lack of success and with my confidence falling through the floor, I put this one down to having been all my imagination. I shoved the piece of paper in my handbag and went home, once again questioning the validity of it all.

The next day, I bumped into a lady in the High Street who I'd met a few times through the spiritualist church. She asked me how I was getting on with my development and I replied that I wasn't doing that well. I told her I'd picked up information that made no sense to anyone and I was frustrated with my progress. We got talking about it, so I mentioned I'd felt a young man, got the name James and had seen a biker jacket, but my partner couldn't think of anyone she knew who fitted the description.

The lady then asked me, 'Do you still have the paper, Claire?'

'Actually, I do. I forgot to bin it,' I said, opening my handbag and handing it to her.

She looked at the paper and then continued, 'May I have this? My friend lost her son and it's coming up to the anniversary of his death. He took his own life and his name is James. She has a photo at home of him dressed in a biker jacket. I'm sure he's orchestrated this meeting because I usually do my shopping on Tuesdays, but had an urge to go out today instead. My friend has been so upset and has been asking me if I've ever heard from James through visiting the church, but so far no joy. I'm sure this is a sign. I'd be so grateful if you'd let me give this to her? I know it will bring her so much comfort.'

What could I do? Whether it was her James or not, if it would bring this mother comfort, then it was worth it, so I gave my blessing. A few weeks later, I saw the lady again at church and she came straight over to tell me that every detail that I had written down could be understood by her friend and that she really felt it was her son. She thanked me because it had given her friend peace of mind and support through a very difficult time.

I was so pleased and amazed at the complex route such a simple message had taken to meet its rightful recipient. I felt that the spirit world had taught me three valuable lessons.

The first was trust: trust in myself, a greater intelligence and the spirit world. I learned I am just the medium through which the message could make its way. I am not an important person in the process and this was a humbling realisation. I would make a concerted effort going forwards not to let my ego get in the way of the message.

The second was not to underestimate the intelligence of spirit. James must have known he could make all our paths cross, and if this was the way of getting his message through, then so be it. As Theresa mentioned in Chapter One, messages from spirit don't always come straightaway in a clear and direct manner; they can be very subtle and it may take years, but when the right conditions present themselves, our loved ones in spirit can – and do – reach out to us, no matter what it takes. We must stay open to possibility and not dismiss the signs.

The third and most important lesson was that those who commit suicide *do* cross into the spirit world and find healing. This was such an important learning that I've since gone on to understand it more deeply. I have come to know that all who pass in such tragic circumstances are offered help and guidance into the spirit world. I've learned that suicide doesn't remove the necessity to deal with our emotions, even in the afterlife. Those who take their own lives must work through their issue from the spirit side of life instead, but the difference is that soul can come from a place of wellness and peace and may experience healing instead of torment. I've also learned that in some respects it does become harder for spirit loved ones once they have physically removed themselves from this world. No longer with those they love, they can't readily ease the pain of family members who often struggle with grief, anger and strong feelings of guilt following a suicide because they were unable to help. If we can try to take on board that those who do take their own lives do so because they are not well and that, in this sense, it's like any other illness that ends a life, we can understand that no one who does so will be judged in spirit. Instead, they are helped and healed. Without the physical impairments that may have exacerbated their mental condition on earth, they can also now see with greater clarity the reason for their suffering, helping them find peace and to be free. In time, if it is possible, they may even attempt to let their loved ones know they are well, as was the case with James.

I should have known from the moment Roberto introduced himself, this would be a connection that would make us all laugh and would lift our spirits (if you'll pardon the pun).

It can be extremely daunting doing a public demonstration. Standing in front of people who are waiting eagerly for something to happen always makes me nervous. As the medium, you have no way of ensuring a successful connection will be made or when. I often question why I put myself through it because who wants to be the person to disappoint and let down a whole audience?

Still dancing on the other side

As I stood alone, in front of a sea of faces that were all looking up at me in anticipation, I waited for my first link of the evening. To distract my mind, I talked about what to expect and how I work, and it wasn't too long before I felt the energy beginning to shift. I took a deep, relaxing breath, entered the stillness and trusted, while my spirit team did whatever it is they do on that side of life to get the communication up and 'online'.

Roberto came bounding into my awareness. Using clairvoyance, he showed me an image of himself cupping my face with his hands and placing a big, overdramatic kiss on my forehead. It took me aback and I laughed out loud. Never had a communicator been so bold! Roberto then sent a wave of emotion over me and I instantly became aware that he was laughing too.

'Oh, my goodness,' I said, chuckling. 'I have a right character here. A very distinguished-looking man with dark hair and darker skin tone who feels to me to be in his late sixties – around sixty-seven, I'd say. He's just bounced into my awareness and cupped my face with his hands, planting a big kiss on my forehead.' I laughed again and this time the audience laughed along with me. 'I can't speak Italian,' I continued, 'but I know this man must be Italian because I can hear an Italian accent in my mind. He's a bundle of energy and has a real sense of fun. I can tell he has a very cheeky nature and is quite the joker.'

Roberto's humour washed over me again and I found I was standing in front of everyone grinning from ear to ear, as his personality brought so much joy with it. 'Goodness me, now he's dancing in front of me here. He's making me aware he wants me to dance with him.' I felt another wash of humour roll over me from Roberto and informed the audience: 'I've just told him, I don't think so. You're not going to get me dancing in front of everyone. That'll make me look a right muppet because they can't see you!' I laughed yet again and the audience laughed with me.

'OK, now I just heard the name Toni being shouted at me here, but I don't feel it's a male name because I actually feel very feminine with this name. So I feel I want to connect with a female in the audience. He's making me want to elongate the name. This lovely man is pointing my attention to the back row, on the left-hand side. Is there a Toni sitting there, by any chance?'

An attractive lady in the back row put her hand up and said, 'I'm Antonia, although everyone calls me Toni.'

'Oh, wow. Thank you so much for speaking up, Toni,' I continued, pleasantly surprised again at how clever the spirit world can be in directing me to the correct recipient of the message. 'Well, I know this man is a family member of yours because as you speak, he connects with your voice. I'm feeling extremely paternal towards you. My heart feels as if it has just expanded right out and I'm filled with love for you. This lovely man must be your dad,' I said.

'No, my dad is alive,' was the answer that came back.

'Oh, I'm so sorry for getting that wrong,' I said. 'Let me go back and ask ... it's just he feels so paternal, just like a father connection,' I explained. Oftentimes, during a message, the general public want me to dot my i's and cross my t's. They don't realise – quite understandably – that it's a big ask. I am not on a direct-line phone call with the spirit world, unfortunately, and mediumship – being a psychic sense – isn't always crystal clear. It's therefore often a challenge in this day and age when I connect with a parental figure because many of us have such extended families. The love these family members in spirit often relay to me is just as strong as that of some biological parents, so many a time, I can't tell the difference between an actual biological parent or an in-law or an adoptive one. I paused to see if Roberto could make it clearer for me. 'Now what's he doing? He's shown me an image of himself stepping to one side.'

'He's my stepdad,' came the reply and the audience and I all laughed again at Roberto's sense of humour.

'I knew it was him right from the off,' said Antonia. 'I got goosebumps when you started because he always greeted people with a kiss on the forehead like that,' Toni said.

'Thank you for explaining,' I said, gratefully.

'He's dancing in front of me again now and making me aware you'll know why,' I stated.

'Yes, I do. He was a dance teacher in Italy.'

'Wonderful,' I replied. 'He's a great communicator and clearly very well in spirit now. He's making me aware he's still dancing on the other side of life.' 'That's great to know,' said Toni.

'Now what's he doing? Oh, my goodness, he's come out here in sequins! Ha ha!' I laughed, Antonia laughed and everyone else laughed out loud again too. 'I take it from this that he must have taught ballroom dancing.'

'That's right, he did,' said Antonia.

'He's showing me what looks like a black sequin mata-
dor jacket now that I believe has been handed down and is
still here. It meant a lot to him. He's making me aware you
haven't got it, though, and once again I feel awash with pride
and emotion. It seems to mean a lot to him that it's being
looked after.' I was feeling the full force of Roberto's strong
emotions waving over me.

'Yes! I know who has that jacket. How amazing he knows
that,' said Antonia. 'He's acknowledging what you just said
and making me aware that the jacket has changed hands;
it's been passed down in the family and he's so pleased.'
'That's right, it has,' Antonia confirmed.

'I feel so much affection for you, Toni. He's letting me
know that he saw you as his own daughter – there was no
difference to him – and that he loves you deeply. He's taking
me back in memory to when he taught you how to dance.'
'Ah, that's lovely. I loved him too and that's right, he did,' said
Antonia.

'I can feel him laughing again and he's joking with me and
affectionately making me aware that you have two left feet.
I hope that doesn't offend you!' I said anxiously.

'Not at all,' Antonia laughed out loud. 'It's completely true!'

'Ooh, he's changed direction with his thoughts and I can
now feel a pain in my head. I feel the pain on the right side
of my own head. I also feel a tingling down my right arm. This
must be a stroke he's trying to show me,' I said.

'Yes, that's right – it was the right side of his body that
was affected.'

'My eyesight just went a little blurred, did he lose his sight
because of the stroke? Does that sound correct?' I asked

because in the back of my mind I was a little unsure if it was simply that my own eyes had gone out of focus for a moment.

'Yes, that's right,' she said again.

'I say this because he's throwing glasses away here now and making me aware he lost them, but he doesn't need them because he can see perfectly well again now. That's funny; I feel your mother must have the glasses. I've just heard, "my wife" and he's making me feel like she stole them, but he finds that so funny as this is passed on with humour.

'Yes!' Antonia laughed out loud. 'That's so true. My mother's glasses broke while my stepdad was in hospital, so she borrowed his reading glasses because he could not use them any more. I don't think he ever got them back.'

'Your lovely stepdad is now making me aware that he knows she read to him after he suffered the stroke. I know it didn't look as though he was aware, but he was, and he's thanking her for being by his side. He felt very safe knowing she had his best interests at heart. I know too that he couldn't speak, as I have a strange sensation in my throat area now. He's making me aware that your mother often wonders whether she did enough for him and he's letting me know that she did, and that he loves her still. He's also showing me a cross and making me aware he received her prayers. Your mother must be religious, as I'm seeing rosary beads now too.'

'Yes, she is,' said Antonia. 'And she prayed for him often. That's so nice to know that he heard her prayers.'

'Who's Robert or Bert?' I asked, as the name randomly floated into my mind. 'It's not Robert, it's Roberto,' said Antonia. 'That's my stepdad's name,' she confirmed.

'Well, that's close enough for me,' I conceded, laughing

again. 'Roberto makes me aware of a distance between you and your family. It's an actual distance. Your family must still be in Italy and you're the only one to come to the UK? He shows me that you couldn't be there when he passed, as you were out of the country and couldn't get home.'

'Yes,' said Antonia.

'Please don't feel bad about that. Your stepdad completely understands, so don't have any guilt because he's OK. He's more than OK, in fact; he's full of life,' I continued. 'Now I do hope he's not giving anything away, but I'm looking at a baby bump. Does that make sense?'

'Yes! That's right,' said Antonia, wide-eyed. 'I couldn't fly because I was heavily pregnant. I felt so bad about not being there,' Antonia confirmed.

I went on: 'Well, please let that go now. It's not helpful to you. Roberto's just completely washed me with feelings of love again and is making me aware he knows your baby. I just heard "He's a lovely boy", and I feel him intimating he's handsome just like him!' I laughed.

'Oh, I'm so happy he knows about my boy,' said Antonia. 'He would have been such a great grandfather.'

'Now Roberto is opening books in front of me here, and I feel as if I'm teaching. He's pointing at you, Toni. He's making me feel as though you're teaching too, and he's giving you encouragement and making me aware he'll be with you always. He makes me feel he enjoys visiting you while you teach at school and tries to inspire you where he can because he loved teaching so much,' I said.

'My goodness, that's right, I'm a primary-school teacher,' said Antonia.

'I do hope you can now see just how close your stepdad certainly is to you, and that he's still interested in all you do. He'll always be there if you need him, just send him your thoughts. What a fabulous communicator he is – such a joyful personality and so much fun. It's been a real honour and a privilege to make this connection. He's blowing kisses to you and your mum now. That's normally my signal he is going to draw back. But just one last thing – he's showing me a red marker pen and, for some unknown reason, as he leaves me, he's drawing on you!' I said in surprise and laughed again at his cheekiness.

'I know what that means,' said Antonia. 'I sat on a red marker pen yesterday and the ink went through my clothes. I was so cross with myself!' Antonia said, laughing. On hearing this, the audience laughed yet again.

'Thank you so much for working with me on this, Toni. Your stepdad is such a joy,' I said as I finished.

'Thank you so much for a wonderful message, Claire. My stepdad was so much fun and I miss him greatly, but you got him to a T.'

I said my goodbyes in my head to Roberto and moved on to the next communication. We continued to experience strong messages that evening. It seemed Roberto's sense of fun and light-heartedness had lifted us all and created the most fantastic energy to work with. At the end of the evening, many people commented to me on how funny his message was and how much they'd enjoyed it.

I took two reminders away with me that evening. Firstly, love has no boundaries and that those in the spirit world are not hindered by distance or language. The language of the spirit is universal and therefore there are no language barriers with mediumship. It is a communication from one being to another being, using concepts and emotions.

Secondly, people often mistake the idea of speaking with the dead as heavy or morbid. That couldn't be further from the truth. In my experience, those in the spirit world are more alive in many ways than a lot of us. They often come through with uplifting humour and joy. Mediumship is a celebration of life, not an obsession with death, and our loved ones return to us to remind us that life is precious and is meant to be enjoyed.

Love, heal my pain

I shall never forget the day Tina walked into my home. She'd never received a reading before and she walked into my dining room very guarded. She was determined not to give me an inch, and her body language showed me she was out of her comfort zone, but nonetheless, there she sat, waiting to see what this was all about.

I, sitting at the other side of the table, sent a silent thought out to my spirit guides asking them to please help me with this reading. I could tell Tina's energy had the potential to block the session altogether. I wasn't sure she even wanted to be here with me and, I had to admit, she made me nervous that the reading was not going to work at all. As with all communication, mediumship always flows better when all participants (including spirit ones) are relaxed and open towards one another. Many a time, messages fail because the conditions aren't right in this respect.

So I closed my eyes, took a relaxing breath, entered the stillness and invited Tina's loved ones from spirit to join us. No sooner had I sent the thought out there, than I realised why Tina had been so guarded. I felt Tina's mother around me. I knew instinctively who she was. She surrounded my senses with a no-nonsense attitude. A strong woman who knew her own mind, her energy commanded my attention. Usually, a maternal connection feels extremely loving and nurturing, but Tina's mum wasn't demonstrating any softness at all. She was tough, emotionally hard and domineering, to say the least.

'I have a lady here with me,' I began. 'I know exactly who she is straightaway because there is no messing with her. She's straight to the point. She's making me aware she's your mum.'

Tina nodded for me to continue, although she was not going to give anything more away.

'Your mum seems very controlling,' I said, as kindly as I could. 'I'm aware she must have had a difficult life, and I don't believe she was shown much love because she doesn't find it natural to express it herself. She's giving me an insight here – I'm aware she had to stand on her own from a young age. It feels to me that she didn't know her own mother's love.'

To this Tina replied, 'My mum was fostered.'

'Ah, OK,' I said. 'Well, I can feel she was quite a large lady in stature and I see she had blonde hair and wore a distinctive red lipstick colour.'

'Mmm,' was Tina's limited response.

I was finding this reading a challenge and the flow wasn't great, but I carried on. 'There was no telling your mum what to do, was there? She is very stubborn-minded even now. She's making me aware that she said things as she saw them. She was very direct and she didn't spare anyone's feelings,' I said, honestly.

Tina was silent and she inadvertently made it more difficult for me to work now, as I was worrying whether she was happy and whether I'd drop the connection. I waited and quietly asked Tina's mum to come even closer to me and to give me some information that would help the sitting.

'I am feeling a wave of emotion now. She is remorseful about that fact. I'm aware she is acknowledging that she hurt you with her words and she wants to make amends. She's holding out an olive branch. I believe she wants to make peace, but she's not sure you'll accept. She makes me aware that she was trying to protect you when you were growing up, the only way she knew how. She brought you up tough to survive in a tough world. Your mum makes me aware she has gained a much clearer perspective now and can comprehend the bigger reasons why she had such a difficult life and why she suffered the way she did. She's not making excuses, but her troubles were inherited ones. She got off to a difficult start from the off, but she's working on her own self-development in spirit and receiving guidance on that. I can feel she now realises she handled your relationship wrongly and she's owning it,' I explained. 'That's a big step in the right direction.'

'That's all well and good,' said Tina, 'but I hold a lot of

anger towards my mum. She was extremely difficult and I suffered much more than I should have done at her hands. I had to walk away from her in the end.'

'OK, that's absolutely fine,' I replied, sympathetically. 'You don't have to accept what I'm saying here. Just because your mum is in spirit now, you don't have to accept that olive branch. I can sense the complexities of your relationship. You need to be ready, and you are entitled to take as much time as you need – or none at all, if you wish. Please just remember, readings are done with love and there is a deeper meaning to our lives than we realise while we are living here. Despite your mother's tough exterior, she loves you in the way that she knows how. She would not be attempting this communication otherwise.'

For the first time, Tina softened a little. 'How do I know this is real?' she asked. 'If this really is my mum, can you tell me how she passed?'

I went quiet for a moment and sent out another silent thought, asking Tina's mum to tell me how she passed. She seemed reluctant, as there wasn't much response. I couldn't feel any conditions or see any illness. Then, suddenly, I saw beer bottles lined up on a bar, and a sense of sadness washed over me. 'I'm sorry. I can't tell you how she died, exactly,' I replied. 'But, I'm looking at alcohol here and I feel very sad.'

'That's it,' Tina replied. 'It's what took her in the end. She was an alcoholic.'

'I'm so sorry to learn that, Tina,' I said, compassionately. 'I can see this reading must be very difficult for you, for many reasons. Please let me know if you wish to stop the sitting.'

'No ... I want to carry on,' she said, and this time, there was a kindness in her voice that hadn't been there before. 'It is the reason why I'm here. I want answers.'

'OK, let's see where your mum wants to take this now, then,' I said, supportively. 'Your mum is making me feel she's very sorry she couldn't be there for you. She makes me aware she was numbing her own pain; it was never your fault, although she made you feel it was. You're a much better mum. She's showing me you have three children. Two boys and one girl?'

'Yes, that's right,' said Tina.

'She makes me aware you should have received her help more, and she's sorry she was not equipped with the right skills.' I paused a moment because I was getting a new insight I found hard to interpret. 'Why is she now separating out your elder two from the youngest? She moves the older two together and then shows me the younger one by himself.'

Tina was taken aback and looked at me, intrigued.

I heard a name. 'Who's Joseph?' I asked.

'That's my youngest son,' Tina answered.

'Your mum makes me aware you must not feel guilty. He is happy in himself. She gives me the understanding that you can't see into his mind, but he is content. He knows he's loved and receives great care. I'm being made aware that he can't show you that in return, bless him. I can't see why, but something prevents him from being able to tell you his emotions. Is he autistic?' I asked. 'Yes, severely,' said Tina. 'I feel so guilty because he stays away from home regularly to give me respite and to enable me to focus time on the other two children as well. That is why you're seeing them separated out.'

'Goodness me, you've had a difficult life, Tina,' I responded. 'Your mum also makes me aware that you are on your own. She's drawing a circle around you. That always signifies independence to me and in your case, I believe that means you're a single parent.'

'That's right.'

'Please know that Joseph is being helped by loving spirit helpers. He has his own spirit team, in fact, and he's quite well aware of their presence. If you'd allow her, your mum would also like to help him, but she's asking your permission first. I know it doesn't help you in practical terms, but the spirit world surrounds Joseph to help him emotionally. I really feel he is happy. He doesn't know anything else. Please know you're a good mum, doing the best you can.'

It was on hearing this that Tina fully opened up to me. 'You have no idea what it means to hear that,' she said. 'I can't express the relief. My heart has been carrying too much pain.'

'I know your mum is returning today to try to rectify some of that. I can also tell this reading is just as therapeutic for her too. She needs to say these things. She needs to heal her own pain. She has some making up to do, but she can see a better way now.' Tina reflected on this while I waited a moment for the next wave of information to come forward.

'Who's Carol?' I asked.

'That's my mum's name,' said Tina.

'I don't think she went by that name, though, because it's strange, she's not identifying with it.'

'That's right, she didn't,' Tina confirmed.

'Do you understand The Bell pub? I've just seen a pub sign. Does that make sense too?'

'Not the name of the pub, no, but my mum did work in a pub for years,' Tina said.

'Ah, OK,' I replied. 'Sometimes I'm shown something that has symbolic meaning rather than actual meaning because it's easier for me to understand and quicker, too.'

'I can sense your mum is trying really hard,' I replied. 'She is letting me see that she's with you more now than she could ever be when she was here. It's ironic, but I feel she'll be a better mum to you in spirit. I just heard "I've got her back", and she's drawing away from me.'

'Thank you,' said Tina. 'I don't know what I was expecting from today, and I wasn't even sure I'd be able to go through with it. I'm sorry if I appeared cold, but this is all new to me. You've given me so much to think about and I appreciate it,' Tina concluded.

Tina left me that day, not saying much more, but certainly much more receptive to mediumship than when she'd first walked in. A medium never fully knows the true extent of the impact of a message and we must be content with that, but a few weeks later I received a lovely email from Tina, letting me know the reading had helped her greatly and been very healing. She wanted to move on with her life now, so had taken positive steps to heal. She'd started seeing a counsellor and she hoped, in time, she would be able to forgive her mum. It touched my heart to read this because, as far as I was concerned, I couldn't have asked for more from a reading.

Tina's mum showed me that we can always take steps to make amends, even after physical death. None of us is perfect, but when we choose love, there is hope. Some of our greatest growth comes from our hardest struggles. Without proper loving guidance in our lives, we sometimes lose our way, but we are never truly alone – even in our darkest moments we are guided and we all have the chance to keep growing, even in the afterlife.

There are countless accounts of readings I could have included in this book, each with its own valuable insights. So, it was incredibly difficult for me to choose just four here for you to read because all the messages I pass on to people are special in their own unique ways. An evidential reading takes time to relay and you can't just hop across as many people as possible in order to fit everyone in and please the crowd. The medium must, instead, carefully build the evidence by passing on piece after piece of information, so that by the end of the message, despite the fact that some errors will most likely have been made through information getting lost in translation, statistically the medium should outstrip chance.

My hope, then, is that the stories in this chapter will go some way to illustrate to you the healing potential of a reading and the uplifting nature of a sitting. Far from being a spooky experience, mental mediumship is a very natural process. Without fail, the vast majority of those who enter my home start out feeling nervous, but leave at the end feeling relaxed and with greater peace of mind. There need be nothing to fear from mental mediumship, and it can, at its best, be an extremely therapeutic experience.

The spirit dimensions are far more wondrous and complex than we can imagine. In the next chapter, I shall show you that it's not just our family members and friends who continue to educate and to guide us from the afterlife. There are other loving beings gently inspiring and guiding us too.

*The flower that blooms in adversity is the
most beautiful flower of them all.*

ANONYMOUS

CHAPTER SEVEN

ANSWERS FROM HIGHER REALMS

The quieter you become,
the more you are able to hear.

RUMI

This book is about seeking and sharing the truth. When I agreed to collaborate on this book with Theresa, I made the decision not to hold back on my experiences because, despite knowing that some people may judge me harshly, I know sharing my truth will help others. Ultimately, that is all I care about, but in the process of sharing, I also hope that my authenticity comes across. I believe that one of the reasons why spirit communication is still so widely dismissed is because not enough of us are brave enough to openly share our experiences for fear of ridicule, but there are many of us with stories to tell. So many that I'm sure if these stories were all shared openly, the tide of public opinion would have to turn.

As Theresa suggested in the Introduction, these stories should be used as data as they are so commonplace. I am therefore going to take a confident step forward and share my whole truth. I'm going to tell you about my spirit guide. He goes by the name of White Feather and, it turns out, he has been watching over me since birth. With hindsight, I realise he tried to draw my attention to his presence many times throughout my teenage years, but it wasn't until 1994 that I was officially introduced to him.

That evening, I sat nervously in a homely living room waiting for my turn to be called in. Adrenaline was pumping through my body and I felt like I wanted to run to the bathroom, so I kept shuffling in my seat. At nineteen years of age, I had no idea what to expect from seeing a medium, but I felt both excited and apprehensive. I had agreed to attend this sitting in support of a friend who had wanted a reading, but didn't want to go alone and now, as I sat waiting, I grew curious. Strange, inexplicable things often happened around me as a teenager and I wondered if perhaps the time had come for me to receive some answers.

'It's your turn,' my friend said brightly, as she returned from her reading to sit and wait in the living room. My stomach flipped as I rose up from my seat and left the living room, entering into the small dining room from which my friend had just emerged. Unbeknown to me, I was about to meet a wonderful woman who would influence my life for the better beyond measure. Sheila Thomas, a highly respected medium in my area, invited me in and beckoned me to sit down with her.

This lovely lady, who was so down to earth, welcomed me warmly and asked me to sit down at her table. Then she gave me a pack of tarot cards to shuffle. When I was happy with my shuffle, she placed down a spread of cards (although I don't think she really needed to do this because she didn't seem to need to refer to them at all during the sitting).

'I have your grandad here,' Sheila began. 'Stocky man. I get the name of Stan.' 'That's right,' I said, shocked.

'He's making me aware he is your mum's dad, and he's sending his love to both your mum and your nan.' She continued, 'What a lovely man he is, and a real joker too. He's making me laugh. He's rolling up his sleeves here now – he would have always worn them like that – and he's making me aware he suffered with a chest condition and with cancer. I've also got a pain in my head.'

'That's right,' I said. 'It was a brain tumour, plus he had respiratory trouble too.'

'Well, he's a good communicator and he's laughing and telling me you're psychic yourself.'

'Well, I don't know about that,' I replied, doubtfully.

'Well, Grandad thinks you are and he knows you well. You've heard from him direct before, he's telling me. He also shows me you've been aware of another spirit being around you, someone who you see at night. Grandad is saying, "Don't be afraid."'

'Yes, that's true,' I admitted. 'I often wake up in the night and through the shadows I see someone standing watch over me. It has frightened me in the past.'

'What's that awful smell too?' Sheila asked. 'I can smell something very strong that I can't quite put my finger on.

The spirit world is trying to get your attention, that's for sure, and the easiest way for you to perceive it is via your sense of smell.'

'Yes,' I said, slightly embarrassed. 'I know exactly the smell you mean. It's been troublesome. Everyone can smell it, not just me – my family and friends have all commented. It comes quickly, travels around the house and then it is gone as quick as that and I don't know what it is. We've searched everywhere but can't find a root cause.'

'You won't,' said Sheila. 'It's your spirit guide. I don't usually give guides in a reading, but he's here now and telling me it's important I pass this information on. He's showing himself as Native American and he's telling me the smell you perceive is a mixture of herbs and plants he used to smoke. He's chosen it deliberately, so you wouldn't be able to explain it and you'd seek understanding. He's introducing himself as White Feather and he's making me aware he's been with you all your life, but the time has come now to get to know him better. He wants you to start training. Grandad's asking me if I will help you with this and I've said to him, if you think you'd be interested in doing that, you are more than welcome to join my development circle. It's held every month at the spiritualist church.'

'Thank you,' I replied, hesitantly. 'I will consider that.'

Sheila then dropped the subject of guides and continued bringing through uncannily accurate pieces of information about my grandad and my own life. I listened to it all, absolutely wide-eyed, and when she finished, I thanked her enthusiastically.

In this short time, my eyes were opened. I now knew that what I'd experienced throughout my life wasn't imagination or wishful thinking. I'd received outside validation from a complete stranger that my grandad was with me and someone else was indeed watching over me. And what's more, we had just been formally introduced.

In that moment, I had the realisation that White Feather had been trying for years to wake me up to his presence. Many times, throughout my teenage years, I'd experienced being watched over, and now he'd finally been given a voice. But, as is often the case with someone so young, I was completely self-centred and thought it was just really cool that White Feather was there for me personally. I didn't consider that he might be showing up because there was work for us to do in the future. So I took my sweet time and did nothing more about it.

That all changed when a well-known medium rolled into town one evening. I went with the family to see him, as I'd read his many books, and after the demonstration, I queued up to get a book signed. As I got to the front of the line, the medium looked at me and told me a Native American guide, much like his own, stood by me. I confirmed proudly that I knew of the guide he was referring to.

'What are you going to do about it, then?' he asked. His simple but powerful reply stopped me in my tracks. I was struck dumb. My teenage self had never considered there might be a reason why White Feather had been so persistent. Could there be a greater reason to his being here other than my own personal guidance? Now, aged twenty-one, and with a little more maturity on my side, I went home and contacted Sheila again to ask if I could please now join her development circle. True to her word, she graciously took me under her wing.

Over the next ten years, I dedicated my time to the development of mediumship. Sitting regularly with Sheila, I learned all I could, soaking up the benefit of her experience until the time came when she informed me that I was ready to become what's known as a fledgling medium. With her assistance, I went out into the world on my own. Over this ten-year period, I'd learned much about White Feather and he soon became a trusted spiritual advisor. I discovered he was always there to help me and share his wisdom, and that together we would work as a team.

Gradually, over the years, and as my mediumship progressed, other spirit guides joined us. Some came to teach only for short periods of time with the purpose of educating me on certain subjects, while others stayed longer. Most recently, for instance, during the development of trance mediumship, White Feather introduced me and my development group to Christopher. We were told that while incarnate on earth, Christopher was a chemist in the nineteenth century and that he now had an interest in helping with our work. I'm told that Christopher's role is to control the atmospheric conditions around us, which fascinates me because it goes to show that even on the other side we choose to have jobs and to work together in teams. I realise this might not come as happy news to all of you currently looking forward to retirement!

The really important thing to emphasise here, once again, is that I'm not special. I've come to understand that we all have spirit helpers and teachers, guiding us through life. You might not have been introduced to your guides in quite the assertive manner I was because, for the most part, it's probably not necessary for you to know who they are. That doesn't mean you can't ask to get to know them or begin to develop your own relationship with those in spirit who walk with you. A guide won't live your life for you or tell you what to do, but they do come and inspire us with their wisdom in the hope that we will receive it and choose to move forward with it. You are not alone and loving spiritual beings do assist you, especially when you're open and willing to ask for their help.

When it comes to guides, I believe that the right teacher with the relevant experience will join you when it's the right time. I have been presented with a Native American as my main guide because the Native Americans were deeply spiritual people who held knowledge that is particularly relevant to my work. A surgeon, on the other hand, could well be guided by those in spirit who were once doctors themselves, or a car mechanic by someone interested in engineering.

Spirit guides are evolved souls. Once incarnate on our planet, they know what it is to live in the physical world and they bring that understanding, coupled with their advanced knowledge, here to help us. They are not invested in their own egos like much of humanity, and they have no need for recognition in this world. Their concern is for the spiritual aspect of life and to help and serve freely. This is enough reward, for they understand that in doing that for us, they do it for themselves. When getting to know a spirit guide, therefore, it's important to know that they present us with an identity and persona that will have meaning, so that going forward we will be able to recognise them and feel comfortable with them. But in truth, a spirit guide transcends the trappings of the material world completely, and so it's most unlikely they take the form of their earthly life when back at home in the spirit dimensions.

CONNECTING WITH SPIRIT GUIDES

Over the years, many people have asked me how they may learn to get in touch with their guides. You may want to ask the same, and so I'm sharing here with you my top five practical steps towards getting to know your spirit guides. This comes with one caveat: guides will ultimately show themselves when they are ready and in a way that they deem best.

1. Learn to meditate

Visualisation is particularly helpful when it comes to giving your guides the chance they need to introduce themselves. I've already explained how important it is that the mind is focused and still during any connection. The great thing about visualisation is that your mind has something to do while you sit, which distracts it from thinking too much. As you create imagery with your imagination during your meditation, your guides can then blend with your mind and literally meet you in your imagery.

At first, you may feel as if you're making the whole thing up because on one level you are! Stick with it though because as you get more proficient at visualisation, you'll start to realise that during your meditation you witness and go through things that you never imagined. You start to collect knowledge that is outside your current understanding. This information can be so accurate that if you research what you have experienced, you will oftentimes discover your insights were absolutely right. The more this happens, the more you will build your confidence in the process and start to trust that those who join you in your visualisation are actual helpers from spirit.

I have received some stunning insights by working in this way and long since let go of the belief that it is just my imagination. Working in this way with your guides is, in many respects, just the same as them visiting you in your dreams. The added benefit is that you're consciously aware during the experience and so are less likely to forget about it.

The lovely thing about this work is that it can be done at home at any time of the day when you find you have some time. Before you enter into your meditation, make sure you're free from all distractions, such as the phone ringing or kids running around.

Get into a comfortable position and then set the intention: ask in your mind or out loud something along the lines of, 'Spirit guides and helpers. I ask that this meditation be carried out in love and protection with my highest interests at heart. Please let me get to know you better through this visualisation. If you are able, please join me here, so I may obtain your wisdom and teachings. I thank you for all you will now show me.'

Next, you can either listen to a meditation that has already been created for these purposes, you can make up your own visualisation or simply sit in the peace and the power until insights come to you. You will find with visualisation that once you really enter into the flow, the meditation will unfold by itself and you'll no longer have to actively use your imagination – you'll be able to just observe.

Once you have finished, write down all that happened – from sensations to imagery to words. You don't have to understand it all straightaway, but by keeping a journal, you'll be able to go back over it in time and notice patterns that start to emerge.

You may wonder how you will recognise that this contact is being made by a guide. First of all, the connection feels incredibly different from that of a connection with a spirit family member. At the risk of generalising, our loved ones present themselves the way they were when we knew them, albeit more worldly, wise and informed. A spirit guide, however, brings with it a powerful energy and confidence that is beyond what we are used to in our world, coupled with a love that is so overwhelming at times, it feels as if your physical body can't actually accommodate it. It's very common, therefore, for people to feel they want to shed a tear as they connect with a spirit guide, as this is the body's way of releasing all that beautiful emotion.

It can also be very hard sometimes to assimilate and grasp the knowledge you've received from a spirit guide as it is usually quite philosophical in nature, cryptic or advanced wisdom. Don't worry if you do not understand what you are experiencing straightaway. All is not lost because at some level, these insights act as a catalyst to open the mind and enlighten the spirit and often, over time, you will find yourself understanding better what was presented to you. For this reason, we normally have greater success in accessing these higher realms of intelligence when we work on our own inner being first and spiritually move towards attuning ourselves to higher energetic frequencies.

2. Pay attention to your dreams

I've already mentioned dreams briefly and, as Theresa has already shown in Chapter Two, they are one of the most common ways for our loved ones to reach out to us. This applies to spirit guides too. Theresa explained that these types of dreams are usually very different from the ones the brain creates to process the day's activities (see p. 66). Known as lucid dreams or, as Theresa beautifully calls them, night visions, the dream will seem incredibly real to you – so much so that on awakening you will remember it for days, weeks, months or even years ahead. Again, I suggest keeping a journal so that you can jot the details of the dream down and always have reference of it, should you need it in the future.

3. Pay attention to the signs

In Chapter One, Theresa called signs from heaven calling cards and I very much like that description. I know we've already emphasised this, but you should pay attention to the signs. (Admittedly, I feel a little hypocritical writing this, having completely ignored them myself as a teenager, but I've learned the hard way and hope you can benefit from my mistakes.)

Guides show themselves in many ways. When White Feather is around, for instance, I often find actual white feathers turn up on my clothes, even though I have been nowhere near anything with feathers. I've lost count of the times I dismissed this sign as a young adult and just dusted them off, thinking some bird had just shed near me (even though the feathers always appeared when I was indoors). White Feather must have been banging his head against the wall, metaphorically speaking.

Another common sign that a guide is trying to influence you and teach you something is if you get a sudden fascination or urge to learn about a particular subject. More than just a passing interest, you feel a real internal pull towards it and, quite inexplicably, you find you can't learn enough about it. If you stopped to pay attention at these times, you'd likely realise your soul was getting deep satisfaction from doing so and that you were experiencing spiritual and mental growth.

I had exactly this happen to me about ten years ago now. Well before mindfulness became the buzzword it is today, I was suddenly drawn from within towards Buddhism and mindfulness in particular. I'm not a religious person, but I couldn't get enough of the subject and then, one day, a fellow medium told me that she could see a Buddhist monk standing right beside me. She asked me if I'd felt a pull towards mindfulness because the monk was making her aware that he'd come forward for this purpose. It was then that it all slotted into place and I understood why I had developed this obsession with understanding mindfulness better. It was the next lesson from my guides on my spiritual journey and I was to integrate it into my practice.

It's also really common for our guides and helpers to inspire us when we are relaxed and it's important to pay attention to any wisdom received spontaneously. We can suddenly find we are holding in our head wisdom beyond our normal comprehension. This usually happens when we are least expecting it. For me that tends to be first thing early in the morning. Just as I wake up and before my mind kicks into gear thinking about the day ahead, I often find I receive downloads of wisdom. I now keep my tablet close at hand by the bed, so I can grab it as soon as a wave of knowledge enters my head and quickly type it up, so it's recorded.

4. Seek out a medium

Let me start this tip by saying that I'm a huge believer in getting to know our own guides *first* before we listen to the advice of a medium. Let's face it – anyone could tell you about a guide, but what proof do you have that this is correct? Without experiential evidence, how would you be able to back up the information the medium has given you?

For the most part, whenever a medium told me about a guide, I'd already been having my own experiences. So the medium validated the evidence I'd received, but was not the first source of it. There's no doubt, however, that spirit guides do connect with mediums and with other energy workers such as healers and therapists during sessions and so as much as I encourage you to keep an open and enquiring mind and to try to test all your connections with spirit, I would also not want you to dismiss their loving wisdom if it comes forth and is helpful to you.

Some mediums offer something called a spiritual assessment, which is different from a normal reading, as it focuses solely on the spiritual aspect of your life. Guides may step forward during these assessments and present their insights or support, which should always be intuitive and helpful to you. Again, should this be the case, try to develop your own relationship with that guide, so that you can substantiate for yourself what the medium has said.

If you have taken steps to meet your guides and given yourself plenty of time to begin a relationship with them, you'll know when the time is right to seek out a medium or energy worker. If they can then endorse the experiences you've been having, there's nothing more amazing. Realising the awe-inspiring potential of consciousness and the infinite nature of yourself within this universe will, more often than not, change you for the better for ever.

5. Seek out a psychic artist

The last of my top five tips in getting to know your spirit guide is to have a psychic artist create a picture for you. The same principle applies here as with seeking out a medium. Psychic artists can usually be found at spiritualist churches, spiritual centres and colleges or mind, body, soul events. Not as common as mental mediums, they tend to be more difficult to source, but should you find a good psychic artist, the reward can be golden.

After many years of knowing White Feather was in my life, I decided to bite the bullet and see what would happen if I had a guide drawn by an artist. I was extremely careful about how I went about this. I told the artist absolutely nothing. In fact, I was at a mind, body, soul event at the time and the waiting list to see the psychic artist was so long, I just popped my name down and disappeared. There was no conversation whatsoever between me and the artist himself; instead, I sent a silent thought out to White Feather, asking him to work with me on this one and then I let the request go. When the allocated time came for me to return to collect my picture, I couldn't believe what I saw in front of me. There was an artist's impression of White Feather. The picture just seemed to jump off the paper at me with some magical quality as I recognised that face instantly. The emotion I felt was pure joy and a love beyond words cloaked me, as the face I'd seen in my own meditations hundreds of times before smiled back at me.

WHY ISN'T IT WORKING?

My understanding is that we are all guided by the higher realms of spirit and we each have our own spirit mentors and teachers, but if after trying all this, you still don't know who your guides are, try to take heart. They are notoriously careful about revealing themselves. White Feather tells me that this is so we don't become reliant on their support and relinquish responsibility for our own lives – for to do that would be catastrophic to our own evolution. Remember too that they often change as *we* change and grow through life.

For most people, guides are content to inspire from the sidelines, through intuition or the subconscious mind. Obviously, for a medium they must take more of an active role, but even then, I know many mediums who say they haven't got to know their own guides, so it really isn't a necessity. And I have come to understand that if your guides perceive it would be a hindrance to your growth for them to reveal themselves, you'll never get them to give in to your requests. As with many spiritual practices, sometimes it's about surrendering to what is and just trusting.

Having said all of that, if your intentions are true and you afford them love, patience and respect, you will quite often be rewarded with small insights that gradually, over time, build a picture for you as to who your guides are and why they visit. Remember, Rome wasn't built in a day. Spirit guides have to learn how best to communicate with you, as you do them, and that takes time.

In an attempt to help you along the way, I have created a Meet Your Spirit Guides meditation and you can find details in the Appendix (see p. 309) of where to go to access this.

ANIMAL SPIRIT GUIDES AND TOTEMS

I couldn't finish this section on guides without giving a nod to our wonderful animal friends in the spirit world. Animals are living conscious beings and, just like Theresa, I believe they have spirits and souls too. I have often experienced clairvoyantly much-loved pets returning to their owners during readings, and I thoroughly enjoyed reading the stories Theresa shared in Chapter Three because I am sure that our beloved animals continue on into the next life. I'm also sure that those animals who loved us continue to stay connected with us because love is a universal emotion and those bonds never die. I can't pretend to understand all the workings of the spirit animal kingdom because I do not. I can only share with you my own experiences and contemplations and leave the rest for you to explore for yourself.

Many animals in this world willingly take it upon themselves to help man, and we often learn of heart-warming stories where animals have formed such incredible bonds with a human companion that they are credited with saving that person – whether emotionally or physically – as you have already read in Chapter Three. If it's possible, then, that consciousness survives physical death, and an animal is conscious intelligence, why should it not follow that animals exist in the spirit world and some choose to help and guide us just the same?

We don't just have to surmise the answer to this question, as there have been many eye-witness accounts by people who report seeing spirit animals. A true story has been handed down the generations in my own family. My nan's grandmother (my great-great-grandmother), Isabella, was a medium herself. One day, while she was out on errands, a large black spirit dog crossed her path. It walked right in front of her and it would not let her pass or continue her journey. Realising something must be wrong, Isabella turned back towards home straightaway, only to discover the police at her front door. They'd come to deliver the worst news: her son had been killed in an accident at work.

As sad as this story may appear, it leaves me in awe. That spirit animal came to assist Isabella and to bring her a warning. The sight of the dog must have prompted some mental preparation for the possibility that all was not well. Strangely, many people report seeing a black spirit dog before receiving news of the death of a family member. I believe this is to help them prepare for the worst.

Happily, however, most support from animal spirit guides is of a much more positive nature. They often appear in our lives at times when we could most benefit from their intelligence or assistance. Each animal has its own unique set of instincts and characteristics, which seems to carry an energetic imprint of its own that can be channelled and used by us as a reminder of who we are and what we could gain from and help us realise our greater potential.

As an example, let us take the wolf. If a person is going through a difficult time in their life, perhaps feeling as though they are under threat and cannot trust the people around them, the spirit of the wolf could show up in their life to assist and inform them. The reason for this is that the wolf is known for its sharp intelligence and deep connection with its instincts – qualities that would be beneficial to a person in this situation. So the essence of the wolf's character comes around the person to help balance out their own emotional state of being and to move them forward in life.

The animal may show itself in spirit form, say, in dreams or in meditation, or it may actually turn up in the person's life, perhaps as a gift with a wolf on it or as an actual physical encounter with the animal itself. The person will likely find wolves showing up in all manner of ways until, after a while, it may dawn on them that they seem to have an affinity with the animal.

Tribal communities have long since respected and revered the spirit animal kingdom and in ancient times many animals were held up and worshipped as gods. Totems are often utilised by indigenous people and I myself was given one by the spirit world.

In my early twenties, I knew absolutely nothing about Native American culture or animal totems. I was too busy being far too intense about life, trying to prove myself in the business world and working hard and long hours. There wasn't time for research on spiritual topics and it may surprise you to learn that I made a conscious decision not to explore the Native American culture in case White Feather was able to inform me through spiritual means. That way, I could once again put my experiences to the test.

This decision paid off quite unexpectedly one day while I was sitting in circle. Theresa mentioned earlier that some people report experiencing an out-of-body experience during meditation (see p. 135) and something very similar happened to me. On this occasion, as was normal, Sheila Thomas led her group in meditation. As I followed her words and gradually transcended all thought, I lost all sensation of my physical body, which was then, quite unusually for me, followed by a loss of awareness that I was sitting in circle. Instead, I became aware I was sitting by a large, open fire, under a blanket of stars in the night sky. The vision was so all-encompassing I could actually smell the fire and what seemed like pine burning, and I could feel the heat of the flames on my face too.

Much in the same way we have lucid dreams, I was experiencing a lucid meditation. I had absolutely no awareness of my physical body, the circle or even my breathing. I was totally and completely immersed in a different dimension of reality. Around me was nothing but dry, dusty red earth and as I sat in front of the fire I wondered why I was here all alone and what the meaning of all this was. Dramatically, the fire then spat and puffed and I noticed great billows of smoke rising up into the air. I was completely surprised when I noticed animal shapes taking form in the smoke as it curled up from the top of the flames. As they rose, they dissipated away into the black background of the sky.

I watched, somewhat hypnotised, and was startled when a voice seemed to come from behind me. Next, a very small woman came into view and when I think about it now she was clearly a shaman, but at the time I can remember just thinking to myself how old and small this woman looked and yet how powerful she seemed. She spoke in a gruff manner. 'Pick your animal,' she stated. At the same time as her words met my mind I became aware that White Feather had now joined us and his familiar strength and presence were next to me too.

I asked, 'Why must I pick an animal?'

'Because it is time and because it is needed,' came the reply.

I focused on the animal shapes and saw an antelope, a squirrel, an eagle, a tiger and a bear all rising up from the flames. 'I'll take the tiger,' I said.

'Not good enough; that's not the one!' said the woman abruptly.

'I don't know what I'm supposed to do,' I replied and I pleaded with White Feather: 'Can you help me?'

'Focus and feel,' was his reply.

I looked again at the smoke animals, which were continually morphing and changing, and this time I felt the essence of their individual characteristics as I watched. Simultaneously, one of the animals, an otter, grew larger and more detailed, and as I became aware of its playful nature, it floated towards me. I was even more surprised when it got near to my face and floated into my nose and I realised instinctively that I needed to inhale it into my body.

I thought to myself, I wasn't expecting that. But while I was pondering on what had just happened and whether or not I was dreaming, the woman exclaimed, 'That's the one!'

'An otter?' I asked. 'Can't I have a tiger or a bear or something strong and protective?' I went on, unable to hide my disappointment.

But it was White Feather who laughed and then said, 'It's time to return.'

And at that moment, I became aware of Sheila's voice once more and I was back in the circle.

It took me a long time to come round from that meditation. I felt as if I'd been anaesthetised and my whole body needed time to wake up. It was as if my mind or my spirit had to realign with my physical body and I had the strangest sensation of actually coming down and becoming heavier. It felt, for all intents and purposes, like an out-of-body experience – but one where I'd visited a different realm. Once fully back to my senses, I relayed what took place to the group. The gentleman sitting next to me said he thought it sounded as though I'd been given my spirit animal totem and to go away and look up the meaning of Otter as an animal spirit guide.

Still new to the world of the metaphysical, I'd never heard of an animal totem before, which sent my logical mind into hyperdrive. I actually had something I could research, and I knew that if it proved correct, it would give me more tangible evidence of the validity of my meditation and of guides. I had no prior knowledge of animal medicine and totems whatsoever and I knew without a doubt that there was no way my mind could have made all this up because the knowledge wasn't in my mind in the first place.

Sure enough, when I researched animal totems, there was Otter. I discovered that when Otter shows up for you, you're being encouraged to find the joy in life through play and to have fun. Otter wants you to lighten up: life is meant to be enjoyed. On reading this I had an epiphany and it all made perfect sense. For a long time, my family had been telling me I'd become too intense. This was partly due to my work/life balance tipping towards all work and no play because I was driven to succeed in my twenties and partly because I was naturally a deep thinker with an analytical mind who could sometimes be too serious and lost in thought. It was then I understood my spirit teachers had given me this experience as a way to wake me up to the fact that I needed to redress the balance in my life. I literally needed to lighten up to become enlightened.

I was so impressed with what had happened to me, I booked a trip away to Norfolk to visit an otter sanctuary there and see for myself their playful nature. I'd never given these animals a moment of my time before now, but I instantly fell in love with their adorable characteristics and couldn't believe I'd overlooked such a creature. Needless to say, I will forever have a soft spot in my heart for otters, and when life gets in the way and it all becomes too intense or too serious, I try to remind myself to be more Otter!

In conclusion, I'd like to suggest to you that the next time an animal shows up in your dreams, your meditations or your physical life repeatedly, or if you feel a deep affinity with a particular animal, pay close attention to what it is trying to teach you. It just might be the animal spirit world helping and guiding your own spirit.

If, after reading this, you recognise having had such experiences or you'd like to learn more about animal totems, there are many very helpful books available on this topic that list all the animals and their meanings in a way that I can't cover in this book. To continue this particular journey, I have pointed you towards a couple of resources in the Appendix to get you started (see p. 324).

IN TUNE WITH THE ANGELIC

Theresa is known for her popular angel and afterlife books, but as someone who left behind all religious dogma and attachment as I grew up, I have to confess that for a long time I didn't put much faith in angels. This was not because I was against the idea of them – I most definitely was not – but purely because they seemed like mythical winged creatures to me and I couldn't logically see why a non-physical being would require wings to fly. So I dismissed angels as a beautiful symbol of a religious faith and, because I am not religious, I gave them no more serious attention. Being brutally honest here, I also thought angels had become over-commercialised in the New Age movement, which also prevented them from resonating with me. My own spiritual knowledge and understanding is based on what I can personally experience, and so because I was never one to blindly follow, I decided the jury was out on the matter until such time as evidence presented itself to me. I know many of Theresa's loyal readers who are drawn to angels may scoff at my stance here, and perhaps deservedly so, but I can only aim to appease by saying that my understanding completely changed when a string of events seemed to provide me with personal insight that angelic assistance does indeed exist.

The first encounter happened nearly ten years ago during a meditation. I was sitting in circle, leading my own students in meditation, when a male who looked like he would have been right at home 2,000 years ago, based on his hair and attire, appeared spontaneously in a vision and introduced himself to me as St Michael. He followed this up by saying that the work I did required careful maintenance of my energy and that he had come to give me healing. He said he needed to release blocked energies and to cleanse my spirit, so that I could continue the important work I'd come here to do, and that he would also provide me with protective assistance going forward. He told me I hadn't realised I could ask for his help, but said I could call on him any time. Following this, I received a wonderful healing experience and at the end of the meditation, I felt physically revitalised and replenished.

It may sound ignorant, but at the time, not having had a religious upbringing and with no proper understanding of saints, I had no appreciation of who St Michael was, so I thanked him for all he had done as the connection faded away. When the meditation concluded, I told my students what had happened and asked them if they knew who St Michael was. I had to laugh when one of them said it could be the spirit of the UK retailer! It was only when I was able to research online that I discovered St Michael was, in fact, an archangel, responsible for protection and healing, just as I'd been told in the meditation. I was excited at this discovery and it certainly made me sit up and pay attention to the power of meditation, but I wasn't yet ready to take a leap of faith in angels, especially as he appeared to me as a man.

Some years later, my second encounter happened, again unexpectedly, when I conducted a reading for a beautiful young lady who, unbeknown to me, was dying of breast cancer. I feel sad even thinking about it today because this kind soul concealed the fact that she was gravely ill throughout the whole sitting because she didn't want me to worry about her. To be honest, she looked so well that I didn't have a clue until the end, when she told me that she was dying. I was shocked and I scolded White Feather afterwards for not forewarning me, but I guess the spirit world was respecting her wishes and they must have known I'd be conflicted about carrying on with the reading. (Had I known in advance I might well have cancelled the appointment because I would have worried whether a reading would be appropriate or beneficial at that time.)

Anyway, the reading did go ahead and after I'd connected with her family in spirit and spent time bringing their loving messages through, I unexpectedly became aware of two angelic beings positioned either side of her – two radiant beings of white light pouring pure love towards my client. It was the first time I'd ever had angelic contact during a sitting and it completely took me aback. Mediums are trained to bring through information that is evidential. We don't usually bring through guides or angels in readings because this information cannot always be substantiated. These particular beings weren't winged, but the experience was unlike anything I'd ever known before, and there was absolutely no doubt in my mind that they had connected with me on an angelic frequency due to the pureness of the connection and the depth of the love they brought forward. I had to trust.

I wasn't quite sure how to present what I was experiencing to my client for a moment, and then I figured I couldn't worry about the ego of man and our ignorant demands for proof. If these angels were here, it was for good reason, so I asked them in my mind what they wanted to relay and I instantly became aware of two miniature angel statues and an image of my client praying to them, followed by a wave of pure unconditional love. I cautiously told my client that I knew she'd been praying to the angels for help, that I could see she had two angel statues at home and that even though I didn't know what she was praying for, there were angelic beings standing beside her now in answer to her prayers. Next, I felt a wave of strength come over me and so I added that these angels had come to bring her strength and that she should not be afraid.

For the first time throughout the whole reading my client looked overjoyed. 'That's why I came today,' she said. 'I needed to know the angels were looking after me, so I can let go of my fears.' She thanked me wholeheartedly and it was then she revealed that she was dying and confirmed that she had been praying to the angels for help. She told me she had great religious faith and that I had now afforded her complete peace of mind; she wasn't frightened any more. I was quite choked up. I couldn't believe this amazing young woman's inner beauty and her complete acceptance of her fate. I learned what true grace is that day; and I also learned that anyone who says faith isn't useful is truly mistaken.

My third and final awakening happened while writing this book. It took place in a way I'm sure many people would least expect it to when considering angelic intervention. It's a fascinating story in itself of how I came to own a talking board, despite having always sworn blind that I would never use one since I felt it wasn't needed to be able to communicate with the spirit world and that it was a long and laborious way of communicating anyway. The full story will have to be for another book, but for now, suffice it to say that in 2016, to my complete surprise, my spirit teachers led me to use the Ouija board.

My reticence had been reinforced in part by my own spirit loved ones when, in my childhood, they got a message to me via a medium my mother went to see (another story for another book) warning me off using a Ouija board my friends were playing with at school because I was sensitive and could experience adverse results. I was so shocked that this lady knew my friends had been playing with a Ouija board (we'd sworn each other to secrecy) that it freaked me out. Even though I hadn't been playing with the board myself, her words led me to develop a fear of using it.

However, they do say never say never – and with good reason. When it came time for me to start writing this book, my spirit teachers did an about turn and I found myself the unexpected owner of a talking board. I soon discovered it was an excellent tool to use while writing because I could ask questions and get answers in a way that I couldn't through other forms of mediumship. It allowed me to interact with White Feather in a way I'd not been able to do before.

Once in possession of the board (no pun intended) I looked online for guidance on how to use it safely and found mostly nothing but nonsense and horror stories. Nevertheless, I knew that I was being gently guided to the board and I trusted my spirit guides and family to protect me from anything negative. So I took control of my fears and put my trust in my own knowledge and in White Feather instead. It took patience to get the board working, but in time, both my spirit team and I got the hang of it and I soon realised I had absolutely nothing to fear. I was able to receive beautiful messages from my guides utilising the board because I'd already attuned to higher frequencies of the spirit dimensions through my many years of spiritual development.

On this one particular day in November 2016, my trusted circle members sat around the board with me and we waited for White Feather to identify himself through the board. Nothing! He didn't show up. Just as we were about to chalk this one down to an unsuccessful attempt, the board spelled out something most unanticipated. It spelled ANGEL and then AURIEL. None of us had ever heard of Auriel, and when we voiced this, the board spelled out: MESSENGER OF THE LIGHT, COME TO ENLIGHTEN YOU.

I quickly grabbed my tablet, which I always keep to hand during sessions for quick research purposes, and typed in the name. I was pleasantly surprised when my search returned Auriel the archangel. More commonly spelled Uriel, the name means 'God is my light', which echoed perfectly what had been spelled out. Our little group sat excitedly for a further hour, as loving wisdom and insights were spelled out across the board.

I later discovered that Auriel is the angel of wisdom. In pictures he carries a scroll to represent the fact that he is a bringer of knowledge. It seemed most fitting that we were gaining wisdom through use of the board from the very angel supposedly responsible for bringing knowledge to earth. What was more impressive, however, was the fact that Auriel is not a commonly referenced angel in religious texts. My research uncovered that he is referred to mainly in Gnostic and ancient Jewish teachings and in the Book of Enoch. He has been dismissed entirely by the Catholic faith as his very existence seems to be debated. Had it just been our subconscious minds working the board, I'm fairly sure we'd have chosen an angel far better known, like the angel Gabriel. None of us had read the Book of Enoch before this and we were ignorant of Gnostic teachings. Between all of us we had absolutely no knowledge of Auriel.

I thought it also impressive that we had been presented with an uncommon spelling of this angel's name adding more weight, in my opinion, to the validity of the communication. If someone in our group had heard of this angel previously and just forgotten they had, they would most certainly have spelled out URIEL on the board instead, as this is the common version of the name used for this angel, but we had received a most uncommon spelling of the name. We'd received AURIEL.

I now had something I could hang my hat on. The fact I'd experienced three different forms of angelic communication and each time had gained information outside of my own personal knowledge, provided me with evidence in favour of the existence of angelic communication. I had to concede that angelic beings do exist and that they can minister to us and do watch over us. For me personally, it was an extraordinary discovery.

I have come to learn that we can ask for help from the angelic realms in much the same way as we do our guides. An absolutely wonderful example of this is a true story from one of my circle members, Jane. The beauty of it shows directly how powerful the presence of angels can be in your life if you ask, and I have included it here in her own words in the hope that it will uplift, comfort and inspire you.

It was a bitter, dark Friday night in late October and I was travelling home from Brittany after a visit to see my family. My plane had been delayed and so I was looking forward to climbing into a warm car for the final leg of the journey home.

Much to my disappointment, when I reached Stansted Airport, my lift had let me down and I was left with no option but to navigate my way across London using the mainline and underground trains with a number of heavy bags.

The train leaving Stansted Airport was old and dirty and was the type that had closed carriages. There were abandoned newspapers and empty beer cans on the seats and an overhead light that flickered as we trundled along.

It may have been the time of night or the fact that I was exhausted, but I felt unusually unsafe. Rather than sharing a carriage with smartly dressed people in business suits as normal, I seemed to be surrounded by unsavoury characters; some were drunk and shouting and a group of men was pressurising passengers to give them money.

Anxious, I messaged a friend and explained where I was and how I was feeling. She messaged straight back and said that she was calling for the assistance of Archangel Michael to be with me and to protect me on my journey. She said I should ask for his protection too. As I texted her I asked repeatedly in my mind for Archangel Michael to come to me and ensure I got home safely.

As I tucked my phone into my bag, a man approached.

He was short and scruffy. And, if I'm honest, I am not sure if given the choice I would have sat next to him. I pulled my handbag closer to me as if to protect it and myself, but then the strangest thing happened. This man brushed the empty sandwich wrapper off the seat opposite me, sat down, looked me straight in the face, smiled and said, 'Hi, my name is Michael. I have come to make sure you get home safely.'

I could have fallen off my seat. His eyes were calm and kind, and rather than feel it was odd, I felt an overwhelming sense of peace. Any fears I had melted away. For the rest of the journey we sat and talked. He asked me about spirituality and at one point he asked me if I believed in angels. I can't really remember my response to him because all I remember is feeling safe and thinking how odd this situation seemed.

Before I knew it we had arrived safely at Waterloo Station, ready for the last leg of my journey. By this time, Michael had travelled with me on one mainline train and two underground trains. As we were about to separate, the sceptical side of me waited for him to ask me for money, but again, much to my amazement, he simply told me that I would now be safe. He wished me a safe onward journey and walked off into the crowd.

I can't explain what happened that cold October night. All I know is that I felt unsafe, asked for divine intervention in the form of Archangel Michael and from nowhere a man called Michael appeared and escorted me safely to Waterloo.

People often ask what the difference is between spirit guides and guardian angels. My understanding is that a spirit guide is a highly evolved being who was once incarnate on earth and can use the benefit of their experience to assist and teach people in this world, whereas an angel is a pure divine being of light who has never required an earthly experience and exists at a high frequency within the spiritual realms. Of course, I don't claim to know everything and wouldn't ever do so. The joy of a spiritual pathway is that just when you think you've got a handle on things, more knowledge and new insights are provided to you. We never stop learning or developing and nor should we. For this reason, I wouldn't ask you to take any of my words in this book on blind faith alone. Rather, I encourage you to explore the truth for yourself and to come to your own understandings.

I asked angel expert Katie Oman (see Appendix, p. 327) to close this section with her thoughts:

Beings of light

The word angel derives from the Greek word 'angelos', which means messenger. Angels are beings of light who act as a link between the Divine and humanity, bringing forth messages of love and peace to all. Angels do not judge us for the things that we do, but they will always try to help us for our highest and greatest good. For me, they have been a source of strength, guidance and love. They have continuously helped me towards both people and situations that have been for my greatest good. Through working with them over the past six years, I have been able to deliver messages of love and guidance to hundreds of people who have been looking for help. More and more people are experiencing a spiritual awakening around the whole world now, like never before.

When we are born, we come into this world only knowing pure and unconditional love. It shines so brightly out of us that it causes everyone to literally light up whenever they're anywhere near us. But, as we grow, we start to learn fear through our family, friends and the world around us. We start to feel separate and different to everyone we see. Our lives suddenly become a ticker-tape parade of judging others and being judged ourselves. Life will never be the same again.

And yet, that initial spark of love is still there! If we can find a way to tap into it again, we will suddenly be able to open our hearts to the compassion, nurturing, kindness and love that never actually left us. We will start to see that underneath all the yellowing, crinkly edges of our lives we are all essentially the same. We all want love. We all have dreams and fears. We all want to feel important and worthy. We are all beings on a planet together, trying our best to muddle through life. If we can open our hearts and minds and let love lead the way, the fear that is permeating the world will start to release its tight grip. Hell, given time, it could even fade away altogether.

And that is the point. Working with the angels and learning to connect with them whenever you need to can help to bring you back to the core of who you are; the love that's inside. The world is a scary place at times, but the more and more of us that consciously come back to love, the more we are able to pour light onto the darkness, and the greater the shifts we can begin to make for all of us. Welcome the angels into your life, and let them help you bring you back to yourself; to the true love that you are.

IS THAT YOU GUIDING ME?

This chapter wouldn't be complete without mentioning the important role our ancestors play in guiding us. Many people ask me if it's possible that their own family members in the spirit world go on to become spirit guides or guardian angels. The answer, strictly speaking, is no because angels have not been incarnate and spirit guides are generally more highly evolved teachers. However, many of our loved ones watch over us and continue to be interested in our welfare long after they have left the physical world so, in a sense, it could be argued that they take on a role of ancestral guide and helper.

To my understanding, family members definitely choose to continue to walk and work alongside us from the spirit world. My conviction is drawn from experiencing the love, support and guidance brought through thousands of messages over the past twenty years. One of my favourite examples of such support was brought through in a reading when a brother returned to his sister to let her know that since his passing he had grown in his own spiritual understanding and he had changed many of his old earthly habits and ways. Now, with greater insight, he was learning that service to others was, in fact, the greatest gift he could give to himself.

His sister, as it turns out, worked in a hospital and during the sitting, her disincarnate brother brought through fantastic evidence of survival when he described the difficult week she'd had due to a patient dying. This loving spirit brother went on to name the patient and how he had died and then to give reassurance that he had been at the hospital with his sister during this stressful time and had assisted when no one else could by helping the patient who'd died to cross over into the spirit dimensions. He even brought the spirit gentleman to the sitting as further evidence of survival.

The wonderful thing about this story is that the brother had experienced such joy in helping from the spirit side of life that he asked his sister to call on him again when such a need arose. He even suggested that they work together as a team, aiding both those in this world and the next. What peace of mind he must have offered her, and strength too, knowing she was supported in what must be a very difficult job at times.

We can all gain reassurance in understanding that while we can't always save everyone, our loved ones in spirit will step in and lovingly care for those making their journey from the physical into the spirit world. This particular spirit loved one has become the true definition of a guardian angel in my mind.

So as I finish this chapter, I find that I join Theresa's chorus. And even though I believe that ultimately we can all access the answers we need from within ourselves, I invite you to call on your guides, the angels and your loved ones if you need their assistance also. Let them know you're willing to accept what help they can give, send them your love and gratitude, make no demands, but stay open to the signs. We have free will and those in spirit respect that, so it's actually right to ask politely, rather than to just expect, but also to trust that they will help if they can. Don't forget they have free will also.

In the next chapter, I shall answer some of the common questions put to me about how to get in touch with those in the spirit dimensions and where to go to explore this field further.

Give me knowledge, so I may have kindness for all.

PLAINS INDIAN

CHAPTER EIGHT

IS ANYBODY THERE?

The reader will judge that I have had many adventures.
The greatest and most glorious of all awaits me now.

SIR ARTHUR CONAN DOYLE, 1930
(WRITTEN JUST PRIOR TO HIS PASSING)

Whether you've found your way to this book because you are new to the idea of afterlife communication or you are already a firm believer, if you are considering the possibility of personally exploring the validity of spirit communication, then you are in good company. Sir Arthur Conan Doyle, physician and esteemed creator of Sherlock Holmes, was an ambassador of spiritualism and even had respected medium Estelle Roberts demonstrate mediumship at his memorial service. He stood up to opposition until his dying day, knowing that in doing so it would damage his reputation, but such was his conviction from his personal experiences, that he could not have led his life any other way.

In the nineteenth century, revered chemist and physicist Sir William Crookes was another believer in life after death; after researching mediums and putting them through stringent testing, he reported his findings to be positive, as did physicist Sir Oliver Lodge. Thomas Edison, inventor of the motion-picture camera and the light bulb, spent time in secret with scientists of his day, designing a spirit phone in the hope of capturing discarnate voices of the dead. In fact, many brilliant minds over the years have pondered the existence of life after death.

More recently a renewed enthusiasm in consciousness studies has arisen, with respected academics such as Dr Dean Radin, Dr Arnaud Delorme, Dr Julia Mossbridge, Dr Bruce Greyson, Dr Charles Tart, Dr Peter Fenwick, Dr Penny Sartori, Dr Sam Parnia, Dr Callum E. Cooper, Loyd Auerbach, Trisha Robertson and Gary Schwartz PhD, to name but a few, carrying out research and presenting their findings. Thankfully, the list of names is growing fast and so is the body of evidence and research. (You can find out more about all these people in the Appendix, see p. 311.)

Arguably, the person who has made the biggest contribution to the scientific study of mediums in recent times is Dr Julie Beischel. She became a personal hero of mine a few years back when I found out about the research she'd carried out through the Windbridge Institute. Here was a highly qualified scientist willing to apply scientific methods to the study of after-death communication and present her findings to the world. For a scientist, that was a very brave thing to do.

Mediums and spiritualists are often criticised for having no empirical evidence to back up their beliefs. I have always found the use of the word 'empirical' interesting, because it means 'based on, concerned with, or verifiable by obser- vation or experience, rather than theory or pure logic', and as I have observed and experienced so much in my lifetime, for me personally the evidence for consciousness surviving physical death does go beyond pure logic, but I appreciate that's still only personal to me.

I'm not a scientist, so do not profess to know anything about that field – in much the same way that the majority of scientists do not know anything about mine – but I do have a very healthy respect for it. I am very fortunate that some of my own circle members are scientists, and in my attempt to understand better the criticisms being made against medi- ums, I sought out as much research as possible in the field of consciousness studies to see if I could get some validation for my own experiences. In doing so, I discovered Dr Beischel, and her work impressed me very much.

It is difficult to provide empirical evidence in a field that hardly anyone in the world with serious scientific credentials will ever consider researching. The chances become slim- mer still when large organisations with the money to back such research are not interested in funding it either. (Why this is, I've never understood, given that the question of life after death must be one of the most important questions to man.)

Despite these challenges, Dr Beischel found a way to

fund research and devise a non-biased scientific process
to test mediums. In a triple-blind test that, as far as I am
aware, was the first of its kind, she managed to successfully
study mediums scientifically and report solid findings.
The experiments were remarkably simple but hugely
effective.

A recipient of a message was first identified. A medium
was then required to give information about a disincarnate relative or friend relating to the recipient. But instead
of meeting or speaking with the recipient in person, the
medium passed the information they perceived to Dr
Beischel direct, who herself had no contact or knowledge
of the recipient.

Dr Beischel then gave the details the medium had provided to an assistant. The assistant had no contact with or
knowledge of the medium, but instead had contact with the
recipient. The assistant gave the recipient two sets of information: the medium's original information and a decoy. The
recipient then had to be able to correctly identify which
reading was for them and which was the decoy, based on
the accuracy of the information. Scores were then marked
and statistically compared against chance.

Remarkably, the results found in favour of the mediums,
who outstripped chance by quite some margin. This simple
yet brilliant system ruled out fakery and cold reading, and
although the study couldn't definitively prove that consciousness survives death, it did prove that not all mediums
are fraudulent. Dr Beischel's work has since been peer
reviewed, and I highly recommend that anyone interested
in learning more should visit the Windbridge Institute's

website, details of which can be found in the Appendix (see p. 299).

Raising awareness of important work like that of Dr Beischel is so important because most people I speak to don't know the data even exists. And Dr Beischel is not alone. Others such as Professor Archie Roy and Trisha Robertson also carried out scientific research on mediums; so too has Dr Callum E. Cooper and his colleagues at the University of Northampton, as well as Dr Gary Schwartz and many more. This book should go some way to spreading the word about all of this because, historically, science and spirituality haven't made the best bedfellows, but I hope that will change going forward and that more scientists like Dr Beischel will take up the mantle from the trailblazers mentioned at the start of this chapter. In the years to come, perhaps we'll see more data published on the study of consciousness, and the body of evidence – which is growing by the day – will be enough to start making many more people sit up and listen.

In the meantime, the beauty of this subject is that we are all qualified to explore the reality of spirit communication for ourselves and we can all be seekers of the truth. Death creates a level playing field. Academia isn't the most important criterion for experiencing a successful communication. In fact, it can quite often be a hindrance. An open mind, a loving heart, honest intentions and bags of patience are all you need and after that, what's required is for you to roll up your sleeves and get stuck in.

THE JOURNEY BEGINS

Once you start down a path of exploration you will find you have more questions than you have answers. I am regularly asked very important questions by students and truth seekers and I'm happy to share some of these with you here now because I know the answers aren't always readily available. I hope they assist you on your own personal path of discovery because spirit communication can be exciting, fun, enlightening and deeply fulfilling if we come to it with the right intention. I would love for you to experience the best of it, as I have.

Q: Where do I go to find a reputable medium?

A: The best way is word of mouth. The psychic industry is not regulated and, unfortunately, it is quite likely that you will come across poor-quality mediumship or psychic ability at least once in your search for the truth. So going on the recommendation of a friend or trusted advisor – someone who has already seen a medium – is preferable.

If it isn't possible to get a word-of-mouth recommendation, organisations in the UK such as the Institute of Spiritualist Mediums, the Spiritualist Association of Great Britain, the Spiritualist National Union or your local spiritualist church are good starting places to enquire about mediums in your area. Spiritualism is a recognised religion in the UK, so there are many centres and churches across the country. In the USA, check out the Windbridge Institute, the Forever Family Foundation, your local spiritualist church or visit Lily Dale, home of spiritualism in America.

In Australia, the Church of United Spiritualism of Australia, Associated Christian Spiritualist Churches of Australia or the Victorian Spiritualist Union are starting places. Of course, there are spiritualist centres throughout continental Europe and the rest of the world too, and the Arthur Findley College in the UK is a great place to meet people from around the world who have an interest in spiritualism. You can find contact details for all these organisations in the Appendix (see p. 311).

Finally, you can tell a lot from a person's website, so an Internet search is also helpful in your initial research.

Be patient and be prudent in your search. When you find a practitioner with the right intention and a good standard of ability it will be worth all the time you took to research.

Q: How can I recognise a good reading?

A: A medium cannot prove life after death scientifically during a sitting. Their intention is to provide evidence for the survival of consciousness after death by offering you proof through experience. You are free to make up your own mind about the validity of this connection. They will have done their job to a good standard if a message consists of the following three components:

- They describe to you a discarnate loved one and you recognise that person. On occasion, this may require you to research an ancestor if it's someone who died before you were born.
- They provide evidence for the survival of consciousness by giving information about yourself and your

loved one in spirit that they could not have guessed. This should be information of which the medium had no prior knowledge. Ideally, this should include knowledge of events that have happened since your loved one's passing as this adds weight to the feasibility of their survival because it shows they still know what's going on. (Remember, the best kind of evidence is that which you yourself didn't know, but must research; so it's quite usual to find you are uncertain about something that's presented, only to discover later that the medium was, in fact, correct.)

- They provide you with a message as to why your loved one has visited and what it is they want to relay to you.

I want to remind you here that no medium I have ever seen has been 100 per cent accurate. Some information does, unfortunately, get lost in translation, and you should always stay mindful of that fact. Mediums are not superhuman or all-seeing oracles. That said, a reading should most definitely contain a *high degree* of accuracy and not be full of generalisations. You will recognise within yourself when the medium goes beyond chance.

This leads me to the subject of names. Naturally, clients hope mediums will provide names – whether of people or places – during a reading. It's often viewed as the holy grail of mediumship and those who are highly successful in the public eye are usually strong on names. However, as impressive as this might appear, it's not the best evidence of survival in my opinion. I believe it's much more evidential when a medium brings the personality of your spirit loved one to life. This is much harder to guess or research; unlike a name, it is unique to your loved one. If the medium can also get a name at some point, that's great, but it's certainly not essential.

Finally, with a good reading you will leave feeling better for having had it. It should be empowering, insightful, therapeutic and uplifting. Naturally, it's disappointing when a connection can't be made, but if the medium remains honest about this fact and doesn't buckle under pressure, the experience can still be a positive one.

Q: What steps can I take to prevent falling foul of bad-quality mediumship or worse, fraud?

A: There are a few things to look out for:

- First and foremost, please do your research. Once you have details of a medium, seek references. A medium working with integrity will have no qualms about putting you in touch with people who have previously received a reading from them. If the medium has a website, check to see if clients can leave testimonials.
- The medium may have voluntarily put themselves through an accreditation scheme with a respected college or organisation. This is not a legal requirement, but it does show their willingness to adhere to a code of conduct and also reflects external validation that they can work to a recognised high standard. It must be said, though, that there are many

good mediums working with no accreditation, so it should not be used as the only deciding factor.

- Some mediums demonstrate to the public. If that's the case, I recommend that you go and see them before you book a reading; that way you can vet them first-hand. It doesn't have to cost a lot (commonly, just a donation at your local spiritualist church during a service in the UK). It can be very much horses for courses with mediums – a medium who resonates with one person may not resonate with another – but if you see them demonstrate in person, you can make a better judgement as to whether or not they are the right medium for you.

- Be aware of false promises. A genuine medium shouldn't make you any promises. They don't have a clue what they'll receive, if anything at all, until the reading begins. Therefore, anyone who promises up front to sort out your life problems or connect you with a specific loved one either isn't an experienced medium or has ulterior motives (namely to make money or stroke their own ego).

- Don't give away any details up front. Genuine mediums do not like to be given any information, as it actually gets in the way of the process by giving their conscious mind something to chew on at a time when they need it to be still. Your first name and a contact number or email address should be all that's needed. And while we're on the subject of emails, please remove any details that give away your work address and title in the signature, for your own peace of mind.

- Sometimes a medium may ask to hold an object of yours, like a piece of jewellery or a photograph to help them focus on making a connection. This is acceptable, but resist giving any information away about the object. During the reading, yes and no answers or I understand or don't understand are all that's required from you, as well as a willingness to take part, of course.

- Be suspicious of anyone asking for personal details. I go so far as to advise my clients not to invite me to become friends with them on social media. I have a Facebook page instead that I ask people to follow if they want to keep up with what I'm doing. I don't make friends with clients deliberately, so I can't inadvertently see news about their lives.

- Genuine mediums should try not to ask a lot of questions; although, of course, there are some occasions when a question is appropriate: for example, during a personal reading they may ask if a client understands a particular name; during a public demonstration, they may make a connection with a spirit being first and then ask if anyone in the audience recognises that person. Remember, mediums don't know what they are giving during a reading. They work blindly and so it's natural they may ask the odd question. But be mindful of too many questions. People who are cold reading or guessing are likely to ask you a lot more questions and make many generalisations.

- Watch to see if the medium can actually describe a spirit person in enough detail for you to recognise or research them. I've seen people give readings where they are unable to describe anything about the spirit being they are supposedly linking with and instead repeatedly say, 'They are telling me this ... ,' without having a clue who the 'they' are. This is a poor-quality reading.

• Finally, please take into account the price. If a medium charges the earth and promises you the moon or promises to give you more information, but only if you return for an exorbitant amount of money, run for the hills. Genuine mediums would never behave like that.

Q: Is there a difference between a psychic and a medium?

A: Yes, there is. A psychic uses intuition to read from the energy field of their client. They do not connect with a third-party intelligence; instead, they may use tools such as tarot cards, runes or even palm reading, for example. Focus during the reading is likely to be on your life and perhaps future predictions. There are some incredibly accurate psychics out there but they are not all mediums. A medium's primary purpose is to reconnect their client with discarnate loved ones and the focus of the reading will be on that. As we are all psychic to varying degrees, some mediums also utilise their psychic ability during their sittings and they should make it clear to you when they are doing so. My advice would be to make sure you know what service you are looking for before you book. One is not better than the other, they are just completely different.

Q: Isn't it detrimental to call up the dead?

A: Mediums never call up the dead. This is a complete misunderstanding. They provide a window of opportunity for your spirit loved ones to come and communicate, if they choose to. There is always free will and for this reason a medium cannot dictate who makes a link with them from spirit side or demand that a particular spirit being turns up. Your loved ones come to a sitting to be with you because they want to, not because they have to. For this reason, mediumship will always be an experimental process.

Q: Will a medium tell me things I don't want to hear, like predicting a death?

A: No, they should not. A responsible medium would never tell you anything that will be detrimental to your peace of mind. They're there to help, not hinder. Plus, the medium can only pass on information your loved ones in spirit give them. Spirit loved ones would not choose to harm you and in my experience, they usually keep very quiet about any information they know which could upset you. Take with a pinch of salt anything that is said to fear monger.

Q: My loved one and I have agreed a code. Will the medium be able to bring it through?

A: Possibly, but it's not probable. It's not really helpful to agree a code with a loved one before they pass. You have no idea if they will be able to use it, and if it's something obscure or unrecognisable, the medium will likely miss it, even if your loved one tries. Codes set you up for disappointment. Your loved one will find a way that is best for them to prove they're around. There is no harm in agreeing with one another upfront that if they can come back and let you know that they are OK, they will, but this is all that's required.

Q: Why do some mediums charge when others don't?

A: This is a personal choice based on a medium's circumstances and beliefs. A medium provides a service and therefore has a right to charge for their time and experience. Those who offer a high level of service will find they are in much higher demand. When this happens, they may choose to leave their day jobs to meet this demand and, of course, we all have to earn money to survive in this world.

There is nothing wrong with a medium charging for their time and experience. How much they should charge is more up for debate and you must decide what you think is fair and reasonable based on your own personal circumstances and the medium's ability.

Other mediums choose to stay with their day jobs and offer readings outside working hours at little or no cost. But, of course, they may have less availability because of this and consequently help fewer people.

Many mediums donate some of their time to charities, so that all people have a chance to receive their services, but again it is a personal choice.

Charging for time and experience does not reflect on a medium's ability or the spirit world's willingness to work with them. You would hope that those with limited or poor ability, who charge, would find they are not in demand as word spreads of their limitations, but there are always those in any trade who offer a poor standard of service and seem to get away with it, so it's key to do your homework first.

Q: What can I expect during a one-to-one sitting with a medium working with mental mediumship?

A: You should expect a medium to be compassionate, kind and have a natural way with people, so you can feel at ease. Many people feel nervous if they haven't experienced a reading before. A good medium will explain to you how they work and what they need (or don't need) from you before they start.

Mediumship is a very natural process. I personally hate the word paranormal. I believe mediumship is normal, albeit little understood. If you are nervous, try to imagine your friends and family sitting around the table for a cup of tea and a chat – how relaxed would you feel in those circumstances? Obviously, sometimes readings are emotional, but they're also very therapeutic and oftentimes there is much laughter shared too. You can expect not to encounter apparitions, tables levitating or other physical phenomena. Sorry to disappoint, but that just doesn't occur with mental mediumship.

Q: Is it OK to receive several readings one after another?

A: Be wary of any medium asking you to return regularly. I never ask clients to return and I have a three-time rule in place to protect my clients from becoming reliant on my readings. In any case, after one or sometimes two sittings, people generally have all they need from me, unless, of course, several years go by or a different loved one passes.

I always advise people to wait at least a year between visits, so life has a chance to move on. That way I can give them something new and they don't pay again for the same information.

There is value in seeing different mediums at work. If different mediums repeat the same information to you about your loved one during separate readings, it builds upon the evidence of survival. This is good investigative research, plus it can be difficult to build your own personal evidence without having experienced a few readings. However, you should avoid having reading after reading when you are desperate for answers. And do not rely on mediums and psychics for decision making; it only disempowers you.

Q: How long should I leave it after my loved one dies before seeing a medium?

A: I would caution that it's much more important to focus on dealing with your own healing in the initial first few months before seeking out a medium. A reading with a good medium can be highly effective in assisting people to move through their grief; however, the grieving process takes time and there is no rush. My personal opinion is that it's good to wrap your head around the fact your loved one has passed first and find some acceptance. The reason for this is that should the medium not be able to make a connection with your loved one, it could lead to greater disappointment for you, particularly if you are pinning your hopes on them giving you total peace of mind in the early days because you are finding your grief is overwhelming. This is not a realistic expectation from mediumship and could leave you worse off.

There is no hard-and-fast rule as to how soon a spirit being may communicate with a medium, but it does appear that many spirit loved ones must learn to communicate through a medium. Once they have adjusted to their new way of life, it becomes more natural to them to work through a medium. I believe that by leaving time between the passing of your loved one and seeking the services of a medium, you allow your loved one a chance to settle and to become a more proficient communicator, while giving yourself a chance to heal.

That does not mean your loved one won't try to contact you directly to let you know they are OK before this. Statistically, high numbers of people report experiencing personal direct contact with deceased loved ones in the first few days and weeks directly after a passing, as Theresa has shown so beautifully in Chapter Four. At this time, people are more likely to receive signs their loved ones are OK – whether in the form of familiar smells, electrical interferences, appliances turning on and off mysteriously, temperature changes, cold blasts on their faces, sentimental songs coming on in the strangest circumstances, visions during lucid dreams, unexplained lights in the room or even telephone calls and apparitions, the list is endless.

Theresa started the book by describing a voice calling out to her while she was in the car, and in Chapter Four she shared Naomi's story about hearing a voice call to her in the mornings. I love the song 'The Rainbow Connection' by the Muppets, in particular the lyrics, 'Have you been half asleep and have you heard voices, I've heard them calling my name.' When Paul Williams and Kenneth Ascher composed that song they were onto something.

Q: What will happen to me if I ignore the advice of my spirit loved ones?

A: Mediums are not all-knowing gurus and nor should they act as such. We are everyday people and any wisdom you receive during a reading should be accepted or rejected as you see fit. Similarly, your loved ones in spirit may have moved on, but they're not necessarily all seeing and knowing either. Take any guidance you receive as you would from anyone you speak to in this world. If it makes sense to you and it's helpful, accept it; if it doesn't resonate with you, reject it. No medium should tell you what to do with your life. You are the only authority on that.

Q: Can mediumship be effective during grief counselling?

A: Everybody's needs and circumstances are different. Mediumship is not a substitute for counselling and if you are experiencing difficulties in life or finding it hard to manage your grief, I recommend you seek out a qualified professional. Mediumship can be highly complementary, however, and research shows a reading with a medium is conducive to improving people's happiness and aiding peace of mind and healing. Whether you agree with the validity of mediumship or not, this fact alone should be taken into account.

Q: Can mediums do readings anywhere and are you picking up on spirits all the time?

A: Yes, in theory mental mediumship can be done anywhere. I personally prefer to be in a space that is familiar to me, where I feel at ease and have peace and quiet. This helps set boundaries and builds the energy, but I have demonstrated mediumship in many different locations. Other forms of mediumship that require more controls usually take place in a prepared seance room.

I don't think it's healthy or appropriate to be tuned into spirits all the time. I'm extremely disciplined about where and when I will work. I control my ability; it does not control me. A simple way to explain how it works would be to use the TV as an example. TV channels are sending a signal all the time through the environment to the TV set in your house. You're not aware of the signal, however, until you tune in. It's exactly the same. Plus, if I were tuned in all the time, I would eventually suffer burnout and be of no use to anyone.

In fact, I am completely against mediums picking up on spirit beings any time, any place. I saw a lady in a shop once choosing a card from the 'With Sympathy' section. I was horrified when another lady came up to her and without even asking if she wanted to know, told the lady choosing a card that she could see a deceased relative standing with her and so she should not be upset. The poor recipient burst into tears and left the shop, while I looked on in shock. There is a time and a place to deliver news that is sensitive and your recipient must be ready to receive it. You might think you're being helpful, but you could inadvertently cause more harm than good or offend someone's religious beliefs.

Q: Why do mediums choose to have readings with other mediums? Can't they just read for themselves?

A: There is stronger evidence for the survival of consciousness if a complete stranger tells you about your spirit loved ones in conjunction with you having your own experiences. When receiving a message from a stranger we are all less prone to just dismissing it as wishful thinking. Mediums do receive direct communication, as I've already shared, especially if they have learned a form of mediumship such as channelling or automatic writing in which direct communication may come forward to them. However, even for them, there is no substitute for having someone who they are aware knows nothing about them tell them about their loved ones in spirit and have them pass on a message. It helps to build trust in an afterlife because to doubt is human, even for mediums. Added to this, it is impossible for a medium to remain unbiased about their own life circumstances. Consulting another medium – someone who has no emotional attachment to their spirit relatives or their life situation – can make for a clearer, more impartial reading.

Q: Why doesn't the spirit world give mediums useful information like the lottery numbers?

A: This seems like an extremely trivial question to me, but it's one I get asked a lot, so I'm attempting to put it to bed by answering it here. The spirit world is not interested in making predictions or in our material gain. It knows all things of the material world are temporary. It is far more interested in giving us wisdom that will help us in both this world and the next. That, in my opinion, is a treasure far more valuable.

Q: Are my family watching me *all* the time?

A: No, please don't worry. They have far more to do than just sit watching you all day. Would you want to do that? They come around you in visitation from time to time, but the rest of the time they're in their own world, doing their own thing and that is healthy.

Q: Where can I go to learn mediumship myself?

A: In my humble opinion, the best way to learn about psychic awareness and mediumship development is to sit in a development group with an experienced medium. (I actually would advise against someone developing solely on their own, purely because there is no one on hand to help them keep a balanced view on the progress made or the information received; but I'm also reluctant to be too judge-mental because I know spirit works in all manner of ways.) Development groups are often called circles and many times they are held in people's homes or at a spiritualist church or centre. Circle groups can be quite hard to find as they are not usually advertised; if there isn't an established circle near you, the Institute of Spiritualist Mediums in the UK runs a programme where you can get advice and guidance for setting up your own circle.

There are two types of circle: open and closed. Open circles are, as the name suggests, open to anyone. They are usually held in spiritualist churches and anyone interested in learning about mediumship can attend for a minimal fee or small donation. Due to the circle being open it does mean that attendance varies from week to week as people come and go, but if you get the right teacher, it can make a wonderful starting place to learn.

Once you show your dedication to your development and your ability starts to progress you may well be invited to join a closed circle. Closed circles do require much more dedication on your part, as the same group of people sits regularly. You need to be sure you want to take on this commitment because if one person is away, it means there are fewer people to work with in the group and the energy within it is altered. This, in turn, has the effect of changing the conditions for the spirit world to work with too. So a lack of commitment obviously affects results. Closed circles are often run in people's homes and can be harder to come by, but once you find the right teacher and you invest in your development you can really begin to reap the fruits of your labour.

I know I've said it already, but finding the right teacher really is key. Look for a medium you respect – someone who is experienced enough to help you develop your own connection with the spirit world.

I know through my friendship with Patrick Keller from The Big Seance Podcast in the USA that circle groups seem to be harder to come by in America than in the UK, so it may also be that your location dictates what's available to you. But don't lose heart. Intention is everything and the spirit world will work with you no matter where you are and what your beliefs or your circumstances. If you have genuine commitment and an interest in learning and exploring this field with an open mind and heart, you have the basis for a connection. You certainly do not have to be a spiritualist to explore mediumship. However, I highly recommend that you don't walk into your experiments blind. Do your best to learn from experienced people first to avoid inadvertently attracting unwanted spirit attention or walking headlong into situations you are unequipped to handle.

You may also choose to visit a college or spiritual centre. Spiritualist churches and other spiritual centres often run workshops. In the UK, the Arthur Findley College in Essex and the College of Psychic Studies in London are both world famous for all types of course on mediumship, psychic awareness and healing.

Finally, many experienced mediums run their own training programmes.

Q: How long will it take to train?

A: It will take your whole life and I'm not joking. We never stop developing, so expect to be in this for the long haul. We each develop at our own speed and we each have our own strengths and weaknesses. It takes the spirit world time to refine working with us and it takes us time to become spiritually aware. I have sat in development now for decades and I'm still learning. The best mediums are the ones who have committed to their development and dedicated their life to their work. The reward for this, though, is tremendous and the good news is it also means time is on your side, as older mediums are just as much in demand as younger ones, if not more so, because they can bring the benefit of life experience to their readings.

Q: Are mediums born mediums or can anyone learn to become one?

A: We all have the potential to develop some level of mediumistic ability. Just in the same way that we may all enjoy taking lessons to learn how to draw or sing, but we won't all go on to become professional artists or performers, we can all benefit from and enjoy learning about mediumship and the world of spirit. However, as is often the case with any skill, some people are born with strong natural ability and it's they who tend to excel at what they do. It is the same with mediumship. I had no conscious awareness myself that I was a medium before I started training. It's only in retrospect that I realise I had been interacting with the spirit world all my life and so the potential to develop into a medium was always there. If we don't try, we don't know. Even the most accurate mediums need to develop. No one is born fully fledged.

Q: How do I build upon my own connection with the spirit world when I'm at home?

A: Meditation is the key that unlocks the door and this is something easily practised at home. When we train the mind to be still and to observe, our spirit friends can inspire us.

Meditation takes practice, so be patient with yourself and allow yourself time. Invite your spirit loved ones and guides to come close to you as you sit. Over time, you'll see the wonder of your connections unfold. Keep a journal and write down any insights you receive, no matter how trivial or small. After a while, you will learn to discern the difference between those times when spirit beings join you and when it's your own imagination. You can then start to develop a relationship with those in spirit who work with you and you will find your journal reflects back helpful insights and knowledge of which you would otherwise have had no prior understanding.

DEALING WITH GRIEF

I touched upon dealing with grief in the questions above and Theresa did the same in Chapter Two, where she wrote about her own mother's transition to spirit, but this book wouldn't be complete without giving this subject a little more attention because, naturally, when we talk about messages from the afterlife, it follows that someone has died and that grief must be a part of the picture. I must stress, however, that I am not a qualified grief counsellor and if you are currently finding it difficult to deal with grief in your own life, I recommend you seek out the help of a professional you can talk to. (You will find details in the Appendix of places you can go to find that assistance – see p. 317.)

All that I write here comes from my own personal journey as a medium and as an everyday person who's loved and lost. It is my hope that what I share will be helpful to you in some small way.

Between 2009 and 2014 seven close family members of

mine passed. No sooner had I nursed one through the dying process and faced letting them go, than the next relative fell ill and the cycle started again. And so it went on each year for five years. Life didn't spare the young; it took those who we thought had decades ahead of them and, of course, it took the old, whose wisdom and life experience were invaluable.

Many times throughout that period I felt as though I didn't have time to process my grief because I was being required to find another dose of inner strength and to push my own healing to one side while the family dealt with the next round of bad news. Not even mediums are shielded from the pain of losing a loved one. Just because we have a knowing that life goes on, it doesn't make us immune to deeply missing the physicality of our loved ones and feeling very sad about that.

Through this time, I leaned on the one pillar of strength that remained constant in my life: my faith in an afterlife. My knowledge of the spirit world was the backbone that kept me standing. I truly don't know how those who have no faith at all manage through such difficult times. My convictions helped me find strength and meaning and, most importantly, they helped me relate to my dying family members with compassion and positivity at a time when they desperately needed it because I was not afraid of death and they knew they could talk to me when they wanted to without fear that I couldn't cope with the subject.

Grief is a strange thing – so full of mixed emotions, ups and downs, highs and lows. In my case, I found it was as though there were two aspects of myself living inside the one body. The surface me, which everyone could see, was full of emotions that rose and fell whenever they chose, taking me on a rollercoaster ride on which I was joined by other family members too. I would fall victim to emotions such as sadness, despair, hopelessness, helplessness, anger and frustration, which were confusingly mixed in with positivity, compassion, laughter, kindness and relief. At times when the strain on the whole family was so great and we were all at breaking point, I'd plead with life that this would all end soon and then immediately feel racked with guilt for having even had the thought, for that would mean letting go of another loved one into spirit, knowing I wouldn't see them again for a long time. This surface me seemed continually torn and pulled in all directions and there was no telling which way I'd go next. One minute I'd be laughing and finding the funny side of life and the next I'd be tearful and sad. There was no predicting it or controlling it. Sometimes I could function well and get on with my life, while at other times I'd stare out into space and whole chunks of time would slip by and I couldn't concentrate on anything. I'd also find myself raising my voice unnecessarily with people because my patience was so thin, something I hated doing.

The deeper aspect of me, however – that which I've come to think of as my soul – seemed more constant and managed to connect to a place of more profound wisdom. At the deeper level, there seemed to be an acceptance that this is life and that ultimately all is well. I began to feel greater contentment for the very fact I was alive and had been given the gift of life. I felt gratitude for the positive impact my relationship with my loved ones had had on my life and appreciation for the love that I'd known. It seemed strange but beautiful that I could live with such contradiction at such a difficult time. Through it, though, I learned that it was possible to feel sadness and contentment at the same time and that, unexpectedly, gave me strength.

This is the thing with grief. It doesn't always make sense and there isn't a right or wrong way to deal with it because it doesn't behave in a rational way. You cannot rush it. It takes its own sweet time. And while for some people that means years, for others it may only mean months. Each person's grief is unique to them. It comes and goes, but it never really leaves you. You can think you're doing really well and then all of a sudden something sparks off a memory and you have an emotional day, week or month. Grief can be uncomfortable and have you wishing you never had to deal with it; then, at the same time, it is the very mark of the fact that you have loved and so you wouldn't exchange it for the world.

The sure fact is we will all experience grief at one time or another, whether that's due to the death of a loved one or through any other kind of loss or challenge in life. The most important thing is to face it and to try to accept it into your life as an important part of the healing process. Problems arise for those people who bury it, run away from it or sweep it under the carpet because it is too painful, so give yourself permission to grieve, pull together with family members and friends, lean on one another and, at the same time, give yourself the space you need to heal. Be kind to yourself just as you would if you were recovering from an illness or surgery. You will move through it and out the other side of it more smoothly if you do.

We are all individual and we have individual needs. What is right for one person may not be right for the next. In her pioneering work as a psychiatrist, Elisabeth Kübler-Ross famously wrote about the five stages of grief being denial, anger, bargaining, depression and acceptance. Through her work with dying patients, she recognised that most people will move in and out of these stages while dealing with grief and so she worked tirelessly to help both those who were dying and those who were grieving come to terms with what they were experiencing. But there isn't any hard-and-fast rule or a process that you can tick off neatly as you make your way through it. Instead, you must go with what feels right to you and accept help when you need it. Try to talk about your emotions to someone you feel comfortable with, enjoy speaking about your memories, express your emotions and allow yourself time to cry. Holding emotional grief inside of you undealt with only leads to health problems further down the line as your body tries to deal with the stress it is under. This is the last thing you need when you're already trying to heal. Instead, try to see grief in a more positive light, as the necessary pathway to wellness.

In my experience, problems with grief arise when people get stuck in it. Many times I've met people who are actually frightened to move through their grief because they feel it is disrespectful to their loved one – as though letting go of the grief requires forgetting their loved one or dishonouring their memory. This is not true. You can move through and let go of your grief and still remember your loved one. This can be done with gratitude instead. When you think of the one you have loved, appreciate all they showed you and all that they did. Honour them by living your life well. Think about their greatest qualities. What was it that made you love them? Vow to be or do more of that in your own life.

Your loved ones in the spirit world are well and still very much alive. Resoundingly, the most common message loved ones in spirit bring is just how well they are and that they live on with vitality. Because of this, they want the same for us. They want us to find contentment, to live happily and to live well. They continue to walk with us and enjoy our achievements and successes. Let your life, therefore, be a celebration of theirs and let the love you shared be the measure of the mark you leave upon this world, not your tears.

In the final chapter, I will share with you ways in which you may achieve a deeper connection to the spiritual dimensions and become more in tune with your own spirit. That way you may go on to discover how you can access answers from heaven – because the answers to all you really need to know can be accessed from within you.

The person who says it cannot be done should not interrupt the person doing it.

CHINESE PROVERB

CHAPTER NINE

YOUR OWN ANSWERS FROM HEAVEN

What lies behind us and what lies before us are
tiny matters compared to what lies within us.

RALPH WALDO EMERSON

Throughout Part Two of this book, I have highlighted the fact that my own understanding of the existence of an afterlife has come from a lifetime of personal experience, coupled with educating myself about the research in this field. I have found that the evidence for the survival of consciousness, taking into account many aspects of the research available (such as near-death experience, deathbed visions, past-life recollection in children and mediumship) is highly persuasive – so much so that I have no doubt that life goes on, even if at times, being human as I am, I find myself questioning the strength of my own ability. This knowledge has enabled me to relinquish fear of death and although I don't relish the idea of the dying process, I no longer hold as truth that death of the physical body results in an annihilation of consciousness. I have no doubt that when my own time comes to exit this world, I will simply transition into a new dimension of reality.

What that reality will be like, I can only surmise, and I certainly don't profess to hold all the answers. In November 2016, when I established a connection with White Feather while experimenting with automatic writing, I asked if he could tell me what it was like where he exists in the spirit world, so that I might gain some insight into what may follow for us all. The answer I received during this session is shared here with you now:

You must understand that the language of words has its limitations. I cannot truly describe to you the beauty of our world, for yours knows nothing of the splendour we have here, and so there are no existing words to fully describe it. It has aspects in appearance that would be familiar to your world – nature, buildings and residences – and yet, at the same time, it is so completely different, your brain could not translate it. I can only point your imagination and your inner knowing to some understanding, but truly, it really must be experienced to appreciate it and there is no hurry for you there, little sister. I shall endeavour to create a picture for you instead, so that you may gain some insight. Just know that all I say pales into insignificance in the light of actuality.

They call it the Summerlands, for it is a world of great

beauty, vibrant in colour and harmonious in sound, where light exists all around like the brilliance of a shining sun on a long summer's day. All who dwell here feel truly at home, nurtured by its warmth and nourished by its rays. We do not rely on an actual sun to create the light, however; rather, it is the pure light of consciousness that resides in all things that lights this land for all to bathe in. It is a light that does not hurt your eyes or burn your skin. Instead, it revitalises and rejuvenates your very essence. It is limitless and timeless here and the soul may know freedom, love and acceptance beyond measure.

Ours is a realm of light so refined, so very much alive, that every aspect of nature is sentient, and all those who dwell here feel intimately connected to the whole. Through hyperawareness, we are attuned to all life, from the humble sunflower to the astute wolf. We experience the vitality and richness of all that resides here, from a simple blade of grass, to the lively hummingbird. We are so keenly aware of our interconnectedness and the love that permeates throughout all creation, we can feel euphoria and joy in abundance here. Our world is more real, more alive than you can possibly imagine; the most vivid of dreams cannot paint it, but if you could see it through your own eyes, you would never again shed a tear for all those who have entered here, for your joy for them would heal the wounds in your own broken heart.

Many in your world call this heaven, and so it is, but heaven is a state of being, little sister, not a destination. Heaven is formed in accordance with your perception and inner progression. Never lose sight of the knowledge that heaven can be experienced on Mother Earth, if you allow it. Those of us who return to your world, do so to remind humanity of this.

The spirit world is far greater than you can imagine, consisting of worlds within worlds, dimensions within dimensions. Ascending in layers, each blends from one reality to the next. Those departing your world transition to their closest reality, one that is in direct relation to the evolutionary frequency of their soul and so there are many routes to and through the Summerlands.

In Chapter Five I wrote that exploring mediumship and evidence for the survival of consciousness raises more questions than it provides answers, but I invited you to open Pandora's box to find hope. Having read the above, you may now see why I wrote this, but the beauty of opening up your mind to the possibility that there is more to life than we can comprehend means that we are also encouraged to keep questioning, growing and developing. Should humanity stop doing that, it could fall into decline.

For my part, despite my extremely analytical mind and desire to understand my experiences on an academic level, I believe I am also beginning to learn that ultimately I cannot intellectualise something that goes beyond comprehension. I must *feel* the truth to recognise it and to know it from within, and that realisation leads me to understand that this is the same for you too.

This is why I would never tell anyone else what to believe or think. Instead, I encourage people to explore the truth for themselves and put it to the test, as I have done. I know my words cannot prove an afterlife to you. They can only point you in the direction of further learning or perhaps turn on a switch within your own awareness, and that is enough. You must find your own answers to life. True spirituality doesn't require me to ask you to follow me and do things my way; rather, it empowers you to follow your own path, to find your own way to enlightenment. If what you have read in these pages has resonated with you, then that is wonderful. But if not, that is also just as acceptable to me because the message in these pages is not about me or Theresa and our needs – it is about you and something far greater than you. It is about us because the greatest and truest connection to spirit comes when we learn to connect to a greater awareness than ourselves.

The journey to spiritual awakening, therefore, takes many different forms. Mediumship is one of those and at its best, it can act as a catalyst to help you access your own answers from heaven. But how do you go on to do that now you have read this book? I know not everyone will become a medium or even want to try, so where do we go from here?

ACCESSING HEAVEN FROM WITHIN

Over the years I have come to appreciate just how powerful meditation and prayer can be. Through them I have gained some outstanding insights and support. Receiving insights from my spirit guide has taught me that higher knowledge is accessible to all of us if we learn to connect within through our own spirit.

In our modern world, where life moves so fast and many of us are hooked into technology for much of the day, we've become completely distracted mentally. We've lost sight of just how much our minds, bodies and souls benefit from quiet time and reflection. We've stopped paying attention to the environment around us. Many of us struggle to be in our own company, especially when we have nothing to do and nowhere to go. We have lost touch with the internal universe accessible to us all, a place where we need never feel alone.

A simple way to rectify this is through meditation and prayer. However, it's common for people to struggle with both of these, particularly the latter if you have no affinity with any one religion. Although both are simple in technique, the majority of us falter because we do not really understand what's required of us. We don't fully understand the true power behind these practices.

Think of them as your direct means of communication with the world of spirit; meditation is the means by which you listen and receive, prayer is the means by which you speak and are heard. Many people do not yet appreciate the immense power behind stilling the mind and taking charge of their thoughts. Thoughts are energy, and when we attend to and direct them decisively, they have the power to create our future, promote healing, shape our world and travel deep within the universe. Like an instant text message, our intentions and emotions can reach out beyond us.

Thoughts carry their own specific energetic frequencies that naturally align with others that match. This is why I have stressed that your state of mind is the most important aspect when it comes to mediumship and why setting the intention affects the outcome of your communication. Your thoughts benefit not only people living in our world – for example, when sending healing prayers – but also those residing in non-physical dimensions. The beauty is that when you focus your mind and expand your awareness, you can open lines or channels for communication, enabling not only your loved ones who have moved into spirit to receive your messages and for them to send their own back to you, but for you also to tune in to the universal mind or infinite consciousness, so you can access wisdom and insights to direct and guide you through life.

Learning to meditate

There are many techniques and practices available to help you learn how to meditate, from visualisation techniques to mindfulness or simple breathing exercises. Even a walk in the park or a round of golf can be a meditation. So you may need to experiment with each practice to discover what suits you best, but once you have found a method that works for you, relax into it, enjoy it and make it part of your life's routine.

Although it's important to practise regularly, it's not necessary to spend hours each day in deep meditation. As lovely as that might be, it's just not practical. A few minutes every day or even every week will begin to train the brain how to become quiet, and the more you do it the easier it will become. You'll then find you can gradually spend longer periods of time in stillness and reflection should you wish to do so.

Get creative and find small ways to introduce peace into your day. A few conscious deep, relaxing breaths, for instance, can be highly effective when done regularly. There are also some great meditations available on YouTube that you can listen to when you have a moment of quiet in the daytime or in the morning upon waking.

In the previous chapter, I wrote that when it comes to mediumship, meditation is the key that unlocks the door, and I encouraged you to keep a journal of your meditations, so that you can begin to recognise when those in the spirit world join you. I also want to add that when developing a link with the spirit world for yourself, for the best experience nothing beats meditating in a group with people you trust. Following a visualisation or sitting in the power together enables you to share what has happened, which can be hugely insightful. It is also highly beneficial because you create together a peaceful and relaxing energy in the room, which in itself is therapeutic. In fact, the health benefits of meditation – no matter which technique you prefer – are extensive. It can help calm the nervous system, improve immunity, maintain the health of your heart, increase concentration, improve creativity and aid restful sleep, as well as helping you to connect with your spirit.

When it comes to meditation, I believe you learn through experiencing. I've therefore included information in the Appendix (see p. 309) on how to access meditations I have created especially for you as an accompaniment to this book to assist you in creating your own connection to spirit.

Effective prayer

As I mentioned at the start of this section, prayer is closely linked to meditation. And, as Theresa pointed out earlier, it need not be confined to the religious. There is so much more to prayer than kneeling with clasped hands and asking your preferred deity for something you want or need. Another word for prayer is intention. There is an immense power in focused thought or intention when coupled with action, which affects both the material and the spirit world. When you realise this, you understand that praying in the conventional way may not be the most effective.

Many people have lost faith in the power of prayer because they're either turned off by the religious connotations or feel their prayers go unanswered. The likely reason for this is that the very act of asking for something you *want* or *need* draws the experience of wanting or needing to you. Your words and the power behind your words – your intentions – matter. A more effective prayer should create the experience of having and being, but many people struggle to achieve this.

This is a real shame because prayer can be so powerful – so much so that, as Theresa mentioned earlier, studies have shown that patients who were prayed for during treatment did better than those who were not, even though none of them knew they were being prayed for. It really is a case of mind over matter. The Global Consciousness Study developed by researcher Roger Nelson in 1997 provides fascinating insight into just how much our collective state of mind may affect our physical world. Through the use of random number generators, scientists have been able to measure the effects of collective thought and concentration on the world during global events such as 9/11 and the death of Princess Diana, and the data collected suggests that our thoughts directly influence our physical world.

Prayer is most effective, then, when you still your mind, focus your thoughts on the result you wish to create and set your intention for your prayer in a confident and affirmative manner. So if you are praying for someone who is ill and you wish for them to get better, an example of a potentially less effective prayer would be something along the lines of: 'Dear God, I need your help. If it is your will, please can you heal my friend, as he is really suffering and I so much want him to get better.'

For a more powerful or helpful prayer, on the other hand, you would take a few deep, relaxing breaths first, fill your heart with love, feel the power of spirit within your own body and then visualise your friend surrounded by beautiful healing rays of light looking well, healthy and happy. Following this, direct these intentions to your friend by saying something along the lines of: 'I trust in universal consciousness. Through it I send my friend these healing rays of light that I have visualised and created. Please direct this healing energy where it will be most effective. Please enhance it, so that the energy is plentiful for my friend whom I love and may they use it to experience health and wellness now. Thank you, for I know all I have asked has been received.'

Finishing your prayer with gratitude in this way affirms the positive emotional power behind your intention and carries the emotion of confidence that the healing is given. You may trust, then, that this positive, subtle energy is now with your friend.

Remember, you can pray for those both in this world and the next because your thoughts are boundless and will be received wherever directed. I often send peaceful healing intentions to those who are transitioning from this world to the next and ask that they be met with a loving embrace in the light because the spirit world has communicated to me in the past that those healing intentions are indeed received and do help.

When it comes to mediumship, before I make any attempt to connect with the spirit world, I always ensure I mentally set the intention for the grounds on which I agree to continue and the manner in which I will allow the communication to take place. I always respectfully ask that my guides in the spirit world come close to assist me and I stipulate that only those in spirit who can come forward in a loving, respectful manner and with my best interests at heart may interact with me. I envision a light around myself, so that I may tune into the higher realms of spirit and receive its protection. Then I give thanks for all the wisdom that is to be imparted upon me and the healing it may bring. At the end of any communication, I always close the session down with gratitude and set the intention that I am now finished and am no longer available to be contacted. In doing this, I take responsibility for myself and my work and remain disciplined and in control of the connection. I would advise anyone else working with the spirit dimensions to do the same.

So in rounding up, it is my hope that you understand that through meditation and prayer it may be possible for you too to make a connection to the spirit realms and, in doing so, continue the dialogue for yourself, so that you may access your own answers and insights, even if you choose not to pursue the topic of mediumship any further.

THERAPY FROM HEAVEN

Both Theresa and I have illustrated the many ways in which those in the afterlife can reach out to you from beyond the veil. Together, we have described how very real these events are and yet how elusive they can also feel. As we near the close of this book, however, we could not complete it without acknowledging the magic that happens within ourselves once we begin to seek the truth and open our minds to an afterworld of possibility.

As I have mentioned, once you let the knowledge of spirit into your heart and expand your mind, you can experience spiritual growth. This often brings with it greater happiness as you let go of fears you held and relieve yourself of unnecessary worries. You may gain a fuller sense of freedom as you relinquish cultural conditioning, allowing yourself to explore new territory and adventure into the unknown. There can be a great sense of wonder as you discover you never stop learning and that the universe holds infinite potential for you. Or, as your world opens up, you may become motivated to serve others and driven to achieve new goals, ones that hold greater purpose and meaning for you and the world. You may find you have greater capacity for compassion and empathy, becoming more caring towards all living things. But by far the greatest personal benefit, in my opinion, is in being able to enjoy life to a greater degree. Rather than taking it for granted, you can now appreciate the wonder of it, giving you access to more joy and contentment. And that, as we now know, is heavenly.

So what are you waiting for? Carry your light out into this world, take the next step and let's continue this journey of discovery together. And now, as I hand you back into Theresa's hands, all that's left for me to do is to thank you deeply from my heart for joining me here and for reading this book. It has been a great honour and a privilege to share information and wisdom with you and I sincerely thank you for the attention you have given it and for your open-mindedness. I hope that together we can continue this dialogue in kindness and compassion.

Meditation, because not all answers
can be found on Google.

ANONYMOUS

THE NEVER-ENDING STORY

A true love story never ends.

ANONYMOUS

Heaven – does it really matter how it speaks to you: through a medium, like Claire, or directly through your intuition or dreams, as I experience it, through afterlife signs or in the guise of other people, a child or beloved pet. It doesn't matter how you receive answers from above as long as the message of love it brings is there and that message is that you are never alone. And it doesn't matter where those answers come from, as long as you are reminded that heaven is not some faraway place you may go to when you die, but somewhere you can connect to anytime in your heart. Whichever way heaven speaks to you it will remind you that it lives for ever in your heart and that the power of love within and all around you is eternal and a source of boundless comfort, joy, hope and inspiration.

Deeply spiritual people have always known that the first place to look for answers from heaven is within their hearts, and a connection to heaven is our birthright, but in the world today so many of us have forgotten who we are. We think status, Facebook likes, money, relationships or material possession will save us and bring us a sense of belonging, validation and meaning. We are all the same: we all want to be loved and to feel fulfilled and that our lives matter, but we are searching outside ourselves for salvation and it can never be found there. We don't realise that although we live in a physical world that feels real, the only reality is our essence or eternal spirit that is deep within us. Afterlife signs can remind us of our true spiritual self, as can visiting a medium who is able to offer clear proof of survival after death.

You are a spark of the divine, always have been and always will be. I hope this book will have reminded you of what you already knew, but may have forgotten along the way, and that is that this life on earth is temporary and your true home is heaven. The key to fulfilment, happiness and meaning on earth is your spiritual growth and that is a never-ending journey that continues when you cross over to the other side. When you live every day with love in your heart for yourself and others you are an earth angel.

Trust that aspiring angel in your heart. It is that angel and the feelings of love, peace, kindness and compassion it inspires within you and others that will always provide the answer and the meaning, guidance and comfort you seek. Believe in that angel of eternal love within you and become the answer you are seeking because you are already, and always will be, in heaven.

*The kingdom of heaven is within you and whoever
shall know her or himself will find it.*

EGYPTIAN PROVERB

WITH OUR LOVE

*At the centre of your being you have
the answer, you know who you are
and you know what you want.*

LAO TZU

Remember, this isn't the end but the beginning of your spiritual journey, which we truly hope you will continue, with us, by reading the Appendix that follows. There, you will find all the information you need about contacting us via our websites and social media, as well as other useful resources.

We both hope you will connect with us online or in person when we do talks or demonstrations, but whether or not you decide to do that, we hope that this book will have reminded you that you already are an answer from heaven. Each one of you is a unique, magical and eternal miracle and we could not be happier and feel more blessed that the love in your heart drew your spirit to this book. Everything happens for a reason. We believe heaven sent you this book.

And we hope it has brought you understanding, comfort, joy and answers.

Always sending you our eternal love and blessings,

Theresa and Claire
xx

APPENDIX 1

THE WINDBRIDGE INSTITUTE

www.windbridge.org

Windbridge is an independent research organisation consisting of a community of scientists from a variety of different backgrounds and specialities. Launched in 2008 and founded by Julie Beischel PhD, the Windbridge Institute, LLC, is currently leading the world in research on phenomena that traditional scientific disciplines currently can't explain. The main aim of the institute is to conduct research to develop and distribute information, services and technologies to help people live happier and more fulfilling lives. Questions that are researched and studied scientifically include:

- What can we do with the potential that exists within our bodies, minds and spirits?
- Can we heal each other? Ourselves?
- Can we affect events and physical reality with our thoughts?

- Can we know things before they happen?
- Are we connected to each other? To the planet?
- Can we communicate with our loved ones who have passed?
- Does visiting a medium help ease the grieving process?

If you've been intrigued and inspired by what you have read in this book, we urge you to check out the Windbridge Institute to see for yourself the cutting edge scientific research it is currently doing on mediumship.

APPENDIX 2

MEDIUMSHIP

Essay written for this book by Windbridge Institute director Dr Julie Beischel

Mediumship is probably as old as humanity itself. Communication with the deceased was a useful social task accomplished by shamans or other individuals in ancient cultures. And it continues to be a common occurrence for modern mediums of various belief systems and cultures all over the world. At some point in Western cultures, we lost touch with that part of our human experience. It only came back with the rise of spiritualism in the mid-1800s and only recently to the American popular culture.

About fifteen years ago, the universe decided that I should dedicate my time, energy and scientific prowess to studying mediums, individuals who communicate with the deceased. Before then, I didn't even know what a medium was. I was on a traditional academic path, finishing up my PhD in Pharmacology and Toxicology with a minor in Microbiology and Immunology, and most likely headed for a career working for a pharmaceutical company (I was young; I didn't know any better).

But then everything changed. Someone close to me died: my mom committed suicide. She was fifty-four. I was twenty-four. I had had grandparents who had died, but they had lived across the country and I didn't really know them. Because there is no formula for grief that fits everyone – no stages, no tasks, no road map – I went through the process my own way, making my own progress and learning to be the new me without her.

A few years later, I saw a medium perform gallery readings on TV. The medium on TV seemed genuine enough. The messages appeared specific and the people looked genuinely moved. Given my recent loss, I was curious, and I decided to test it out for myself. I received a reading from a local medium and the universe seemed to be watching and steering.

The reading contained far too much specific information to dismiss. It included information I didn't know but later verified with members of my extended family. The medium accurately conveyed the cause of death and specifics about my childhood. (I have shared the complete details of this story in *Among Mediums*, so I won't repeat it here.)

The reading convinced me that something I couldn't easily explain had happened, but what really hoisted me on the mediumship research train was not the content of the reading but some of the responses to it. It might have stopped there and just been an interesting story I sometimes told at dinner parties. But when other scientists I knew claimed that all mediums were con-artists and that I had somehow been duped by this charlatan, I got mad. Really mad.

I found this view insulting to my ability as a scientist to objectively observe a phenomenon and felt it was illogical of my peers to make sweeping generalisations about an entire group of people with no data. (To be clear, I only encountered this ignorant viewpoint a couple of times. Most people I knew responded like good scientists: 'I don't know anything about mediums personally, but it sounds like you had a very interesting experience.') I soon learned that this negative opinion about mediums was widespread, also with little to no data to back up the scepticism. That seemed so unfair to me. I decided to bring mediumship into the lab and put it to the test using modern research methods.

Within a few years, I got married and my husband, Mark Boccuzzi, and I started the Windbridge Institute in order to perform research on the potential of the mind. I concentrate on mediumship and Mark focuses on related phenomena, like using technology to interact with the deceased. We work with a handful of other researchers on specific projects and have a few volunteers but, for the most part, it's just the two of us.

When we study mediumship at the Windbridge Institute, we study it as it actually works in the real world and not how people think it should work. Often, sceptics – or, more accurately, 'deniers' – criticise mediums for not being able to complete tasks the deniers think they should be able to do (for example, acquiring lottery numbers). However, those tasks do not reflect what a medium actually does. A medium is not a fortune-teller. A medium experiences communication from the deceased and shares the messages he or she receives with living sitters. That's it. And it's a lot, so expecting more is unreasonable.

I have used different analogies for deniers' claims over the years, but I think my favourite is this: calling a medium a fraud because she can't win the lottery (or guess the number you're thinking of or get rich in the stock market or tell the future) is like calling an acorn a fraud because it can't turn into an oak tree in your hand. In order to effectively study a phenomenon, you need to let it be itself, not what you think it is.

At Windbridge, we work with a team of about twenty secular American mediums. Secular means they are not members of an organised religion or belief system and practise their mediumship independently of any larger organisation. The Windbridge Certified Research Mediums (WCRMs) on our team were each screened, tested, trained and certified over many months, volunteer their time to research and agree to specific standards of conduct, including not giving messages to someone unless specifically asked to. At Windbridge, our research with mediums can be categorised into three programmes: Information, Operation and Application. The Information research programme looks at the accuracy and specificity of mediums' statements. For most experimental study readings, it's only a medium and me on the phone, and the only information we have is the first name of a deceased person. The sitter associated with that deceased person then scores the transcript of that reading (called a target reading) and another sitter's reading (called a decoy reading) for accuracy without knowing which is which. (The transcripts don't include the names or words like 'target' and 'decoy'.)

It's a very complex protocol. My peer-reviewed journal article describing it is roughly thirty-five pages long. Nearly everyone who has tried to summarise the protocol has failed. Suffice it to say, the protocol optimises the research environment to allow the medium to do her thing, while maximising the experimental blinding. The protocol eliminates fraud, cold reading, rater bias, and information leakage as explanations for where the mediums get the information they report. In a recent study of ours using this protocol, twenty mediums performed fifty-eight readings and received statistically significant accuracy scores.

The accuracy of readings is judged by the sitters for whom they were intended. The only person truly capable of determining the quality of the messages a medium provides is the sitter. What might seem trivial or nonsensical to you, me or other outside observers, may, in fact, be profoundly meaningful to the sitter. And since a mediumship reading is a private conversation reflective of a relationship between the living sitter and the deceased, only the sitter can determine if it contains accurate, specific and meaningful information. This is why we don't publish the transcripts of our study readings. It would be like publishing someone's love letters.

However, while the only person who can determine if you had a good mediumship reading is you, it is important to remember that there are three people participating in a mediumship reading: the sitter, the deceased and the medium. If a reading is not successful, any one of those three people or the dynamic between them could be responsible.

On that topic, here's some advice you didn't ask for: anyone can call herself a medium and charge sitters for readings, so it is important for sitters, who are often influenced by their grief, to be aware of red flags such as mediums fishing for information or agreeing to provide them with many readings in a short time. To help people find a medium, prepare for a reading and be a good sitter, I wrote a short Kindle book titled *Meaningful Messages: Making the Most of Your Mediumship Reading*. For example, I suggest that if during a reading a medium asks the sitter questions, the sitter should try to only respond with: 'Yes', 'No', 'Maybe', 'Sort of' or 'I don't know'. (It's harder than it sounds.)

Our second mediumship research programme, called Operation, examines the mediums' unique experiences, psychological characteristics and physiology. For example, when asked about their experiences when communicating with the deceased, the mediums describe a 'multi-modal' scenario. That is, all of their mental senses seem to be engaged. A medium may see the deceased in her mind's eye, hear words or sounds, taste certain foods, smell certain odours and feel specific ailments in her body.

Because I, like Theresa, am not a medium, when people ask me about the experiences of mediums, I have to defer to the experts. In *From the Mouths of Mediums*, I collected and organised Windbridge mediums' descriptions of their experiences and their suggestions for how non-mediums could have similar ones. For example, Ginger noted, 'I am shown images of things the discarnate did in life, I hear the music they liked, taste the food they ate, see where they spent a lot of their time. I am shown where they are now in regard to the sitter, and I feel what they felt before they passed.' Similarly, Joanne shared: 'I will hear names and dates, see numbers and letters and places, feel their personality, get a sense about their life with their hobbies or career, see memories connected to the deceased or the sitter, see objects that are connected to the deceased or have meaning to the sitter.'

Another important factor of mediums' experiences is that the deceased come to them to communicate, rather than the mediums 'reaching out' to find the deceased. We call it 'receive vs retrieve'. This is how our research readings can work with only the first name of the deceased: the right Jack finds the medium, rather than the medium having to locate the right Jack. In fact, the right Jack often shows up and communicates with the medium before our scheduled study reading even starts.

The third mediumship research programme at the Windbridge Institute is Application. In these studies, we are interested in the practical social applications of mediumship readings. For example, can the deceased provide wisdom to the living to help solve problems? Can mediums share information that could benefit law-enforcement cases? Do mediumship readings help with grief?

Currently, we are focusing on the potential of mediumship

readings for bereavement within what is called the continuing-bonds model of grief. The continuing-bonds model demonstrates that the key to getting past grief is recognising that your relationship with the deceased isn't over, it has just changed. What was once physical is now spiritual. This is a realisation that can be accomplished through after-death communication experiences, which come in several varieties, including spontaneous and assisted.

Research has demonstrated that spontaneous experiences of the deceased are common and beneficial. These can include sensing the presence of the deceased, multi-modal sensory phenomena, powerful dreams, music associated with the deceased, lost-things-found and other unexplainable phenomena.

I have a friend (OK, he's an ex-boyfriend) who works in law enforcement and he was going through some rough patches at work. Often, during times when he was feeling most lost and in need of comfort, he would see a penny on the ground nearby. It happened so many times that he recently contacted me to make sure that it wasn't 'weird'. As the resident expert in all things weird, I assured him it was not. 'Pennies from heaven' is a saying for a reason, I reminded him. When he checked with his parents, he found out that this was something right in line with his grandmother's personality. So now he is able to experience the pennies as messages letting him know he's not going through the hard times alone. Spontaneous experiences like these, and the others explored in this book, allow the living to recognise their continuing bonds with the deceased.

Another way this is possible is through the assisted after-death communication that occurs during a mediumship reading. The reading may include information effectively identifying the deceased (evidence that it's the right Jack), about the presence of the deceased in the sitter's life since their death and specific, often encouraging, messages for the sitter. This seems like a good formula for demonstrating continuing bonds, but no research has been done in this area. We are currently working on a clinical trial where instead of a treatment or drug, it's a mediumship reading. It's called the Mediumship and Bereavement (BAM) study and is being funded through crowd-funding and support from the William H. Donner Foundation. The aim of the BAM Study is to determine, using appropriate research methods, if receiving a mediumship reading is helpful, harmful or neither for the grieving.

Books like this one by Theresa and Claire are crucial for normalising the experiences of mediums and sitters. Similar to cooking shows, it never turns out the way it looks on TV. The more people who understand mediumship and how it works in the real world, the less frustrated the sitters, the mediums and the deceased will be. Like our study reading protocol, a mediumship reading in reality is a complex situation that is drastically hampered by unrealistic assumptions and expectations.

Whether this is your first, tenth or thousandth step on a path of learning about the reality of mediumship, I welcome you.

19 March 2017
Julie Beischel, PhD
Director of Research
Windbridge Institute
www.windbridge.org

APPENDIX 3

GIFTS FROM THE AUTHORS

Theresa's gift: http://noetic.org/theresa-cheung. This link takes you to a page created by The Institute of Noetic Sciences (IONS) for Theresa Cheung readers and references seven videos in the video library of my Theresa Cheung Author Facebook page where the science team, led by president Dr Cassandra Vieten, speaks to my readers. In the videos, they talk about their encouraging research into mediumship (Dr Arnaud Delorme), precognition (Dr Julia Mossbridge), channelling (Dr Helane Wahbeh), mind–body healing (Dr Garret Yount) and mind influencing matter (lead scientist Dr Dean Radin). The aim of the videos is to show my readers that the gap between science and spirit is closing fast. The page also includes three free gifts from IONS exclusively for readers of this book to download.

Claire's gift: http://www.clairebroad.com. This link takes you to my website where you will see directions for accessing two free meditations that I have created especially as an accompaniment to this book. The first is a guided visualisation to help you develop your own connection with spirit. The second is a guided visualisation to help you meet or connect with spirit guides.

APPENDIX 4

KEY ORGANISATIONS

The Institute of Noetic Sciences (IONS)
www.noetic.org
Science-based, non-profit research, education and membership organisation, dedicated to consciousness research and educational outreach and engaging a global learning community in the realisation of human potential.

The Parapsychological Association
www.parapsych.org
International professional organisation of scientists and scholars engaged in the scientific study of PSI (or 'psychic') experiences.

The Rhine Research Centre
www.rhine.org
Advances the science of parapsychology, provides education and resources for the public and fosters a community for individuals with personal and professional interest in PSI.

Forever Family Foundation

www.foreverfamilyfoundation.org

Furthers the understanding of afterlife science through research and education, while providing support and healing for people in grief.

The Windbridge Institute: Applied Research in Human Potential

www.windbridge.org

Independent research organisation investigating the capabilities of our bodies, minds and spirits, and attempting to determine how the resulting information can best serve all living things.

The Institute of Heart Math

www.heartmath.org

Provides free education and training programmes, services, research membership and tools and technology to transform people's lives by deepening their connection with their own hearts and the hearts of others for a peaceful future.

Australian Parapsychological Research Association (APRA)

www.parapsychology.org.au

Founded by neuroscientist Vladimir Dubaj, the APRA is a non-profit, Australian-based organisation dedicated to the research of parapsychological phenomena through scientific research and education.

Association for the Scientific Study of Anomalous Phenomena

www.assap.ac.uk

UK-based charity and learned society founded in 1981 to

investigate, research and educate on a wide range of anomalous phenomena. Also carries out paranormal investigations and trains members to become accredited investigators.

The Global Consciousness Project
www.noosphere.princeton.edu
The Global Consciousness Project is an international, multidisciplinary collaboration of scientists and engineers. They collect data continuously from a global network of physical random number generators with the purpose of examining subtle correlations that may reflect the presence and activity of consciousness in the world.

Koestler Parapsychology Unit (KPU)
www.koestler-parapsychology.psy.ed.ac.uk
Research group based in the psychology department of the University of Edinburgh. Established in 1985, it consists of academics who teach and research various aspects of parapsychology.

The College of Psychic Studies
www.collegeofpsychicstudies.co.uk
Founded in 1884 by a group of eminent scholars and scientists. Based in Kensington, London, and runs cutting edge courses in psychic development where modern methods are used.

The Society for Psychical Research
www.spr.ac.uk
Founded in 1882, the SPR was the first organisation to conduct scholarly research into human experiences that challenge contemporary scientific models.

Scottish Society for Psychical Research
www.sspr.co.uk
Founded by Professor Archie Roy, the Scottish Society for Psychical Research is a registered educational charity dedicated to investigating the paranormal in a scientific manner.

The Spiritualist National Union
www.snu.org.uk
The UK's largest spiritualist charitable organisation, set up to unify and support the 350 spiritualist churches nationwide. Find churches in your area.

The Arthur Findley College
www.arthurfindlaycollege.org
The world's foremost college for the advancement of spiritualism and psychic sciences.

The Institute of Spiritualist Mediums
www.ism.org.uk
Educational charitable organisation set up for the promotion, teaching and development of spirit communication and excellence in mediumship.

The Spiritualist Association of Great Britain
www.sagb.org.uk
London-based spiritualist organisation where you can attend spiritualist services and demonstrations of mediumship, attend workshops and receive training on a vast number of subjects relating to spiritualism, sit in development circle, receive energy healing with trained healers or book a reading with a medium. Grief counselling is also offered through the organisation. To understand more, visit its website.

Alternatives

www.alternatives.org.uk

The longest running mind–body–soul event in London, at St James's Church, Piccadilly since 1982, hosting world leaders and visionary teachers in the field of spirituality

Respected spiritualist organisation dedicated to spiritualism and its philosophy.

The Church of United Spiritualism of Australia

www.spiritualist-church.org.au

Website for spiritualist churches in Australia.

Associated Christian Spiritualist Churches of Australia

www.spiritualistchurch.com.au

Website for Christian spiritualist churches in Australia.

The Victorian Spiritualist Union

www.vsu.org.au

Serving spiritualism since 1870.

The Leslie Flint Educational Trust

www.leslieflint.com

The Leslie Flint Educational Trust was created to preserve, record, authenticate and promote the work of the independent direct voice medium Leslie Flint.

Helen Duncan, the Official Pardon Site

www.helenduncan.org.uk

Website dedicated to the life and work of medium Helen Duncan.

Sir Arthur Conan Doyle, official website
www.arthurconandoyle.com
Website dedicated to the literary work of Sir Arthur Conan
Doyle.

APPENDIX 5

BEREAVEMENT SUPPORT

Cruse Bereavement Care
www.cruseorg.uk
Not in any way connected to spirituality or research into the afterlife, but a nationwide charity that exists to promote the well-being of bereaved people and to help anyone suffering a bereavement to understand their grief and cope with their loss. Offers confidential counselling and support and advice about practical matters.

Bereavement Advice Centre
www.bereavementadvice.org
Free UK helpline and web-based information service provided by Simplify, which gives practical information and advice on the many issues that face us after someone dies.

GriefShare
www.griefshare.org
US-based online support group and advice centre.

My Grief Angels

www.mygriefangels.org

Comprehensive list of links to resources and groups to help cope with the grieving process. The resources are organised by type of loss and there is a section, by country, on international resources.

Robin Grey Counselling

www.robingreycounselling.co.uk

robingrey62@gmail.com

Robin Grey is a qualified bereavement counsellor who offers advice about grieving with spirit or developing an ongoing relationship with departed loved ones. He regularly posts on Theresa's author page on Facebook.

APPENDIX 6

SPIRITUAL RESEARCH AND READING

Healing at a distance/prayer

Masters & Spielmans, 'Prayer and health: Review, meta-analysis, and research agenda', *Journal of Behavioral Medicine*, 2007, October; 30(5):447

Schlitz et al., 'Distant healing of surgical wounds: An exploratory study', *Explore* (NY), 2012, July–August; 8(4):223–30

Radin et al., 'Distant healing intention therapies: An overview of the scientific evidence', *Global Advances in Health and Medicine*, 2015, November; 4(Suppl):67–71

Radin et al., 'Compassionate intention as a therapeutic intervention by partners of cancer patients: Effects of distant intention on the patients' autonomic nervous system', *Explore* (NY), 2008, July–August; 4(4):235–43

Survival of consciousness after death

Van Lommel, P., 'Near-death experience, consciousness and the brain. A new concept about the continuity of our consciousness based on recent scientific research on near-death experience in survivors of cardiac arrest', World Futures, *Journal of General Evolution*, 2006; 62:134–52

Van Lommel, P., 'Near-death experiences: the experience of the self as real and not as an illusion', *Annals of the New York Academy of Sciences*, 201; 1234:19–28

Van Lommel, P., 'Nonlocal consciousness. A concept based on scientific research on near-death experiences during cardiac arrest', *Journal of Consciousness Studies*, 2013;20:7–48

Greyson et al., 'Seeing dead people not known to have died: "Peak in Darien" experiences', *Anthropology & Humanism*, 2010, November; 35(2):159–71

Beischel & Schwartz, 'Anomalous information reception by research mediums demonstrated using a novel triple-blind protocol', *Explore: The Journal of Science and Healing*, 2007; 3(1):23–7

Kelly & Arcangel, 'An investigation of mediums who claim to give information about deceased persons', *Journal of Nervous and Mental Disease*, 2011, January; 199(1):11–7

Kelly & Kelly et al., *Irreducible Mind: Toward a Psychology for the 21st Century*, Rowman and Littlefield Publishers, 2009

Nahm et al., 'Terminal lucidity: a review and a case collection', *Archives of Gerontology and Geriatrics*, 2012, July–August; 55(1):138–42

Facco & Agrillo, 'Near-death experiences between science and prejudice', *Frontiers in Human Neuroscience*, 2012, 18 July

Parnia et al., 'Awareness during resuscitation – a prospective study', *Resusitation*, December 2014; 85(12):1799–1805

Beischel, J. et al., 'Anomalous information reception by research mediums under blinded conditions II: replication and extension', *Explore: The Journal of Science and Healing*, 11(2), 136–42. doi: 10.1016/j.explore.2015.01.001

Beischel, J. et al., 'The possible effects on bereavement of assisted after-death communication during readings with psychic mediums: a continuing bonds perspective', *Omega: Journal of Death and Dying*, 2014–15; 70(2): 169–94, doi: 10.2190/OM.70.2.b

Beischel, J., *Among Mediums: A Scientist's Quest for Answers*, Windbridge Institute, 2013

Beischel, J., Investigating Mediums: A Windbridge Institute Collection, Blurb, 2015

Moody, Raymond, *Life after Life: The Bestselling Original Investigation Which Revealed Near Death Experiences*, Harper, 2015

Cooper, Callum E., *Telephone Calls from the Dead*, Tricorn, 2012

Alexander, Eben, *Proof of Heaven: A Neurosurgeon's Journey into the Afterlife*, Piatkus, 2012

Moorjani, Anita, *Dying to be Me*, Hay House, 2014

Van Lommel, P., *Consciousness Beyond Life: The Science of the Near-Death Experience*, HarperOne, 2010

Sartori, P., *The Wisdom of Near Death Experiences: How Understanding NDEs Can Help Us to Live More Fully*, Watkins Books, 2014

Fenwick & Fenwick, *The Truth in the Light, An Investigation of Over 300 Near-Death Experiences*, White Crow Books, 2012

Tart, Charles T., *The End of Materialism: How Evidence of the Paranormal is Bringing Science and Spirit Together*, New Harbinger, 2009

Precognition

Radin, 'Predicting the unpredictable: 75 years of experimental evidence', Institute of Noetic Sciences, November 2011

Mossbridge et al., 'Predictive physiological anticipation

preceding seemingly unpredictable stimuli: a meta-analysis', Institute of Noetic Sciences, 2012

Bem et al., 'Feeling the future: a meta-analysis of 90 experiments on the anomalous anticipation of random future events', PubMed, version 2, F1000Res, 2015, 30 October [revised 2016, January 29]; 4:1188

Science meets spirit

Radin, D. & Schlitz, M. J., 'Gut feelings, intuition, and emotions: an exploratory study', *The Journal of Alternative and Complementary Medicine*, 2005;11 (1):85–91

Nelson, R. & Bancel, P., 'Effects of mass consciousness: changes in random data during global events', *Explore (NY)*, 2011; 7(6):373–83

Schmidt, 'Can we help just by good intentions? A meta-analysis of experiments on distant intention effects', *Journal of Alternative and Complementary Medicine*, 2012, June; 18(6):529–33

Radin, D., *The Conscious Universe: The Scientific Truth of Psychic Phenomena*, HarperOne, 2009

Tart, C., *The End of Materialism: How Evidence of the Paranormal Is Bringing Science and Spirit Together*, New Harbinger, 2009

Carter, C., *Science and Psychic Phenomena: The Fall of the House of Skeptics*, Inner Traditions, 2012

Targ, R., *The Reality of ESP: A Physicist's Proof of Psychic Abilities*, Quest, 2012

Sheldrake, R., *The Sense of Being Stared At, and Other Aspects of the Extended Mind*, Cornerstone, 2013

Radin, D., *Supernormal: Science, Yoga, and the Evidence for Extraordinary Psychic Abilities*, Deepak Chopra, 2013

Dossey, L., *One Mind: How Our Individual Mind Is Part of a Greater Consciousness and Why It Matters*, Hay House, 2014

Buruss, I. & Mossbridge, *Transcendent Mind: Rethinking the Science of Consciousness*, American Psychological Association, 2016

Kübler-Ross, E., *On Life After Death*, Celestial Arts, 2008

Robertson, T., *Things You Can Do When You're Dead*, White Crow Publishing, 2013

Spiritualism and mediumship

Williamson, L., *Contacting the Spirit World*, Piatkus, 2010

Smith, G., *Developing Mediumship*, Hay House, 2009

Conan Doyle, A., *History of Spiritualism*, Echo Library, 2006

Findley, A., *On the Edge of the Etheric*, Book Tree, 2010

Barbanell, M., *This is Spiritualism*, Spiritual Truth Press, 2000

Weisberg, B., *Talking to the Dead: Kate and Maggie Fox and the Rise of Spiritualism*, Harper, San Francisco, 2004

Hardinge Britten, E., *Autobiography of Emma Hardinge Britten*, Spiritualist National Union, 1996

Brealey & Hunter, *The Two Worlds of Helen Duncan*, Saturday Night Press Publications, 2008

Fuller, J. G., *The Airmen Who Would Not Die*, Book Baby, 2014, Kindle edition

Flint & Montgomery, *Voices in the Dark, My Life as a Medium*, Macmillan, 1971

Roberts, E., *Fifty Years a Medium: The Autobiography of Estelle Roberts*, SDU Publications, 2006

O'Brien, S., *Visions of Another World*, Aquarian Press, 1989

Borgia, A., *Life in the World Unseen*, CreativeSpace Independent Publishing Platform, 2015

Greaves, H., *Testimony of Light*, Rider, 2004

Dahlman, K. A., *The Spirits of Ouija, Four Decades of Communication*, Creative Visions Publications, 2013

Soloman, G., *The Scole Experiment: Scientific Evidence of Life After Death*, Campion Books, 2006

Halliwell, K., *Experiences of Trance, Physical Mediumship and Associated Phenomena with the Stewart Alexander Circle: Part One – Evidence of Survival After Death,* Saturday Night Press Publications, 2008

Farmer, S. D., *Animal Spirit Guides,* Hay House, 2006

Andrews, T., *Animal Speak,* Llewellyn Publications, 1994

Roman & Packer, *Opening to Channel: How To Connect With Your Guide,* H. J. Kramer, 1987

Dealing with grief

Kübler-Ross, E., *On Death and Dying, What the Dying Have to Teach Doctors, Nurses, Clergy and Their Own Families,* Scribner Book Company, 2014

Kübler-Ross, E., *On Grief and Grieving, Finding the Meaning of Grief Through the Five Stages of Loss,* Simon & Schuster, 2014 edition

APPENDIX 7

ENDORSEMENTS

These enlightened souls regularly post on our Facebook pages or work alongside us and we do hope you will visit their websites or social media to connect with them further, follow their spiritually and psychically empowering online courses or request readings.

Loyd Auberbach
Director of the Office of Paranormal Investigations and president of the Forever Family Foundation, Loyd has been investigating psychic phenomena for over thirty-five years. He is a professor at Atlantic and JFK universities, teaches parapsychology (local and distance) through HCH Institute in Lafayette, California and online courses through the Rhine Education Center. He is on the board of directors of the Rhine Research Center and the advisory board of the Windbridge Institute. He has made thousands of appearances on TV, radio and in print, including ESPN's *SportsCenter*, ABC's *The View*, *Oprah* and *Larry King Live*. He works as a parapsychologist, professional mentalist/psychic entertainer, public speaking and media/social-media skills coach and as a professional chocolatier. Visit his public-speaking site at www.speakasyourself.com and his main website

at www.mindreader.com to find out about his online psychic-development courses.

Jo Angel
Jo is an intuitive psychic coach and NLP practitioner with twenty years of experience in helping people in reaching their true potential. She uses a combination of tools to give accurate readings, while calling upon her intuition, energy and psychic abilities. She combines this with practical life coaching to create a plan for her clients' next steps, so they do not feel alone in figuring it all out on their own. Jo contributed a story for this book, 'We need to talk about Jenny' (see p. 43). You can connect with her at www.joangel.co.uk or visit her on Facebook.

Dr Callum E. Cooper
Parapsychologist and author of *Telephone Calls From the Dead* (Tricorn, 2012), based at the University of Nottingham Centre for the Study of Anomalous Psychological Processes (Fawsley, Park Campus, Northampton, NN2 7AL), Callum is always interested to read about afterlife experiences and can be contacted at: callum.cooper@northampton.ac.uk.

Tina Read
Tina Read is an animal advocate and an ambassador for 'The Prayer for the Animals in our World'. She works as an animal reiki practitioner and teacher and volunteers reiki with Feline Care Cat Rescue and UK German Shepherd Rescue Angels. Tina regularly posts on the Theresa Cheung author page, sharing her interactions with the animal kingdom, heaven and the angels. Tina writes magazine articles for various publications, drawing on her experiences with her own pets, volunteering and working with animals over many years. You can read several of her wonderful animal stories

in Chapter Three and connect with her on her animal tranquillity page on Facebook or via www.animaltranquillity.co.uk.

Tania Poppleton

Light worker Tania Poppleton offers advice and support for those grieving the loss of a loved one on both Theresa's author page on Facebook and her Heaven and Angels Facebook page. Her inspiring 'Life carries on' story can be found on p. 137 of this book and her email contact is heavenandangels1@outlook.com.

Katie Oman

Website: http://katieg81.wix.com/littlewhitefeathers
Email: kateoman@yahoo.co.uk
Katie is a qualified angel worker who is able to channel messages direct from the angelic realms to those in need, using her own psychic abilities and angel oracle cards. Alongside this, she can also show you how to connect with the angels yourself, so that you can bring miracles into your life every day. Katie is a regular featured writer for two national magazines, *Soul & Spirit* and *Chat – It's Fate*. She has self-published two books – *Chasing Rainbows* and *Little White Feathers* – and is currently working on her third. See also p. 327 for Katie's explanation of angels and their meaning.

Shirley O'Donaghue

www.luciscollege.com
Director of Lucis College and author of *Live Better: Crystal Therapy* (Duncan Baird), *Working with Crystals* (Capall Bann) and *Working with Natural Energy* (Capall Bann), Shirley is an authority on crystal healing and a true spiritual crusader, bringing knowledge of holistic and spiritual therapies and the nature of spirit to a wider audience and empowering those she teaches to take this knowledge out into the world to help others.

APPENDIX 8

INTERESTING PODCASTS AND YOUTUBE VIDEOS

Podcasts

Jim Harold
www.jimharold.com
The Paranormal Podcast guy since 2005, Jim is host to *The Paranormal Podcast* and *Jim Harold's Campfire*. He is also author of a collection of books titled *True Ghost Stories: Jim Harold's Campfire 1–5*.

Patrick Keller
www.bigseance.com
Patrick Keller is the host of the popular paranormal podcast show *The Big Seance Podcast*, where he covers subjects such as spirit communication, mediumship and anything else that pops up in his paranormal world.

Howard Hughes
www.theunexplained.tv
Howard Hughes is host of popular podcast *The Unexplained*, covering diverse subjects right across the field of the paranormal. Howard also has a weekly version of *The Unexplained* on national radio in the UK.

Heather Wade and Art Bell
www.midnightinthedesert.com
Midnight in the Desert is a late-night talk-radio station in the USA, also available to listen to online, created for legendary US radio host Art Bell and now hosted by Heather Wade.

Alex Tsakiris
www.skeptiko.com
Host of popular podcast *Skeptiko*, exploring science on the tipping point, Alex interviews leading academics about the science of human consciousness and is author of *Why Science is Wrong about Almost Everything*.

YouTube

Bob Olson
www.afterlifetv.com
Host of *Afterlife TV*, searching for evidence of life after death.

Kevin Moore
Host of *The Moore Show*, covering spirituality and the unexplained.

Jeffrey Mishlove, PhD
www.thinkingallowed.com
Popular psychologist of the paranormal field and host of *Thinking Allowed*.

Jimmy Church
www.jimmychurchradio.com
Popular radio host of *Fade to Black* and *Coast to Coast*.

Spirit Science Central
www.thespiritscience.net
Discussing ancient spiritual philosophies with a modern physics understanding of the universe.

HOW TO CONTACT THE AUTHORS

You can contact Theresa via her Theresa Cheung author page on Facebook or email her at angeltalk710@aol.com or via her website www.theresacheung.com

You can contact Claire via her Claire Broad mediumship page on Facebook or email her at claire@clairevoyant.co.uk or via her website www.clairebroad.com

Both authors can also be contacted c/o Piatkus Books at:

Little, Brown Book Group
Carmelite House
50 Victoria Embankment
London EC4Y ODZ